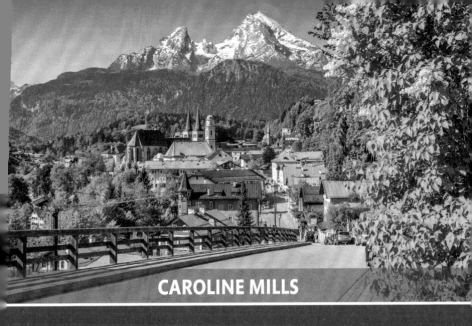

CAROLINE MILLS

CAMPING
ROAD TRIPS
FRANCE · GERMANY

30 ADVENTURES WITH YOUR CAMPERVAN, MOTORHOME OR TENT

GW00535552

Bradt Travel Guides Ltd, UK
Globe Pequot Press Inc, USA

First edition published February 2021
Bradt Travel Guides Ltd
31a High Street, Chesham, Buckinghamshire, HP5 1BW, England
www.bradtguides.com
Print edition published in the USA by The Globe Pequot Press Inc,
PO Box 480, Guilford, Connecticut 06437-0480

Project Manager: Anna Moores
Cover research & design: Ian Spick

ISBN: 978 1 78477 810 1

British Library Cataloguing in Publication Data
A catalogue record for this book is available from the British Library

Photographs
Photographers & picture libraries all credited alongside individual photos

Front cover Top image: Sylvenstein Reservoir (Westend61/Alamy.com); Bottom image:
Journey along the Côte d'Azur (Roman Babakin/Shutterstock)
Back cover Admiring the views over the Col d'Aubisque (Caroline Mills)
Title page Berchtesgaden, the beginning (or end) of the Deutsche Alpenstrasse
(canadastock/Shutterstock)

Map David McCutcheon FBCart.S

Typeset by Ian Spick, Bradt Travel Guides
Production managed by Zenith; printed in the UK
Digital conversion by www.dataworks.co.in

AUTHOR

Caroline Mills (⊘ carolinemills.net) is an experienced travel writer, and has spent a lifetime camping, caravanning and motorcaravanning. Her travels in campervans and motorhomes have taken her extensively throughout the UK and mainland Europe, from Portugal and southern Spain to the Baltic States, Scandinavia, Eastern Europe and Russia.

For the past 20+ years most of these European camping road trips have been either alone or companioned by her three young children, most often wild camping. They have experienced all kinds of adventures, now brought together as a collection in this book.

Caroline writes extensively on the subject of camping, caravanning, campervans and motorhomes. She contributes regularly to magazines, national newspapers and websites in the UK and abroad, such as *Practical Motorhome, Practical Caravan, Camping & Caravanning*, and *Touring* magazine, of which she is the freelance editor. She is author of *The Camping Pocket Bible, Cool Caravanning* and *Slow Travel: The Cotswolds* and contributes to many other travel guides. Caroline is a member of the British Guild of Travel Writers. You can follow her on Twitter at 🐦 @CarolineMills99.

ACKNOWLEDGEMENTS

A hearty thank you to all the wonderful team at Bradt Travel Guides for bringing this book to fruition: to Adrian for taking the book on at one of the most difficult times in history for the travel industry, to Hugh and Laura for marketing and publicity, to Claire for proofreading, Ian for creating the fabulous design, David McCutcheon for the map design and, most of all, to Anna Moores for editing, and providing lots of thoughtful advice and perceptiveness.

To the magazine, newspaper and web editors that have commissioned features over the past 30 years and provided opportunities to create exciting road trips, thank you.

DEDICATION

This book is dedicated to Kate, Dominic and Lara, the best, most enthusiastic, inspiring and responsible travelling companions anyone could hope to have. And to Paul, who always gets left behind yet is the rock that keeps things going while I'm travelling, or hidden in my office writing. Thank you.

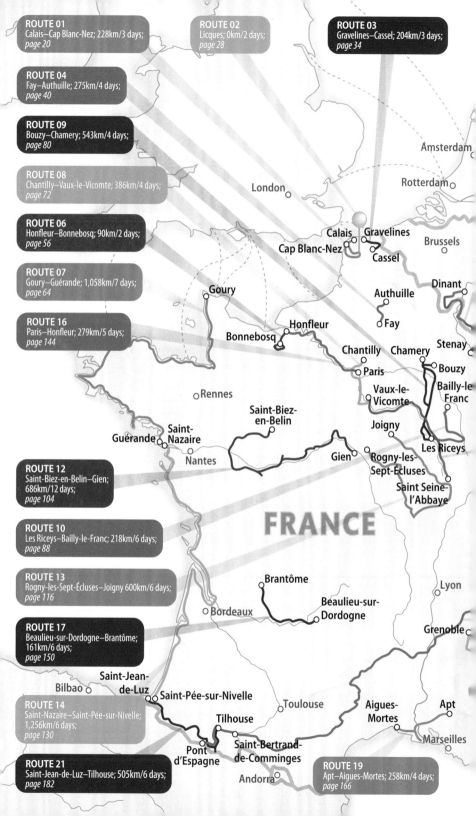

Amsterdam

Rotterdam

London

Calais   Gravelines
Cap Blanc-Nez   Brussels
Cassel

Dinant

Authuille

Fay

Goury

Honfleur   Chamery   Stenay
Bonnebosq   Chantilly   Bouzy
Paris   Bailly-le-
Vaux-le-   Franc
Vicomte

Rennes   Joigny

Saint-Biez-
en-Belin   Les Riceys

Saint-
Guérande   Nazaire   Gien   Rogny-les-
Nantes   Sept-Écluses
Saint Seine-
l'Abbaye

FRANCE

Brantôme   Lyon

Beaulieu-sur-
Bordeaux   Dordogne

Grenoble

Saint-Jean-
Bilbao   de-Luz
Saint-Pée-sur-Nivelle   Toulouse   Aigues-   Apt
Tilhouse   Mortes
Saint-Bertrand-   Marseilles
Pont   de-Comminges
d'Espagne   Andorra

ROUTE 05
Stenay–Dinant; 489km/4 days;
page 48

ROUTE 23
Papenburg–Ahlbeck; 1,760km/21 days;
page 210

ROUTE 24
Celle–Bad Iburg; 423km/6 days;
page 226

ROUTE 25
Monschau–Mendig; 209km/4 days;
page 236

ROUTE 29
Passau–Bad Brückenau; 732km/5 days;
page 270

ROUTE 26
Mannheim–Pforzheim; 341km/4 days;
page 242

ROUTE 27
Herxheim (bei Landau)–Baden-Baden;
316km/6 days;
page 250

ROUTE 28
Sasbachwalden–Blansingen; 234km/3½ days;
page 262

ROUTE 15
Saint Seine-l'Abbaye–Vaux-le-Vicomte;
310km/3 days;
page 138

ROUTE 30
Berchtesgaden–Lindau; 450km/5 days;
page 280

ROUTE 11
Toul–Rodern; 507km/4 days;
page 94

ROUTE 22
Pont d'Espagne/Saint-Bertrand-de-Comminges–
Chamonix-Mont-Blanc;
1,255km/6 days;
page 196

ROUTE 20
Saint-Laurent-du-Var–Grenoble; 427km/4 days;
page 174

ROUTE 18
Castellane–Comps-sur-Artuby; 230km/3 days;
page 158

Ahlbeck
Hamburg
Szczecin
Papenburg
Celle
Berlin
Bad Iburg
Essen
GERMANY
Leipzig
Monschau
Laacher See
Bad Brückenau
Mendig
Frankfurt
Luxembourg
Mannheim
Nürnberg
Herxheim
Pforzheim
oul
Baden-Baden
Baiersbronn
Sasbachwalden
Passau
Rodern
München
Blansingen
Lindau
Salzburg
Zurich
Berchtesgaden
Innsbruck
eneva
Chamonix-
Mont-Blanc
Milan
Venice
Turin
astellane
Comps-sur-Artuby
Saint-Laurent-du-Var
Florence

N

Bradt

CONTENTS

INTRODUCTION

There cannot be a child that hasn't, at some stage in their childhood, draped a duvet cover over a couple of chairs and 'camped'*. That hasn't created a den in their bedroom or garden, had a picnic – pretend or otherwise – or a midnight feast and devoured an entire packet of Wotsits and Jammie Dodgers by torchlight or attempted to sleep in a makeshift tent. That was me. That was my children.

A new camping shop opened up close to home when I was six years old and my birthday present was a proper tent and camping tableware. I already had the sleeping bag. The tent was bright blue, with orange doors, and I loved it. It stayed up in the garden all summer and the summer after that, until, when I was ten, I was allowed to go on my first week-long camping holiday with a friend away from home. The tent blew away.

Camping, in all its guises, became a part of my life and defined many moments. Childhood weekends were spent sitting in caravans on airfields around the UK. I spent teenage years moodily listening to compilation cassettes through my Sony Walkman on the overcab bed of a motorhome while recuperating from long-term illness, and received exam results while touring France on a road trip through the Champagne region. I learned to fly and camped beneath the wing of an aircraft in northern France. At 17, I took my first lone-female trip overseas, on a culture binge of art and architecture in Florence. A tent in Picardy was my first ever holiday with a boyfriend (now my husband).

This all seems quite ordinary now, but it took place when even much of France seemed quite 'exotic', when the package holiday on a Spanish costa was just

↑ Peaceful riverside camping in the Ardennes (Caroline Mills)

beginning its rise to becoming the norm, before seatbelts, before the internet when any kind of travel was booked through a travel agent using a brochure, before mobile phones, when a 5p piece for the telephone box sufficed, before Glasnost and the Fall of the Berlin Wall, when a trip to East Germany was unthinkable, and before young females went travelling alone that much.

And then came children.

I'd been told that life changes when you have children and not to expect travel to be the same again. Gone were the camping trips, self-guided tours and independent adventure; in would come package deals and bland family-friendly hotels to family-orientated destinations… so I was led to believe. Three months pregnant, I thought I'd better do my last-ever trip away 'before children' and booked flights to Toronto, travelling alone. The helicopter flight over Niagara Falls made me feel incredibly sick, but that was more to do with banking hard right to get a decent photograph than an otherwise uneventful pregnancy.

Eighteen months after our daughter was born – and four months pregnant with our second child – a friend living in the USA needed support. My toddler and I flew to the Mid-West, with a few days in Iceland on the return. Here, we picked up a hire car and little Kate and I, complete with emerging bump, took a road trip. The roads and the landscape were deserted, often nothing more than a volcanic black track. We were miles from anywhere with no mobile phone (they barely existed except as a 'brick' attached to your car). I thought nothing of it and we had a fabulous time together, witnessing a country long before it became a tourism hotspot. Returning home, people questioned the soundness of the mini adventure, of a lone, pregnant female taking a young child to 'such a place'.

Ten months after my son Dominic was welcomed to the world, with the two toddlers in tow, I headed off in a motorhome on an independent road trip around Nova Scotia. The children loved the rental 'van but the trip was memorable for the wrong reasons. I'd planned everything down to the last detail – except Immigration on arrival in Canada. After hours of interrogation (with two toddlers needing a nap) and questions like 'Where's the father?', delays, flights cancelled, connections missed and a motorhome supplied that was much larger than I'd envisaged, I began to question the wisdom. To top things off, I bought the wrong teabags. Without a cup of tea to make things right, everything was wrong. Package holidays and family-friendly hotels in predictable locations were looking a sensible option.

Despite the mistakes of that trip, the sense of freedom and adventure was still there and an extended road trip across Europe was planned before the children would be in school full-time. My husband and I bought an inexpensive secondhand motorcaravan, we packed in work for a few months and took off through 15 countries and two continents. The plan was to sell the 'van when we returned home. It never did get sold, except to part exchange it for something larger when child number three came along.

Eight weeks after Lara was born, the three children and I took off on a camping road trip across Europe alone. It was the first of many road trips that we've since taken together as mother and son/daughter(s), with all three children, or I alone, touring across Europe from France and Germany, to Italy, Slovenia and Croatia, Eastern Europe, Spain and BeNeLux to Scandinavia, Finland, Russia and the Baltic States. Most of the time, we've 'wild camped' legally, stayed in *aires* and *Stellplätze* or pitched in permissive private spaces, all in addition to campsites. We never book ahead; rarely do we know where we're likely to be or stay until

↑ Camping in the pine forests of Les Landes, southwest France (page 134) (MilaCroft/Shutterstock)

we choose to pitch up for the night. We don't think anything of it; it's what we do, but plenty of people have commented on the mettle to get-up-and-go, to camp, to drive a motorhome in a foreign country 'without a man'. It's simply the man in our lives unfortunately can't come with us.

In terms of adventure these road trips don't compete with a solo round the world yacht race, or extreme sports. They're not meant to. But we've been on cable cars, mountain railways, boats, buses, trains and trams, travelled mountain roads with enough hairpin bends to rival any rollercoaster, walked on glaciers, swam in several seas, rivers and lakes, kayaked, seen the weird and the wonderful – architecture, countryside, gardens, paintings and people, witnessed different cultures, walked through bulb fields, lavender fields, vineyards and lemon groves, climbed windmills, sand dunes, castles, bell-towers, hills and rocks, watched ski-jumpers, snake charmers, camels, Barbary apes, nesting storks and soaring eagles, sampled dozens of new foods and, simply, eaten breakfast in the sunshine of a quiet market square. It should be enough to stop any child, of any age, from becoming bored.

I'm so excited, therefore, to share with you *Camping Road Trips: France and Germany*. It offers a mere selection of some of the best trips that we've been on in these two countries, and they're suitable for anyone that likes to camp, whether in a small campervan, a motorhome or tent and car/bicycle/motorbike (and, if you don't like to camp, I've provided the websites to find alternative accommodation).

If there's purpose to this book, it's to encourage you – young families, single parents or solo travellers as well as couples of all ages – that *anything* is possible, to get out and explore. It's as much about slowing down, getting to know places and spending time on foot, by bike or boat as it is about spending time on the road.

↑ Col d'Aubisque, Pyrenees (page 188) (Caroline Mills)

These are not journeys to be rushed. If travel is not possible, I hope it provides an armchair opportunity to come along on the ride. I recommend that you have a look at the *How to Use this Guide* section before you find yourself whistling down the autobahn on your first road trip. Hopefully its use will be more than a convenient levelling device for a rocky camping table. If not, at least you'll be able to eat your camp meal without food sliding into your lap.

Happy travels!

*I'm well aware of the sad fact that some children don't have the opportunities to do something as innocent and child-like as pretend camping and creating a tent, let alone the opportunity to go on holiday. For these children, I'd encourage any reader to take notice of the Family Holiday Association (⊘ familyholidayassociation.org.uk), a national charity in the UK dedicated to 'providing short breaks and day trips for families coping with some of the toughest challenges life can bring.'

HOW TO USE THIS GUIDE

I'm not going to tell you how to go camping or how to buy a motorhome. For this type of general information, I recommend reading the excellent advice and articles in the numerous camping and motorhome magazines/websites or, if I may, even lead you to one of my other books, *The Camping Pocket Bible*.

There are 30 road trips within this guide: 22 in France (one of which begins and ends in Belgium) and 8 in Germany.

For each trip, introductory information indicates the region/s and departments (France) or federal state/s (Germany) through which you'll travel, the start and finish locations and the distance and time. At the end of each trip, is an **Essentials** box with information on getting there and around, parking, accommodation and a list of recommended websites where you can find out more information about a region or specific location/attraction.

Look out, too, for **Top tips** across the book, which provide extra information on detours, recommended tour extensions or the use of public transport, and **Souvenir** boxes, offering suggestions to keep memories of your travels alive.

TIME The time is the minimum number of days you should allocate to each trip; I really want you to be able to enjoy being on the road and take time to savour moments, and you may well wish to spend more time in certain locations than we did. Bear in mind seasonality for mountain regions, too.

ROAD TRIP PLAYLISTS

No road trip is complete without a music playlist. I'm from an age when compilation tapes, especially those you've put together yourself, ruled. I listened to them during camping trips then. And, for every trip we've been on, a new playlist would be created and sung along to... badly. Many define a trip, a particular place or a memory. Many would be played on repeat! Here are some of the tracks on our road trip playlist (which you can find on Spotify by searching 'Camping Road Trips: The Playlist'). I hope you have many more to add.

5.A.M, David Gilmour
99 Miles from L.A., Art Garfunkel
A Song for Lovers, Richard Ashcroft
Airport, The Motors
AKA... What a Life!, Noel Gallagher's High
  Flying Birds
Another Love, Tom Odell
Anywhere, Rita Ora
Attention, Charlie Puth
Ave Maria, Franz Schubert
Ballad of the Mighty I, Noel Gallagher's
  High Flying Birds
Black Out The Sun, Darren Hayes
Blinding Lights, The Weeknd
Breakfast in America, Supertramp
Call the Shots, Girls Aloud
Chained to the Rhythm, Katy Perry
The Chamber, Lenny Kravitz

The Closest Thing to Crazy, Katie Melua
Comptine d'un autre ete, Yann Tiersen
Dancing On My Own, Calum Scott
Dare, Shakira
Demons, Brian McFadden
The Devil Went Down to Georgia, Charlie
  Daniels
Don't Know What Came Over Me, Mike &
  The Mechanics
Don't Let Me Down, The Chainsmokers ft. Daya
Dribbles of Brandy, Eliza Carthy Band
Eye in the Sky, Alan Parsons Project
The Fallen, The Wishing Well
Feeling Good, Nina Simone
Fields of Gold, Eva Cassidy
Fire, Gavin McGraw
The Flood, Take That
Gravity, Embrace

DISTANCE These are not exact to the last mile or kilometre (remember that all road signs in France and Germany indicate kilometres), so please use them as a rough guide only and please don't use them to set your petrol gauge by. I start and stop the mileometer for each trip and – by the time I've taken a couple of wrong turns, gone round the roundabout an extra time before deciding upon an exit, pulled into a petrol station or supermarket with a massive car park and hunted down a parking space – the distance of any trip won't be exact.

GETTING THERE & AROUND Allow me to let you into a secret: I hate Satnav. I've used it a couple of times in the UK and I find my brain switches off; it

Here With Me, Dido

Holding out for a Hero, Bonnie Tyler

Home, Michael Bublé

Hometown, Andy Burrows

The House of the Rising Sun, The Animals

Hung Up, Madonna

I Can Change, Brandon Flowers

I'll Be Here Where the Heart Is, Kim Carnes

I'll Get Over You, Dj Cramp

Idlewild, Travis

Jolene, Dolly Parton

Juliet, Lawson

Kings, The Pierces

Kissing in the Wind, Travis

La Serenissima, Rondò Veneziano

London Calling, The Clash

Lost, Michael Bublé

Modern Love, David Bowie

Need You Now, Lady Antebellum

Northern Star, Melanie C

The Ocean, Mike Perry

On a Night Like This, Kylie Minogue

Only You, Jack Savoretti

Ordinary World, Duran Duran

Perfect Strangers, Jonas Blue

Picking Up The Pieces, Paloma Faith

Poison Prince, Amy McDonald

Pretty Amazing Grace, Neil Diamond

Roxanne, The Police

Rule the World, Take That

Run, Snow Patrol

Save a Prayer, Duran Duran

Serenade No. 10 in B flat, K361 'Gran Partita', Wolfgang Amadeus Mozart

Shape of You, Ed Sheeran

Skyfall, Adele

Slavonic Dances Op. 72 B147 no 2 in E minor, Antonín Dvořák

Summer Son, Texas

This is the Life, Amy McDonald

Ticket to the Moon, ELO

Titanium, David Guetta feat. Sia

Tragedy, Bee Gees

True Faith, New Order

Under the Makeup, a-ha

Voulez Vous, Abba

We are the People, Empire of the Sun

What About Now, Westlife

What Goes Around, Justin Timberlake

What's All the Fuss About?, Stereophonics

Will You?, Hazel O'Connor

You & Me As One, Sigma & Jack Savoretti

stops me from being alert, from tuning in to my immediate location and noticing landmarks, because I know that someone else is doing the navigating for me.

Please use **Satnav** if you need to, but – to get the most out of these road trips – I encourage you to switch it off and get out a good road atlas or map. I'm not the only one concerned that we're losing our map-reading and natural navigation skills or sense of direction. Besides, much of the fun of a road trip is plotting a route, joining the dots and locating where you are in relation to other places (did you know that the most northerly point in Germany is in line with Newcastle, or that the mouth of the River Loire, only a third of the way down France's west coast, is not that far north of the most southerly point in Germany?). Neither does Satnav tell you whether you like the look of the terrain you might be driving through.

Road signage in both France and Germany is excellent, but if you take a wrong turn and you can't spin round for a couple of miles, don't worry about it; that's when you spot the lake you like the look of sitting by for lunch, or the ruined *schloss* on the hilltop tucked among the trees.

Neither does it matter if you don't follow these routes exactly. You may be more interested in steam trains than I am and prefer to take the road that's signposted to a heritage railway. You may not feel the need to take a detour to the summer toboggan run if you're not touring as a family. You may also find a road closure that forces a diversion – or you may well find a prettier route. Please use these road trips as inspiration to create your own itinerary, based upon your own interests and your own timescale. Hence, I've included a general set of directions but, often these tours include back roads and lanes without a name or number. That's when you get the road atlas out and plot the route!

My preference for a good **road atlas** of **France** is the AA's *Big Easy Read France*, which covers three miles to the inch (1.9km to 1cm) and utilises IGN, France's official mapping agency. For **Germany**, I prefer *Michelin's Touring & Motoring Atlas: Germany (plus Benelux, Austria, Switzerland & Czech Republic)*. This has a scale of five miles per inch (3km to 1cm). Do make sure the road atlas is up to date; France has recently changed many of its road numbers, downgrading N roads to D roads, and Germany seems to be in a constant state of road building.

If you're not familiar with driving in either France or Germany, I recommend taking a look at the **compulsory kit list** drawn up by The AA: ⊘ theaa.com/

↑ France Passion site in Grane, Provence (page 203) (Caroline Mills)

european-breakdown-cover/driving-in-europe/what-do-i-need. Also here is useful general information about driving in Europe, speed limits, and the travel documents required. Bear in mind the need for winter tyres/snow chains in mountain regions during winter.

Both France and Germany have **environmental anti-pollution schemes** in various parts of each country, particularly major cities. More locations are being added or extended each year. Some are fixed, others come into force depending on daily conditions and also take into consideration the age and type of your vehicle and engine. For more information on Germany's Umweltzone and France's Crit'Air, a good website to visit is: urbanaccessregulations.eu.

One thing to consider when driving and planning your day, especially if you wish to be pitched before dark and only drive in daylight hours: both France and Germany are an hour ahead of the UK. It's darker for an hour longer in the morning but lighter for an hour longer in the evening, except, the further south you go, that extra evening light diminishes.

Notes on **parking** are devoted to coachbuilt motorhomes and campervans that require extra-long or wide spaces, or need to avoid height barriers.

ACCOMMODATION In addition to campsites, I frequently use the excellent system of **aires** *de service de camping cars* in France and *Reisemobile/ Wohnmobile* **Stellplätze** in Germany. These are dedicated places for tourist campervans and motorhomes to park up, either during the day if you're only visiting a town or village for a brief stop, or overnight (a few don't allow overnight parking).

They vary tremendously in size, location and style; some may be very basic and utilise a dedicated space of a more general parking area, others are set up like campsites and provide electric hook-ups. Most offer basic essentials such as

↑ Follow the sign to a France Passion site (Caroline Mills)

emptying grey-waste water and cassette toilets, and have a fresh water tap. Many are free of charge to use, some charge a few euros; keep a supply of change for meters.

Many offer outstanding locations, such as beside a lake, river or with a mountain view, though there are some that don't offer the finest situations. Be prepared to move on if you don't like the look of a location. That's the beauty of *aires* and *Stellplätze* – they provide far more freedom than campsites. However, not everyone likes using them and, as they are exclusively for campervans/motorhomes (a few in Germany also allow caravans), I've also included recommended campsites.

My **go-to bibles** that are an essential part of planning any road trip are *All the Aires France*, which details every *aires de service* in the country (written in English), and the annual *Bord Atlas Deutschland* (written in German, though non-German speakers will soon pick up standard terminology). Another useful guide is the annual *Le Guide Officiel Camping Caravaning*, which lists all campsites in France. All these guides are available to order online from ⌀ vicarious-shop.com.

When in France I also use the **France Passion Scheme**, which allows you to stop overnight free of charge on private property throughout the country. It also creates an opportunity to meet wine producers (or indeed producers of other goods such as cider, cheese, jam or honey) and purchase their products. There is no obligation to buy, but it is an enjoyable way to spend the same money you would otherwise have spent on a night at a campsite.

Visiting France Passion sites is only possible by purchasing the annual guide that provides the details of all the producers signed up to the scheme; ⌀ france-passion.com/en.

FEEDBACK REQUEST

Have you been inspired to drive one of Caroline's recommended routes? Or want to suggest one that you feel should have been included? Or fancy sending an update about conditions along the way. Why not write and tell us about your experiences using this guide? You can send your feedback to us on ☏ 01753 893444 or ✉ info@bradtguides.com. We will forward emails to Caroline who may post updates on the Bradt website at ⌀ bradtguides.com/updates. Alternatively you can add a review of the book to ⌀ bradtguides.com or Amazon. Please also communicate your adventures on Twitter, Instagram, Facebook and YouTube and remember to tag us!

▦	BradtGuides	▣	@bradtguides
◤	@BradtGuides &	ⓟ	bradtguides
	@CarolineMills99	▶	bradtguides

FRANCE

Cycling over the Col du Soulor, Pyrenees (page 188) (Caroline Mills)

1 CHANNEL HOPPING

EXPLORE BEAUTY & FAMILY ATTRACTIONS IN FRANCE'S MOST NORTHERN NATURAL PARK

WHERE	Hauts-de-France (Pas-de-Calais)
DISTANCE/TIME	143 miles (228km)/3 days
START/FINISH	Calais/Cap Blanc-Nez

There's a soft wind drifting up the Aa valley. Its warmth is carried from the west, tumbling first over sand dunes, rich in buckthorn berries. The airstream makes itself visible as it shifts the shoreline with every gentle puff.

It lifts up over hedge-lined hills, the Collines du Boulonnais, before it descends to help push the Aa's playful trickle of water towards Saint-Omer and the Audomarois wetland.

To the north, two headlands, defined by monotones, push their way into the English Channel. They are breezy at best, blustery most of the time. Poppies, wild carrot, chicory and gleamingly yellow vetch hold their heads up among the wild grasses here. There's nothing rare about their beauty, but it is a beauty to behold, nonetheless.

How often have you trundled off the ferry in Calais and put your foot down on the *autoroute* south, barely taking a second glance at those initial views of France? You've just bypassed a large area with designated natural park status, a landscape full of character and historic places to visit.

Similar to British AONBs (Areas of Outstanding Natural Beauty), France's regional natural parks celebrate an area's natural and cultural distinctiveness.

↑ The coast road between Calais and Boulogne (ID-VIDEO/Shutterstock)

Taking the time to explore the Parc Naturel Régional des Caps et Marais d'Opale, we found it to be a really beautiful area with rolling hills, agricultural plains, forests and a remarkable coastline.

It's this that we began to explore first, touring along the curvy, contoured coast road from **Calais** to Boulogne; through the elegant Belle Époque coastal resorts, once made popular by English Edwardian aristocracy, of Wissant, Ambleteuse and Wimereux. These are charming little villages, each with colourful beachside villas sat beneath pointy turrets and rust-coloured roofs, and collectively known as **Les Site des Deux Caps**. They deserve greater recognition than a passing glance from the ferry to England.

Wissant, the first of these villages, sits between two headlands. Cap Blanc-Nez is a no-go area for motorhomes so, to survey passing ships and the white cliffs of Dover from this blustery viewpoint, it's best to walk. There's an agreeable (on a sunny day) footpath across fields from Sangatte to the headland. which is topped by a prominent obelisk dedicated to the Royal Navy's Dover Patrol during World War I. But first you'll come across a memorial dedicated to Hubert Latham, an early aviation pioneer with several world records to his name, including the first person to attempt to fly the English Channel prior to Louis Blériot's successful crossing from Wissant.

↑ Cap Blanc-Nez (Caroline Mills)

You can walk right the way along to Cap Gris-Nez, southwest of its white-nosed neighbour via the GR120 Sentier du Littoral (Coastal Trail). This cap's prominent focal point is its lighthouse though our clifftop walk spied dozens of locals along the shoreline, out scratching the rocks for the renowned Côte d'Opale mussels.

The **Opal Coast** is also known for its sand dunes that run along much of the coastline. The Dunes de la Slack, between Ambleteuse and Wimereux are the most well known; they're teeming with wildlife and flowers, and are an important, protected ecological zone. There are plenty of parking areas along the coast road to pull across and admire the view, or take one of the circular walks on dedicated footpaths around the dune system.

No sooner had we arrived in **Boulogne**, we made directly for Nausicaä, France's National Sealife Centre, which sits right beside the beach. As a centre for research and conservation, in addition to education, its permanent and temporary exhibitions focus the mind on the health of oceans around the globe.

Lara (six at the time) came face to face with fish that were far larger than her; a shark appearing to aim straight towards you is a formidable sight. So, too, the impressive tropical lagoon full of electric-coloured creatures, with a backdrop of Boulogne's beaches and sea beyond the room-height windows.

As France's leading fishing port, Boulogne-sur-Mer has an industrial flavour around its western docks, and much of the central port area has seen a loss of grandeur since the last passenger ferries docked in 2010. But the old town is quite beautiful. Situated on a hill, the Haute Ville is surrounded by walled ramparts from which are inimitable views across the coast. The walls offer a peaceful and leafy tree-lined walk to Boulogne's moated medieval château and to the Notre-

↑ Wildflowers on the Opal Coast (Superstock)

Dame Basilica, a structure that we'd often noticed while charging by on the A16 *autoroute* but never visited. It is worth the stop, the building and huge dome were inspired by St Paul's Cathedral in London and St Peter's in Rome.

Within the ramparts too, the narrow, atmospheric streets are filled with little cafés and bistros; you can't help but find time to watch the world go by from the central Place Godefroy de Bouillon. We had just enough time to visit Boulogne's daily fish market on the Quai Gambetta and the Wednesday market in Place Dalton before leaving town to explore the outskirts. A visit to Philippe Olivier's cheese shop on Rue Thiers, is a must, too. With several shops across northern France, it's famous throughout France and supplies leading restaurants. It sells many regional cheeses, including its own Vieux Boulogne. It stinks, but it's divine!

I can't keep my children out of a swimming pool for very long without them clamouring for water so a visit to Helicéa in **Saint-Martin-Boulogne** was a must. This futuristic structure also houses an ice-rink, but it was the numerous pools, diving boards, waterslides and jets, wave machines and lazy river that got them excited. Anyone with a family looking to let off steam will find this a blessing.

Barely able to move one foot in front of the other from the day's activities, we just had time to visit the Colonne de la Grande Armée at **Wimille** as the sun set to silhouette the stately figure of Napoleon, casting his watchful eye over Boulogne and the Channel (he raised a 180,000-strong army to invade England in 1805).

↑ Place Godefroy de Bouillon in the Haute-Ville, Boulogne (Superstock)

At more than 50m high, it's a notable landmark and, if you brave the 263 narrow steps inside the marble column, you can see for miles. Our legs had had enough exercise for one day so, avoiding the long climb, our choice was to find somewhere to pitch and clamber briskly into bed instead.

A stay at the cliff-top *aire* near **Wimereux** set us up nicely for the next stage of our tour. We moved inland, via Marquise, to **Guînes**, passing cornfields rich with blood-red poppies. Other war-like memories are stirred with the numerous World War II bunkers that dot the landscape. At Guînes, the Tour de l'Horloge museum recreates the 1520 scene of the Field of the Cloth of Gold, an event when Calais and its hinterland belonged to England and King Henry VIII met with the French King François I for an ostentatious show of opulence and short-lived solidarity.

Following the small canal north from Guînes, on the road towards Calais, is really quite pretty, but we took a detour to **Le Marais de Guînes** (the marshes) to visit Saint Joseph Village. It's a simulated hamlet that has been recreated from 19th-century France in order to preserve local traditions and includes an old windmill grinding corn, a garage complete with ancient Citroëns sinking on their axles, and a fully functioning *estaminet*. This is France's best equivalent to an English pub, long associated with the Flemish part of the country, serving beer and traditional food from the region.

↑ Saint Joseph Village (Caroline Mills)

Crossing the regional park from Guînes to **Lumbres**, we uncover beautiful views and classic Artois villages like **Licques**, France's sacred home to the free-range turkey where farmers celebrate their breadwinners with a pre-Christmas parade each December (page 28), **Clerques**, on the River Hem and **Bonnigues-lès-Ardres**, approaching the **Forest of Tournehem**.

While Saint Joseph Village represents a rose-tinted view of history, on the east side of the regional natural park is a more sinister site of European history, **La Coupole**. Tucked amid trees south of the pretty town of Saint-Omer, this giant concrete dome, as if erupting like a volcano from the forest, was the launching point for Hitler's V2 rockets.

Despite the 200km that separate the site from London, a mere five minutes' flying time was all the rocket took before destroying the capital's streets. The museum is astonishing, with some unsanitised film footage that's uncomfortable to watch, and some unpleasant facts to come to terms with – such as the V2 inventor, Wernher von Braun's employment by the USA after the war to put Neil Armstrong on the moon; Braun invented Saturn 5. As a tour guide put it, 'It's the dark side of the space race.'

As an antidote, our final destination for the day was the **Audomarois**, the marshlands around Saint-Omer where market gardeners have been tilling the fertile soil for generations, using the waterways as transport. It's the perfect excuse to hop into a boat and explore a fabulous, little-known corner of France that's so important ecologically, especially for its migrating birds, the entire area is protected as a UNESCO Biosphere Reserve.

Many of the marshlands around Saint-Omer are only accessible by boat and the best way to see this beautiful area is to hire a boat or canoe, possible from Salperwick or Clairmarais.

↑ La Coupole (Caroline Mills)

With little time left on this short family-excursion trip, we had one more essential thing to do: a cycle ride with a difference. **Rando-Rail** uses the disused Saint-Omer to Boulogne railway line as a cycle track. It's not uncommon for former railway lines to be used in this way these days, except that here, the railway track is still in place and the 'bicycles' run along the line.

The bikes carry five passengers – two pedal and up to three people sit behind. You can choose one of two 5km railway routes to pedal along – west through the gladed woods around Nielles-les-Bléquin (our choice) or east, along the more open valley with a view of the Artois hills.

Lara and I were in safe hands on the uphill route through the forests around Nielles-lès-Bléquin as Kate and Dominic chose to pedal. It's a gentle climb that provides the opportunity to get close to nature – and it's an enthralling free-wheeling ride on the return. Take a water bottle with you, though; the exercise isn't like a normal 5km bike ride and really pulls on the legs.

Back at **Cap Blanc-Nez** that evening, we watched the ferries come and go and wondered how many on board gave a second thought to the little villages, the wild headlands and the sand dunes they were passing by. The wind was no longer soft and white horses pummeled the shoreline. It was time to cross from one white headland to another; the White Cliffs of Dover, shining brilliantly in the evening light, were beckoning.

↑ Rando-Rail (Caroline Mills)

ESSENTIALS

GETTING THERE & AROUND

The D940 is the coast road between Calais and Boulogne; follow signs for 'Boulogne par la côte'. Returning to Wimereux having visited Boulogne, we took minor roads cross-country to Marquise, then the D231 to Guînes and the D215 (Licques) and D217/D225 to Lumbres. La Coupole is 6km southwest of Saint-Omer, near the village of Helfaut. Salperwick lies just north of Saint-Omer. Nielles-lès-Bléquin is on the D202, southwest of Lumbres.

Many of the **car parks** in Boulogne specifically forbid motorhomes. One car park open to 'vans during the day is on the Quai Gambetta. It's reasonably priced and is convenient for both Nausicaã and the town centre. The best option, however, is the dedicated cliff-top *aire* approximately 2km north of Boulogne on the D940 towards Wimereux; bus route F between Boulogne town centre and Wimereux stops right outside the *aire*. Otherwise, all the attractions mentioned have plenty of easily accessible parking for 'vans, with the exception of Cap Blanc-Nez (height barrier). Here, park at the Hubert Latham parking area (also an unofficial overnight motorhome *aire*) west of Sangatte and take the very pleasant off-road footpath to the headland.

In July and August, the Div'in bus connects Calais with Cap Blanc-Nez and Escalles. The cheapest service stations to pick up fuel is the Auchan hypermarket in Calais Coquelles or in Saint-Martin-Boulogne. Both are open 24 hours.

ACCOMMODATION

We stayed on *aires* at Boulogne-sur-Mer and Saint-Omer. There are several other pleasant *aires* in the area at Wissant, Tardinghen and Équihen-Plage. Attractive **France Passion sites** are at Leubringhen and Brunembert; The tourist attraction Saint Joseph Village is also a member of the scheme.

The Pas-de-Calais region is awash with **campsites**. On the coast, Camping Municipal Les Ajoncs, Audresselles; Camping Municipal L'Olympic, Wimereux; Camping Municipal de la Source, Wissant. Camping Côte d'Opale le Blanc Nez, at Escalles, is a basic site, but has an excellent village centre location within metres from the beach and walking distance to Cap Blanc-Nez.

Inland, Pommiers des Trois Pays, Licques; La Bien-Assise, Guînes; Le Camping grand Large, Salperwick; Camping Les Genêts, Helfaut.

FIND OUT MORE

Au Bon Accueil ⊘ bonaccueil-marais.fr
Boulogne-sur-Mer ⊘ boulonnaisautop.com/en
Calais Côte d'Opale Tourist Board ⊘ calais-cotedopale.co.uk
La Coupole ⊘ acoupole-france.com
Helicéa ⊘ elicea-cab.fr

Nausicaã ⊘ nausicaa.fr
Parc Naturel Régional des Caps et Marais d'Opale ⊘ parc-opale.fr
Rando-Rail ⊘ rando-rail.com
Saint Joseph Village ⊘ st-joseph-village.com
Saint Omer ⊘ tourisme-saintomer.com

2 TURKEY TWIZZLERS

EAT, DRINK, DANCE AT A WINTER FESTIVAL IN HOMAGE TO A TURKEY

WHERE	Hauts-de-France (Pas-de-Calais)
DISTANCE/TIME	0 miles (0km)/2 days
START/FINISH	Licques

If you're exploring the Pas-de-Calais using 'Channel Hopping' (page 20) during winter, you may wish to add a visit to the village of Licques and this festival to your itinerary. For December sees the most important festive celebrations for the village of Licques, when 'The Fellows of the Order of the Turkey' (yes, there really is such a thing) dance and twirl their way through the streets. Paying homage to the Christmas bird, locals celebrate in style. The village and its surrounding area are famous in France for rearing free-range table poultry – its status an assurance of provenance, quality and flavour, the producers justly proud of their livestock.

Held on the last weekend before Christmas, the annual Fête de la Dinde (Turkey Festival) draws thousands from the surrounding regions – Paris, Normandy, Picardy and the Pas-de-Calais as well as visitors from abroad, the village fit to bursting while sightseers line the streets. It's a festivity that has run for 30 years, organised by the poultry farmers who make up the Coopérative de Licques; all

↑ Turkeys at the Fête de la Dinde (Garnett/Alamy.com)

help out – while some erect the marquees, others are making and serving soup (turkey of course), preparing gala dinners and arranging musicians.

Activities focus around the High Street and Place de l'Église. Saturday attracts shoppers for an indoor Christmas market held in a large marquee opposite the church, the stallholders selling regional produce from bread, artisan chocolates and local beers to wines, snails and strawberry products from a nearby strawberry farm. But the highlight of the market is the Licques Volailles stall, selling the sought-after Licques turkeys, capons and chickens. Within the marquee a restaurant sells tempting local dishes, perfect to keep the winter frost away.

On the Saturday evening a huge meal and dance is held, the last partygoers departing as the first cockerel crows. As one of the *confrérie* (fellows) told me, this evening is for *les jeunes* (the young) and a second, more decadent lunch is held the following day for those who can't handle the late night.

And, it's Sunday that really draws the crowds. We braved the icy cold to witness the event, a day that, while the warmth of the winter sunshine glowed on our faces, required much stamping of feet to keep warm as the frost rose through the soles of our shoes.

↑ Licques Abbey (Caroline Mills)

SOUVENIR

The whole festival focuses on food. Create your own lunch from produce at the indoor Christmas market, dine at the accompanying market 'restaurant', or book a place to eat at the dinner/lunch-dance in the separate tent (in the grounds of Licques Volailles) on either the Saturday evening or Sunday lunch. Anyone may join the two dinner-dances, the atmosphere that of a fantastic community-based party. Tickets for the dinner-dance can be purchased on the door. Don't forget the free soup and barbeque on the Sunday morning, too.

Free soup was distributed from an enormous cauldron, heated by an open fire, the bowl so large that the *confrérie* had to stand on steps to reach in with his giant ladle. The crowds gathered fast. Chicken wings and barbecued *boudin blanc* sausage, all donated by the poultry farmers and served from various 'stations' along the street, warmed their bellies while they too joined in with inevitable feet stamping exercises. Musicians from the band Fanfare Licques began to congregate, attempting to tune their instruments but struggling with the cold temperatures and I felt for their fingers, poking out from fingerless gloves in order to play for the crowd's benefit.

And so began the procession, majorettes from the village heading the parade, batons twirling, as the musicians played. Then the stars of the show, a small flock of quiet and well-behaved turkeys, unaware of their celebrity status, followed their leaders up the street towards the church while the 'Knights', dressed in full regalia, kept order. There was no panic, no coercion, the Confrérie de l'ordre de la dinde de Licques (Fellows of the Order of the Licques Turkey) honouring the bird that pays their wages. Joining them on the procession were other brothers including the Confrérie de la chou-fleur de Saint-Omer (Fellows of the Cauliflower of Saint-Omer), a bizarre sight to see ladies dressed as cauliflowers ambling along the road.

Once at the church the turkeys left the limelight, returning to their orchard to reflect on the day's events (and the few remaining days ahead?) while visitors moved towards the market to buy their Christmas bird, or the short walk to the grand Sunday lunch-dance arranged in a large heated tent a few metres away. Located in the grounds of the Licques Volailles headquarters, the rolling hills of the Parc Naturel Régional des Caps et Marais d'Opale as a scenic backdrop, the tent sat a thousand people, and was full, an indication of the appeal and regard that the nation has for the quality of the Licques turkey. The dishes celebrate the turkey, in various guises – simple but filling fare. The dessert complete, the wine flowing, the accordion-playing Michel Pruvot with his dance band struck up and, just as the Saturday evening, the twirling began again.

But visitors not taking in the sounds of Monsieur Pruvot at the lunch-dance were not left out of the turkey tasting. The separate market restaurant continued to supply local dishes simultaneously, and a *confrérie* cooked up an enormous pan of turkey in white wine and crème fraîche for free tastings. If the lunchtime-dance yards away was civilised, the stampede to try the concoction was anything but, arms thrust forward for a taste like something from a Dickens novel. Were the pan not steaming, I fear less-refined souls may have been seen licking the rim for the remnants of cream sauce.

↑ Dishing out free samples of turkey in a cream sauce (Caroline Mills)

Licques is known around the whole of France as 'the turkey capital' and, once the tourists have left the village, the professionals arrive on the Monday for yet another feast – farmers from other poultry-producing areas of France (such as Périgord geese and Bresse chickens) congregate as local celebrity chefs prepare further culinary turkey delights. By the end of Monday more than 3,000 turkey meals are served throughout the festival weekend.

Licques Turkeys are not a recent phenomenon. They were introduced by the l'Abbaye de Licques in the 17th century, when the monks would walk the birds along pathways to reach the meadows. In doing so, the turkeys would eat the grass, berries, herbs and vegetation along the way and the abbey farmers realised that was how the birds were picking up their flavour. The abbey now gone, it is this tradition that the procession of turkeys harks back to in today's festivities; the birds fed today with 'the tastes of Christmas'– nuts and berries added to their 100% vegetarian diet. A Licques turkey is an indication of the best quality in France.

↑ Musicians parade through the streets at the Fête de la Dinde (Caroline Mills)

Once the turkey chicks have feathered, they are reared outdoors in free-range shaded pastures. No antibiotics or growth stimulants are given. Bronze turkeys are selected for their superior meat quality and slow growth, the birds reared for a minimum of 140 days. Quality and traceability is of the utmost importance and every bird sold can be traced back to its origins and farm. The 'Licques Volailles Label Rouge' is the assurance scheme of the Licques Volailles Cooperative. It guarantees the quality of every bird sold.

Julien Saint-Maxent farms in Licques with his son Nicolas, who showed me around. The turkeys (the very same ones that were on parade) enjoyed the dappled sunshine that flickered through the old apple orchard as we talked. The merry sound of gobbling couldn't help but stutter the conversation. 'The bronze turkey (actually black feathers) comes from the Périgord region and we choose it because of its exceptional quality,' he said. 'These turkeys have been reared since August. They are a very slow-growing breed and that is what produces the flavour.'

Certainly I had to agree with him. The flavour is delicious and having looked the turkeys so closely in the eyes as they trooped along the village street, and witnessed first-hand the homage paid to them by both the *confréries* and all the visitors each year, I too will honour and be a little more thankful for my Christmas lunch each and every year.

ESSENTIALS

GETTING THERE & AROUND Licques is 21km south of Calais. From Junction 43 on A16, the D305 to Guînes, and the D215 to Licques. **Parking** is roadside during the festival.

ACCOMMODATION The following **campsites** are open all year: Le Beaucamp, Ambleteuse; L'Ermitage, Helfaut; Domaine des Palominos, Marck (Calais). Camping Pommiers des Trois Pays in Licques is not open officially during December. However, upon application, we were able to stay both the night before and the day of the festival.

Aires and **France Passion sites** are the easier option during winter as they tend to stay open all year (see page 15 for details). There is no *aire* in Licques; the closest *aires* are in Calais (Cité Europe), Wissant and Tardinghen. There are France Passion sites at Fréthun and Guînes.

FIND OUT MORE

Licques Volailles licques-volailles.fr
Pas de Calais Tourism pas-de-calais-tourisme.com/en
Pays d'Opale Office de Tourisme paysdopale-tourisme.fr

3 CAROUSING AT THE CARNIVAL

WAKE UP IN FRENCH FLANDERS
FOR CARNIVAL SEASON

WHERE	Flanders (Hauts-de-France: Pas-de-Calais & Nord)
DISTANCE/TIME	127 miles (204km)/3 days
START/FINISH	Gravelines/Cassel

Gazing out from my hilltop viewpoint, I can see Belgium, an arrow-straight Roman road to Dunkerque, La Manche and I think I can see Paris. Well, perhaps not, but the panoramic map in front of me points in the right direction and, with the TGV whistling past in the vale below, I know that all of France is there for the taking.

I'm standing on top of Mont Cassel, one of the only hills in northeast France. It's one of four in France and a couple in Belgium – merely hummocks really – that make up the Monts de Flandre. The rest of the land is below sea-level flat.

Mont Cassel is reputedly the hill that the Grand Old Duke of York marched his 10,000 men up and then back down again according to the nursery rhyme. They

↑ Reuze Papa stands tall above the crowds at Cassel's summer carnival (Superstock)

must have grumbled. It may only be a hummock, but on foot it's quite a march. I'm here for a reason though. To witness the 20,000 strong army of visitors that march to a more recent tune for the town's arrival-of-summer carnival.

For most, Flanders is predominantly and poignantly linked to the horrors of the Great War. The locale, which crosses the French–Belgian border, is quite distinctive in its quiet, rural outlook, the agricultural plain, ditches, dykes and canals, steepled churches and stepped gables. Many villages and towns are designated as Patrimoine, indicating they're of historical interest within French and Flemish culture. And, indeed, a part of that culture is Carnival. The region is awash with such colourful events.

We all know the French like to party and Flanders is right up there with its collection of carnivals. The tradition within the area dates back to the 17th century. Dunkerque is one of the largest centres hosting numerous carnivals throughout the early weeks of the year, though many of the villages and other

towns of Flanders throw their own celebrations. The carnival season runs from January until Easter, with the 'carnival to end all carnivals' taking place in Cassel on Easter Monday. The event waves goodbye to winter and heralds the arrival of summer. And it's a carnival of giant proportions, beginning at 6am and lasting a mammoth 16 hours.

Our tour of the area begins in **Gravelines**, west of Dunkerque. It's a near-coastal town on the banks of the River l'Aa, and with star-shaped fortifications. Moated by the sea, the town walls provide a great viewpoint of the central core that they protect, a pleasant town square with attractive Hôtel de Ville (town hall), belfry and arsenal, which is used as an art gallery. From there we move inland to discover the agricultural plain where the soil, in a *chocolat au lait* brown is always ever so slightly sticky regardless of the time of year and where village names sound very Flemish. Where barns are typically laden with two-pitched gambrel roofs, churches have steeples that rise effortlessly skyward and windmills remain to look pretty as a legacy of a vibrant medieval cloth industry, when the surrounding fields were covered in the pastel blue flowers of flax.

One such is the Moulin du Nord at **Hondschoote**. The timber windmill, dating back to the 12th century, is the oldest in Europe and lies on the northern edge of the once-prosperous cloth town. Hondschoote's attractive 16th-century town hall and the collections of crow-stepped houses indicate a continued wealth, with community pride remaining today throughout the attractive town square. A further windmill – the Moulin de la Victoire – sits to the north of the town, next to an *aire* for motorhomes.

↑ Moulin du Nord, Hondschoote (Superstock)

Through the tiny village of **Killem**, we see the first signs of carnival as feather-tipped festival-goers appear on street corners while we sidle through to our next destination, **Bergues**. This fortified town also has moated ramparts that you can walk. Alternatively climb the distinctive belfry to gain an idea of the medieval layout. By far the prettiest – and arguably most Flemish – of streets is the Place du Marché aux Fromages, where attractive terraced houses line the town-centre canal.

Our route to Cassel takes us through Le Pays des Géants, a commune of seven villages, the largest of which is **Steenvoorde**, again with an impressive church steeple and clutch of neighbouring ancient windmills. Each village has a friendly giant that comes out to play at carnival and festival time, though none are as old or as recognisable as the faces of **Cassel**.

Anxious to take our place ready for the big day, we choose to arrive early in the hilltop town, which proves quite a landmark in such a horizontal landscape. By far the prettiest of all the towns in the area, we find, Cassel's cobbled centre thrives with restaurants and cafés, shops and the Musée de Flandre, a museum that's home to the original Cassel giants, too frail to be paraded outdoors now on carnival day.

Artists from the town created the two gigantic sculptures: Reuze Papa dates back to 1827; his wife, Reuze Maman originates from 1860. The pair, now registered as French Historical Monuments and on the UNESCO World Heritage list, are based upon a traditional legend that Mont Cassel was created when two giants carrying a clod of earth tripped, dropping the sods and so forming a hill.

We climb to the very pinnacle of the hill to gain the best views before descending for a walk out into the countryside. With celandines and periwinkle littering the woods and the sound of birdsong accompanying every footstep, we wander along quiet country lanes with Cassel always in view. An early night is deemed necessary for a long day ahead.

And then it starts. At first it's just a hum. Distant. Then the metrical thump, thump, thump. Dreaming? No. Opening the skylight high, frost glistens on the rooftops. This is not summer. And yet the drums are definitely calling. This *is* summer; the summer carnival.

I lay slumbering, listening as the rhythmical beat entrances me back to a doze. It's the chattering birds that wake me a second time, as the drums grow louder. At last we cannot ignore the beat any longer. It, they are telling us, is time to party.

By 6.45am we're steadily climbing the hill into town. The moon is a shade off round, the dawn mist lingers across the vale below. All is still and calm but for the tender call of the drums. As we arrive in the Grand Place some, it seems, have been partying all night and could well be just returning home. They throng the boulangerie, soaking up the party juice with a fresh-baked brioche.

Drums? Well, some resemble instruments. Other festival-goers are simply banging and bashing anything their kitchens could offer up. Pans that will never lie flat on the stove again are indented hard with wooden spoons, egg whisks and potato mashers. Fluorescent pink leg warmers seem to be *de rigeur* coupled with floral hats, feather boas and holey tights. We feel very underdressed, very reserved in our attire for seven in the morning. If only we'd packed kitsch rather than cagoules.

At 6am there had been a platoon of revellers. By 10am, when we return to join the party post-breakfast, there's an army of carnival-goers marching to the tune of whistles, kazoos and *cuillers* (spoons). Families dressed in matching

↑ Grand Place, Cassel (Caroline Mills)

garb, children adorned with toy drums, painted faces, patterned tights. It's all here. The drums keep beating and some, we think, will never make it through to 10pm. This really is a test of endurance. We temporarily bow out by midday for R&R back in the 'van.

We return at 3pm to find many of the early morning revellers have indeed retired, exchanged for a much more sober-looking, plain-clothed bystander enjoying the atmosphere and the music from the eight bands that parade before us. Les Musiciens en Folie (Musicians in Madness), we deem, are the best, attired in green-hooped dresses, pink tights, purple socks and orange plaits. They are the warm-up for the giants who come, metres taller than the crowd, parading along the street. Bringing up the rear, like a Roman legionary with his Byzantine princess, come Reuze Papa and Reuze Maman, Cassel's very own six-metre giants. Rising above the rooftops, they are the most gargantuan of them all.

By dawn, the dancing and the carousing of the previous day appears to have performed its magic. Summer has arrived – on the town at least. Mont Cassel awakes to warmth and bright sunshine while a wintry mist shrouds the vale all the way to the coast.

ESSENTIALS

GETTING THERE & AROUND French Flanders covers a relatively small proportion of northeast France that can easily be covered in a short break. The A16 runs between Calais and Dunkerque while the N225/A25 from Dunkerque will take you direct to the south of the area. The best way to see the landscape and the interconnecting web of villages is along the country lanes, which are wide enough and sufficiently quiet to enjoy from the comfort of a motorhome or, preferably, by bike. We approached the villages, first on the D947 (off the A16) to Hondschoote, then Killem and Bergues, before taking minor roads south to Steenvoorde and Cassel.

Motorhomes should **park** in the dedicated *aire* in Cassel, which is on the road to Oxelaëre. There's a steep, ten-minute walk to the town centre. Note that there is only room for six to seven 'vans so arrive early for the carnival. If the *aire* is full, parking during the carnival is roadside.

ACCOMMODATION We stayed at *aires* throughout our tour at Gravelines, Bergues and Cassel. **Campsites:** Camping Vauban, Bergues; Camping des Dunes, Gravelines; Camping Le Romantic, Steenvoorde.

FIND OUT MORE

Cassel ⌖ coeurdeflandre.fr
Musée de Flandre ⌖ museedeflandre.fr

Northern France Tourist Board
⌖ northernfrance-tourism.com

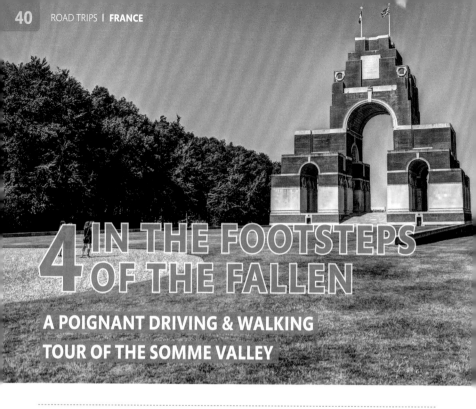

4 IN THE FOOTSTEPS OF THE FALLEN

A POIGNANT DRIVING & WALKING TOUR OF THE SOMME VALLEY

WHERE	Somme Valley (Hauts de France: Somme & Pas-de-Calais)
DISTANCE/TIME	171 miles (275km)/4 days
START/FINISH	Fay/Authuille

At 7.20am birdsong awakens my senses on a morning that's blisteringly blue, the sun already spreading sprinkles of light like shimmering stars over the surface of the River Somme. The landscape is still and restful save for the twittering of the hedgerows. Luscious greenery erupts from skeletal branches on this peaceful spring morning and the surrounding fields flutter with the rich golden glow of rapeseed flowers.

But 7.20am is a notable time here in the Somme Valley. I doubt that my grandfather would have heard the birds sing at this moment on 1 July a century or so ago, or indeed much else from the natural world except the cacophonous thump of his beating heart and those of his platoon near Beaumont-Hamel. Not least this rhythmic thud would have been deafened by the explosion of Hawthorn Ridge Mine, at the start of the Battle of the Somme and the signal for my grandfather to go 'over the top'.

I've come here with my youngest daughter on a very personal walking tour. Together we want to see where my grandfather fought in the Battle of the Somme. The battle is wretchedly marked as the most deadly episode in the history of the

↑ The Memorial to the Missing of the Somme at Thiepval (Todamo/Shutterstock)

British army and this region of northern France, northeast of Paris, will forever be synonymous with this devastating interlude.

Prior to World War I, the Somme was just a river valley – and an attractive one at that, amid gentle rolling countryside, chalk cliffs and agricultural plains. We're keen to appreciate the natural beauty of the area, aided by a collection of 19 circular walks and hiking trails that have been created by the Haute-Somme tourist board. Off the beaten track, these signposted walks guide you through the countryside, extending the scope of a battlefield tour by road. Of the 19, we walk six trails that lead us along ancient sunken lanes, old bridleways and deserted tracks.

Our introductory walk begins at the remains of the former village of **Fay**, 14km southwest of Péronne. Situated along the French section of the front line, Faÿ was totally destroyed during World War I and, while the ruins are still visible, it became the only settlement never to be rebuilt in situ, with a new village created metres away.

Leaving the fallen village behind us, the dappled sun glistens through the arched canopy of new leaves above our heads with the high hedges of a peaceful sunken lane sheltering us from the chilly spring wind. South of the Somme river valley, our walk extends out on to the open agricultural plains of the area. It has recently rained and the sticky folds left by the farmer's plough make us appreciate the months of mud that troops endured. But we are soon passing beside woodlands bursting with bluebells and celandines before arriving in the pretty **Vallée de Chuignes** and the tiny hamlet of **Fontaine-lès-Cappy**, where a picnic

↑ Ancient sunken lane in the Somme (Caroline Mills)

bench becomes our lunchtime location. The first of the Brimstone butterflies greet our arrival in the neighbouring **Vallée de Fontaine** on our residual walk back to the campervan.

By late afternoon we're on our second walk, a short and easy 'Stroll around **Péronne**'. The walled town, which sits astride the River Somme, was nearly destroyed during the war but liberated by Australian troops in September 1918. Our route takes us past the numerous Art Deco buildings, a style that's repeatedly seen in towns within the vicinity as each community rebuilt during the post-war period, together with the Hardines, small 'floating' gardens on the banks of the Somme's reclaimed marsh lands.

However, it is Péronne's **museum** that is the biggest tourist draw here. The Historial de la Grande Guerre is a moving introduction to World War I with artefacts and images illustrating the effect on society. Uniforms of various soldiers and their belongings are laid out within recesses on the floor, rather like a simplified model-making kit. Initially alarming, the approach is attention grabbing but effective and succinct.

The River Somme, 245km long, begins life near the town of Saint Quentin and enters the English Channel at the Baie de la Somme, having flowed through the city of Amiens. The river is renowned for its marshland, island woods and numerous streams; hence it is a haven for wildlife.

Our next walk is based around the river at **Eclusier-Vaux**, a tiny village that was on the front line during the Battle of the Somme. Indeed, a section of the river formed No Man's Land between French and German troops. The walk begins at the **Belvédère de Vaux**, a magnificent viewpoint high on the chalk slopes above the river. Interconnecting streams and lakes form a lacy web of water, a fisherman's

↑ Historial de la Grande Guerre, Péronne (Caroline Mills)

paradise today but a horrific scene of fierce fighting just over a century ago.

From the viewpoint our trek descends across fields to the village and river below. It's a place where eels are known to congregate before migrating on a perilous journey to the Caribbean's Sargasso Sea to spawn. We see no such slippery creatures, just the occasional moorhen or mallard looking to create a nursery nest amid the reeds and rushes. Besides, wandering along the banks of the meandering river, our eyes are kept aloft at the chalky slopes (known as Larris in Picardy) of the valley, where grazing 'wild' goats have been reintroduced.

Our self-guided tour takes us on to **Albert**, a town that suffered destruction during World War I, in particular the Basilica Notre-Dame de Brebières, whose glistening golden statue of the Virgin Mary and baby Jesus is a notable landmark from afar.

Next to the Basilica is Musée Somme 1916, a poignant museum that utilises underground chambers to replicate dugouts and trenches while highlighting the Battle of the Somme's timeline of events. It's a chilling reminder of the horrendous conditions under which troops were living on the front line.

Of all the walks that we do, it's the two around **Auchonvillers** and **Beaumont-Hamel** (the pair in allied and German-occupied territory respectively during 1916) that are the most personal. For it was here that my grandfather was involved in the Battle of the Somme alongside many others of the 29th Division.

At 7.20am on 1 July 1916 a mine was detonated beneath the heavily fortified Hawthorn Ridge Redoubt occupied by the Germans – an event filmed by the official war cinematographer Geoffrey Malins. At 7.30am the vast contingent

↑ Belvédère de Vaux, overlooking the River Somme (Superstock)

of British troops assaulted, backed up by the Newfoundland Regiment later in the morning. My grandfather's platoon, however, was the first to advance five minutes prior to this, expected to rush the Hawthorn Ridge Mine. He was one of 591 casualties from the 2nd Royal Fusiliers that morning.

The first of our two walks near the villages begins at the Newfoundland Memorial site. Dedicated to the 1st Newfoundland Regiment, which also suffered devastating losses on the 1 July, the landscape of trenches and disturbing shell holes (one of which miraculously saved my grandfather's life) has been preserved. Visitors can see the layout of trenches (each one identified on the Allied side of the front line with London street names), the front lines, No Man's Land and Y Ravine, where the German army was positioned. Monuments to the 1st Newfoundland Regiment and the 51st Highland Division (which ultimately liberated Beaumont-Hamel in November 1916) are within the grounds, alongside several military cemeteries. A small exhibition at the visitor centre provides insight into the events of 1 July around Beaumont-Hamel.

We extend our walk of the area beyond the boundaries of the memorial park with the Circuit du Caribou, one of the tourist board's signposted walks that begins in **Auchonvillers**. The walk skirts around the Newfoundland Memorial before entering Beaumont-Hamel.

↑ Reconstructed trenches at Beaumont-Hamel (Caroline Mills)

The countryside is soothingly gentle. A chorus of skylarks harmonise as they soar above our heads, innocent violets litter the shell holes and the heady scent of pine trees planted within the memorial park perfume the air. From Beaumont-Hamel, the route returns via the Sunken Lane, an old cart track where British troops from the 1st Lancashire Fusiliers waited in the early morning sunlight to advance. We take a slight detour to visit the **Hawthorn Ridge crater**. Now filled with hawthorn, blossom prettily diverts attention from the atrocities that once took place here.

My grandfather barely spoke of his time in the Somme. Though in his final hours as an aged man he cried, regretful of the imposed decision to lead his men over the top to a certain death. Some 60 years from the battle, the horrors of a handful of hours remained with him, as it did for so many of his compatriots.

I am fortunate that my grandfather returned home. So it seems fitting that our final walk is around the **Thiepval Memorial**, the Memorial to the Missing of the Somme. The monument, designed by the celebrated architect Sir Edwin Lutyens and standing 45 metres high, bears the names of more than 72,000 men from the United Kingdom and South Africa who died in the Somme but have no known grave.

Our walk takes us from the hilltop memorial beside the once heavily occupied village of Thiepval down the hillside to the **River Ancre**, a strikingly pretty valley of lakes and marsh, just like the Somme but on a smaller scale.

Listening to the sounds of nature as we amble beside the playful river towards the tiny village of **Authuille**, it's difficult to contemplate that, once upon a time, this landscape of the Somme was not so restful. May it rest in peace now forever more.

↑ Walking along the River Ancre (Caroline Mills)

ESSENTIALS

GETTING THERE & AROUND We approached the area from Calais on the A26/A1. All roads are easily accessible. We had no problems **parking** at any of the start points for the walks, though this can be on-street parking (there is off-road parking for the walks at Fay and the Belvédère de Vaux while there are large off-road parking areas available at Thiepval and the Newfoundland Memorial Park. There is free, on-street parking in both Péronne and Albert though vehicles over 7m may prefer to pitch at the campsite first before walking into town.

ACCOMMODATION There are many **campsites** and motorhome *aires* within the Somme Valley and the area around the Battlefields.

We stayed at: **Camping du Port de Plaisance, Péronne** (pleasant campsite with some pitches overlooking the Canal du Nord and the marina. The site is a 10-minute walk to the town centre); **Camping le Vélodrome, Albert** (attractively landscaped on two levels with grass pitches and gravel tracks – the River Ancre and several fishing lakes are adjacent); **Aire, Bapaume** (four overnight bays for motorhomes within the town centre. Its location has the potential to be noisy).

FIND OUT MORE You can download directions and maps (in English and French) for all 19 walks around the Haute-Somme from the Somme département website: ⌖ somme.fr/services/loisirs-et-sports/sports-et-loisirs-de-nature/les-randonnees-a-pied-et-a-velo/. Click on 'Exploring the Natural Site' for directions in English.

The poppy is the flower of, and symbolises, the historic region of Picardy, through which the River Somme flows (Ruth Swan/Shutterstock)

Each walk is graded as easy, moderate or challenging and gives the distance and estimated time allowed. We didn't find any of the walks 'challenging' though a good pair of walking shoes is essential as we found some of the routes muddy in places. All the walks that we covered were on well-made tracks and lanes (rather than across ploughed fields) and were well signposted.

Cyclists that wish to explore the area can do so using both the Véloroute Vallée de Somme (Somme Valley Cycle Path), which follows the river along a 120km traffic-free route between Péronne and Saint-Valery-sur-Somme. This route also links with the signposted Remembrance Cycle Route, which links the cities of Arras and Amiens and passes by many of the sites of remembrance throughout the Somme.

Haute-Somme Tourist Board
⌁ hautesomme-tourisme.com
Historial de la Grande Guerre, Péronne & Thiepval ⌁ historial. fr/en

Musée Somme 1916, Albert
⌁ musee-somme-1916.eu
Visit Somme ⌁ visit-somme.com

Finding the graves of relatives involved in World War I
Commonwealth War Graves Commission ⌁ cwgc.org
The National Archives
⌁ nationalarchives.gov.uk
National Army Museum ⌁ nam. ac.uk

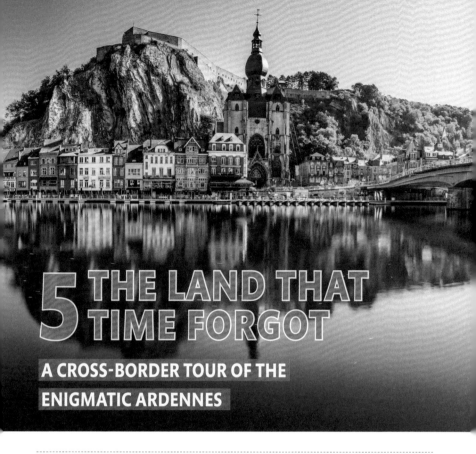

5 THE LAND THAT TIME FORGOT

A CROSS-BORDER TOUR OF THE ENIGMATIC ARDENNES

WHERE	Ardennes (Grand Est: Ardennes & Meuse)
DISTANCE/TIME	304 miles (489km)/4 days
START/FINISH	Stenay/Dinant (Belgium)

When Belgium and France joined forces to promote a new Beer Route in the cross-border region of the Ardennes, it moved up my list of places to go.

Don't expect to turn up in the region and follow a brown-signposted tourist trail though; this route is of the modern age, downloadable on to a smartphone, where you create your own itinerary. We did just that, taking in 490km of the 560km beer tour. Unlike the high-tech world of mobile apps, we found a region that was anything but.

Other than a slice of pâté (of which we saw none), I had no pre-conceived ideas of what to expect from the Ardennes. As it happens, it's a tale of remoteness, peaceful solitude and a land that time – and the world – seems to have forgotten about.

↑ Dinant, Belgium (Pajor Pawel/Shutterstock)

Covering a large chunk of southeast Belgium and a splinter of France that pokes its way into its neighbour's back yard, the Ardennes is made up of a series of river valleys with mountain-high sides and shiveringly tight bends, of forlorn-looking villages and alluring crumbling towns. And in among, are springing up dozens of microbreweries, adding to the weighty collection of well-established Trappist beers and village brasseries.

You'd barely realise it, such is the apparent isolation of the region and the mile upon mile of dense forest, but the Ardennes was, allegedly, second only to Britain as the world's leading player during the Industrial Revolution. That's due to its trees. Indeed, the Ardennes' industrial history goes back to the Middle Ages when the woods were an important commodity to make charcoal, which in turn was used for the iron foundries in the area. Metallurgy became the region's biggest industry right through until the 20th century. At which point, it would seem that workers simply downed tools and walked away, leaving behind the scars of a once-booming trade. The Ardennes, in its own way, is a museum to all this and, with little commerce (other than beer) to replace it, has become a silent ghost of its former self, to the fortunes of the tourist looking for a quiet place to retreat.

We began our tour in the French town of **Stenay**, home to the Beer Museum, which seemed an appropriate starting point to delve into the world of hops and malt. It's a great introduction, guiding the visitor (including families) through the history of brewing and how techniques – and drinking habits – have changed.

Thereon, we crossed the Belgian border to the tiny town of **Ethe**, where our first glimpse of the Ardennes' past industry was soon upon us.

In the middle of nowhere (but then almost everywhere in the Ardennes seems to be in the middle of nowhere), hidden cosily amid beech woods on the road between Ethe and Buzenol, are the roofless walls of an ancient charcoal market. This lakeside idyll may be silent now but for 350 years it thronged to the resonant clanking of ironworks that were sited here. The shadowy pool on which shiny dragonflies now flourish once used to feed the foundry. Contemporary art installations, made from iron and steel, pay homage to the area's former life.

Our route took us through the forests of Neufchâteau and Chiny where, crossing first the River Verre at Suxy, we stumbled across the **River Semois**. It's the Ardennes' greatest asset. Following the river for the next 64km as it capriciously came and went amid its secret world of silent valleys, we became ever fonder of the Semois, for it has an enchantment that is unassuming and mesmerising in equal measure.

At **Chiny** it's possible to hire kayaks and canoes to experience the Semois' charms at deck-level. The 8km paddle finishes in Lacuisine, and is arguably one of the prettiest stretches of the river. It was not until **Florenville** that we came across any particular sign of human life, though. From villages with shuttered windows and deserted streets, it was a shock to find a bustling town with a central square packed with diners enjoying a low-lying sun on their alfresco backs. Perched high above the Semois, we could look out across the Gaume landscape, where an agricultural plain breaks up the uniform realm of trees.

Further downstream near **Sainte-Cécile**, the river squeezes its way between the pillars of the viaduct that soars 35m above. The viaduct no longer accommodates trains, rather the gentle patter of feet and the swoosh of a cyclist's wheels passing overhead to visit parts of the Ardennes that you can't see by road.

While the stretch of river between Chiny and Lacuisine may be the prettiest, it's a hard one to call, for the section between Herbeumont, where we joined it next, and Cugnon is arguably prettier still.

Many villages within the Ardennes show signs of lifeless decay and a sense that the region has long been abandoned, shy of aesthetics when it comes to recent building and unashamedly void of being house-proud. **Herbeumont** is not one of those villages. The gaping moss-covered, precipitous ruins of its 13th-century fortress provide magnificent views over the river. The village centre is rich with stone architecture, coloured up by well-tended window boxes, and is worthy of a stopover. Herbeumont's neighbour, **Mortehan**, offers more sightings of the river.

↑ Bouillon and the River Semois, Belgium (Tatiana Popova/Shutterstock)

Here crooked stones, ravished by algae in a long-lost waters-edge graveyard, provide evocative beauty from a mystical world when the river's vapours rise. It is, naturally, a restful place to sit and enjoy the peacefulness of the Semois.

Our steep descent into **Bouillon** came something of a surprise. After the wilderness of the region beyond Mortehan, with seemingly limitless woods, Bouillon is a vibrant resort and a tourist magnet. Brushing aside the plastic swan-necked pedalos, it's also rather appealing. The Semois snakes its way around the town, providing a natural moat. Little wonder then that Godfrey, Duke of Bouillon, built his imposing fortress here in the 11th century during the First Crusade. You can't miss it.

Stopping overnight, it's here that I tried my first Ardennes beer, having missed out on several microbreweries along the way: a taste from the Brasserie de Bouillon. In truth, I found most of the beers from the region too strong for my liking – most are between 8 and 10%. That didn't stop a few purchases – for they are perfect to make a flavoursome beef in beer.

As the mist descended, our first stop the following day was **La Tombeau du Géant**. Passing muscular Belgian Blue cattle in the fields around Botassart, the beauty spot is another of those middle-of-nowhere moments. Here, the Semois has hairpins to rival those of any alpine road and the loop near Botassart is so sharp, it has virtually created an island, upon which, fable has it, is the tomb of a giant said to have been struck down. A similar hairpin can be seen from the village of Rochehaut, which looks down upon the ring-fenced hamlet of Frahan.

↑ La Tombeau du Géant (Thomas Dekiere/Shutterstock)

Crossing the border into France, we reluctantly said goodbye to the Semois at Monthermé, where the river meets its mightier counterpart, the **Meuse**. Though no less tortuous, the Meuse appears more immense, stronger and more industrial. Like the Semois, it too is flanked by gorge-like hillsides, with each town along its banks backed by a wall of trees.

The towns – Monthermé, Deville, Revin, Fumay – being larger than any we'd passed through in the Belgian Ardennes, also showed more of an industrial past – and an industrial decline. **Revin**, however, is a town of two halves; on one side of the river there's a mass of archaic factories, derelict, stark and tumble-down, while on the other, a gentler old-town quayside with a hotchpotch of 16th- to 18th-century buildings. **Fumay** too, has a similar context, the elegance of the town hall in contrast to dereliction elsewhere in the town.

Our favourite, however, was **Haybes**. In August 1914, as the German army swept through the Ardennes, the town suffered a massacre with 52 civilians shot and buildings razed to the ground. The British town of Stockport assisted in the rebuild in 1920. The town's microbrewery, the Clos Belle Rose, makes a 'Stockport' beer in tribute to the town that gave a helping hand. The beer is sold solely for the neighbouring Saint-Hubert Hotel where the brasserie is cosy and snug, a great place in which to try a glass – or you can purchase the beer by the bottle to take away.

Back in Belgium, we visited a different artisan brewery close by, the **Brasserie des Fagnes**. Popular with tourists, the brasserie has been making beer for more

↑ The town of Revin, on the River Meuse, France (Caroline Mills)

than 150 years and you can follow the brewing process in the small viewing area. You can also taste beers on site that are not available to purchase anywhere else – the tanks are pumped direct to the bar!

Our next stop, however, was somewhat more disturbing. Southwest of Nismes, hidden in dense woodland, is the tiny village of **Brûly-de-Pesche**. It comprises little more than a small church, a couple of houses, and a reinforced, concrete bunker. Adolf Hitler chose the site in which to lead a swift offensive against France. He arrived in the village in June 1940, naming the spot as the 'Wolf's Ravine', living in a specially built cabin in the woods. Here he directed the French campaign and received important military guests associated with the Third Reich. A small but fascinating museum has been erected in two chalets, identical to the one built for Hitler (which were taken down by the German army upon his departure) next to the bunker. In two parts, the first houses a collection of period photographs, film footage, letters, plans and drawings from Hitler's time during his stay in Brûly while the other commemorates the efforts of the resistance movement.

In sombre mood and with drizzling rain, the province turned grey. Wallonia, the district within which the western Ardennes falls, is grey. The buildings are made

SOUVENIR

Rochehaut is a good place to buy beer and other *produits de terroir* (local products), such as cheese and hams. The village is a prime example of a settlement hell-bent on overcoming the scars of yesteryear and has redeveloped several buildings to provide an assortment of shops, restaurants and cafés serving regional produce.

↑ Belgian beer on sale in Rochehaut (Caroline Mills)

from a silvery-grey limestone, they're roofed with a dark-grey slate and under grey skies, it is a very monotone world. With the renowned Ardennes forests and river gorges left behind, the countryside here is flatter and more open. We took a brief stop in the town of **Chimay**, where one of two Trappist beers in the Ardennes is made, but rain stopped play at the vast **Lacs de l'Eau d'Heure**. The lakes are a favoured attraction in this land-locked part of Belgium, with every watersport imaginable on offer.

Despite flickers of interest with towns such as Walcourt and Cerfontaine, we came to the conclusion that the eastern Ardennes is the more attractive. That was until we turned into the **Molignée Valley**. Just a handful of miles long, the river valley is steep-sided and winds through the trees once more. Along its route are two abbeys, Maredret and Maredsous. One, Maredret, sells jams and apple juice while the other, Maredsous, makes the perfect combination of beer, bread and cheese. There's a one-hour off-road walk between the two.

Were it not for the rain we'd have enjoyed a rail-bike cycle ride that uses a disused railway track through the valley between Maredret and Anhée. Instead,

↑ Monthermé lies beside the River Meuse (hal pand/Shutterstock)

we descended on **Dinant**, the largest town on our tour. On the banks of the Meuse Dinant has a giant rocky fortress, accessed via a cable car. The town has a vibrant cosmopolitan buzz, and provided a good contrast to the silent woods and river valleys experienced earlier in the tour. Cross the main bridge, the Pont Charles de Gaulle, and you'll pass by a collection of animated giant saxophones. They pay homage to the town's most famous son, Adolphe Sax, who invented this musical masterpiece. His birthplace, close to the larger-than-life Notre-Dame Collegiate Church, is free to visit and you can while away an hour listening to a jazz concert – the perfect accompaniment to a beer. Dinant's offering is from the Leffe Abbey, perhaps fittingly for the end of our tour – the world's most well-known abbey beer.

ESSENTIALS

GETTING THERE & AROUND We began our tour of the Ardennes at Stenay, 23km southwest of the Belgian border. The D947/D981 (France) and N88/N82 (Belgium) takes you to Ethe in southeast Belgium. If approaching from Belgium, without taking in the Beer Museum at Stenay, Ethe is accessed by the N82 off the E25 motorway. We had no particular problems **parking**, though most is on-street. In Dinant, we found it easiest to park on the northwest side of the River Meuse (the road from Anhée) and walk into the town centre across the Pont Charles de Gaulle as there is no motorhome *aire* or dedicated parking. Alternatively, park in the car park next to the entrance to the Citadelle on Chemin de la Citadelle and use the cable car to reach the town centre.

ACCOMMODATION We stayed at *aires* throughout our tour at Stenay (beside the river), France; Bouillon (a very attractive location on the banks of the Semois with views of the castle ruins and pleasant riverside walk into town centre), Belgium; Nismes (in the town square, overlooking the River Virois), Belgium. We also passed *aires* in Herbeumont, Poupehan, Monthermé and Haybes. Recommended **campsites**: Camping Le Canada, Chiny; Camping Champ le Monde, Sainte-Cécile; Camping les Ochay, Mortehan; Camping de Devant-Bouvignes, Dinant, Camping de la Citadelle, Montmédy (for Stenay).

FIND OUT MORE

Ardennes Tourism ⊘ visitardenne.com/en

Beer Museum, Stenay ⊘ museedelabiere.com

TOP TIP: CYCLE THE VOIE VERTE It's possible to cycle along the riverbank from Charleville-Mézières to Givet on the Voie Verte Trans-Ardennes cycle route.

6 SEARCHING FOR CIDER

LOOK OUT FOR APPLES AS YOU FOLLOW NORMANDY'S CIDER ROUTE

WHERE	Normandy (Calvados, Pays d'Auge)
DISTANCE/TIME	56 miles (90km)/2 days
START/FINISH	Honfleur/Bonnebosq

A late September sun flickers through rows of gnarled apple trees bursting with birdsong, casting long shadows from tree to tree. Glossy berries ripen across thorny brambles alongside hushed country lanes and wispy old man's beard scrambles over hedge tops and into ancient oak trees, creating a squirrel's climbing frame. I wind the window down and, even though a rosy apple won't be pressed for at least another fortnight, I'm convinced there's a scent of cider in the air.

I still can't quite put my finger on why I like the Pays d'Auge so much. It might be the timber-framed houses within an unpretentious Anglo-French landscape that reminds one of Norman England, of temperate undulations and smooth valleys, grass pastures and field upon field of aged apple orchards. It's also quite possible it has something to do with the bottles of amber-coloured nectar available at every turn. Most likely, it's a combination of the two.

I've visited the area many times and upon each return it feels like visiting old friends, be that farms, buildings, viewpoints, a favourite apple tree (actually, a glorious pear tree smothered with delicate pale blossom in spring, dripping with fruit in autumn), or cider producers and their families.

↑ Domaine Dupont, one of many producers on the Route du Cidre (Caroline Mills)

The Route du Cidre is a signed tourist trail, a 40km ring in the Pays d'Auge area of Normandy, roughly midway between Caen and Honfleur. Taking in narrow hedge-lined lanes (not all suited to the largest or longest of motorhomes), it links villages and farms that produce the best quality cider the region can offer, and is surrounded by some of the most exquisitely rustic countryside, I believe, in France. The scenery is not challenging to the eye, it's simple, gentle and relaxing.

Like much of France though, this is a 'doing' place – things happen. The orchards that dot the countryside are here for a purpose, not simply to make the scenery look pretty. This is cider country or, as the name of the *département* foretells, the countryside of Calvados: apple brandy.

We were already staying in Honfleur (page 148), a town where the local beverage is served in every restaurant and where you can pick up a bottle or two from several dedicated shops selling local produce. But nothing beats buying direct from the farm and seeing where and how it's made. Hence our arrival at the Route du Cidre (at Bonnebosq) was from the coastal town via **Beaumont-en-Auge**, a hilltop village that overlooks the therapeutically soothing Touques valley. It's a village that makes one gasp as you round a corner to find its near-perfect timber-framed style, and is situated in a landscape where one really begins to notice apple orchards appear.

The Cider Route is easy to follow; converging on the villages of **Cambremer**, **Bonnebosq** and **Beuvron-en-Auge** – used as entry and exit points – a series of 'apples'

signpost you, anticlockwise, round the circuit. These are fun too – the children love searching for and seeing who can be first to spot the next apple while counting how many they can find in total; they always finish with a different number.

On the route are 18 or so cider producers who compete annually for the coveted reward of displaying the Cru de Cambremer sign, an esteemed mark of quality and provenance within the Appellation d'Origine Protégée (AOP) Cidre Pays d'Auge zone. Those certificated are strictly controlled; everything concerning production is checked including the orientation of the orchards and the varieties of apples used.

What makes the route so pleasant is that all the farms, the producers and their products are each very different; it's not difficult to become transfixed with nomadically walking, cycling or slowly touring from farm to farm, collecting booty on the way. Just nominate a driver if you're on four wheels – each producer is proud of their vintage, rightly so, and they anticipate that you'll taste it. Depending on your preferences, they can offer you either dry (*brut* or *bouché*) cider or a slightly sweeter option, *demi-sec*. Both are equally refreshing, chilled on a hot summer day or cooler autumn evening. This golden nectar is pure, there's no comparison to the chemical-tasting commercial brands sold on supermarket shelves.

The route being circular, it's possible to start as and where you wish, and stop off at any one or more of the producers along the way. One of our favourites is **Calvados Pierre Huet** in Cambremer. Run by Philippe Huet with the fifth generation of family members, he manages 30ha of orchards at La Brière des Fontaines, a magnificent *manoir* with roaming peacocks and the opportunity

↑ Manoir de Grandouet (Caroline Mills)

to visit the apple press and cellars. 'We produce 500 tonnes of apples every year from 40 different varieties,' says Cyril, Philippe's nephew. 'All the family work in the business including my sister and my cousins.' The *manoir* is conveniently within 200m of an overnight motorhome *aire*, allowing drivers the chance to taste the outstanding selection without issue.

My favourite location on the route is **Stéphane and Lucile Grandval's farm**, tucked into a charming, steep wooded valley and opposite the pretty Gothic church and tranquil hamlet of **Grandouet**. Here you can visit the ancient *pressoir* (the apple press) and watch a presentation on how cider and Calvados are made.

The cider farm, with 30ha of traditional, organic orchards, together with a herd of Normande cattle, was set up by Stephane's grandfather, who also helped to instigate the Route du Cidre in the 1970s. Says Lucile, 'To make an AOP cider, we must respect the rules and only use certain varieties of apples grown within the Pays d'Auge. We don't add sugar or water; the cider is made from pure apple juice and the yeast that is naturally present. After pressing, there are three to four months of fermentation before we filter the juice and then do a second fermentation, in the same way that Champagne is made.

'The Cidre de Tradition is the Pays d'Auge cider, granted AOP status – not too sweet or too dry. A brut (dry) cider, which has a longer fermentation to provide more alcohol and less sugar, is too dry to be considered as a Pays d'Auge cider. The brut is the oldest cider while a young cider is usually more fruity.'

↑ Barrels of Calvados (Natalia Bratslavsky/Shutterstock)

We enjoy visiting the farm of **Alain Sauvage**, also at Grandouet, where his cows are the first to greet us and his cider is tasted in a rustic barn. Alain and his wife are of an age to have perfected the art of cider-making and he has one of the driest ciders that I've tasted on the route.

Equally we enjoy visiting the home of the **Giard family**, set high on a hill above Grandouet, amid orchards full of cows that are privileged with their grass-fed view; the **Denis household**, ornamented from top to toe by brilliantly carmine and blue-painted implements; or **Madame Desvoye**, who potters out to greet you with an inquisitive grandson from her house in St Aubin-Lébizay. Madame also sells her own jams made from the orchard fruits, including a delicious *gelée de pommes*. As we leave her, we say *au revoir* to the chickens, happily feeding on the windfalls in the dappled sunlight of the orchard.

In contrast to the rustic charm of the Sauvages, or another cider farm, owned by the Helie family, where you're cordially greeted in their front room, the **Dupont's establishment** is a professional and commercial affair; a grand house symmetrically positioned down a long drive with a purpose-made boutique and tasting room. The ciders are many and varied: an organic Bouché; a Triple fermentation cider, strong like a Trappist beer to achieve more alcohol; Cuvée Colette, like a Champagne; and Cidre Reserve, a vintage cider matured in Calvados barrels for six months.

Every producer sells cider. Most also sell their own pure, non-alcoholic apple juice (a perfect prize for the children's 'spot the apple sign' contest), *poiré* (perry), a pear equivalent to cider and made the same way, the famous Calvados and

↑ The colourful home of Cidre Denis (Caroline Mills)

SOUVENIR

CIDER The pure apple juice, pressed from a mixture of later-developing apple varieties (picked from October until the end of December), is slowly fermented. As it purifies, the natural sugar changes to alcohol and the cider becomes more fruity and fragrant. The sugar content (and therefore the alcoholic proof) determines the final sweetness or bitterness of the cider. Once bottled, the fermentation continues creating the sparkling juice. *Poiré* (perry) is made in the same way with pears.

CALVADOS Calvados uses early-fruiting cider apples (September–October). It is made from cider left in casks, distilled in two separate stages several months later and then left to mature in oak casks for a minimum of two years. In time the colourless liquor of the apple brandy acquires colour and becomes smoother. It is possible to buy Calvados in ages varying from two to 50 years on the Route du Cidre.

POMMEAU Made from a blend of cider and one-year old Calvados, Pommeau must age for at least 18 months in oak casks before being bottled. As it matures this still apéritif takes on an amber colour and is much less 'fiery' than Calvados.

↑ Purchasing cider at Pierre Huet (Caroline Mills)

Pommeau, Normandy's own *apéritif*, a blend of cider and Calvados – quite delicious when served chilled.

When all the tasting and prospective purchasing has been done, there are plenty of other attractions on the Route du Cidre. **Cambremer**, the village which lends its name to the quality mark, is also home to Les Jardins du Pays d'Auge (next door to the Huet's cider farm), a collection of different garden 'rooms' interspersed with half-timbered Normandy buildings, many taken down piece by piece from their original sites when obsolete and lovingly restored in situ.

Beuvron-en-Auge, a village listed with L'Association des Plus Beaux Villages de France (The Most Beautiful Villages of France) contains many a striking 17th- and 18th -century timber-framed house. As a tourist attraction, the village can be unfavourably busy on warm summer days; I prefer visiting on a damp off-season day, when the locals frequent the snug Colomb'Auge Crêperie. We sit at one of the rustic wooden tables, watching *crêpes* being prepared while soaking up the atmosphere of three-generational families out for Sunday lunch. Minutes later we're experiencing flaming Calvados ladled over pancakes filled with apples and Normandy *crème crue*; well I am, at least, the children opt for a choice from the 20 or so other fillings.

Afterwards, before we return to Bonnebosq, a short detour drive to an exit (or entrance) of the Route du Cidre, between Cambremer and Sainte-Laurent-du-Mont reveals very agreeable views over the countryside below, to **Crèvecoeur-en-Auge** with its medieval château and the cheese town of Livarot beyond.

I come to the conclusion it must be the bewitching combination of rural beauty and its golden liquors that brings me back repeatedly, but when is the best time to visit? Spring, when the pink-tinged blossom erupts over the orchards? Summer, when there is nothing more attractive than to break open a baguette and local cheese (choose between Camembert, Livarot or Pont L'Évêque – they're all within a few kilometres of the Route du Cidre) under the shade of an apple tree, washed down with a glass of cider, of course? Or autumn, when the trees are covered in wondrous rosy gems and the orchards are buzzing with reapers? They're all ideal, and the cider producers welcome you at any time of year.

ESSENTIALS

GETTING THERE & AROUND Honfleur is easily accessible at Junction 3 off the N1029, which is essentially a short section of the A29 autoroute between the A13 and Le Havre. From Honfleur to the Route du Cidre, take the D579 and D58 to Beaumont-en-Auge, followed by the D16 to Bonnebosq.

The Route du Cidre is circular, with main 'entrances' and 'exits' at Bonnebosq (D16) in the northeast, Beuvron-en-Auge (D49) in the west, Cambremer (off D50) in the south and La Boissière (D50) in the southeast. Note that Route du Cidre signposts are marked anticlockwise only. For a useful map of the route, locating the various cider producers, visit the Route du Cidre website (below). There is space to **park** motorhomes at all of the cider route producers (a little tight at Cidre Denis). Use the dedicated *aires* at Cambremer and Beuvron-en-Auge for motorhome parking in these villages.

ACCOMMODATION We stayed on *aires* at Honfleur and Cambremer. There is also an attractive *aire* at Beuvron-en-Auge. Ferme Cidricole Desvoye and Ferme de la Vallée au Tanneur, both on the Route du Cidre, are part of the France Passion scheme.

There are no **campsites** directly on the Route du Cidre. Take advantage of Camping de la Vallée at Lisieux to visit this beautiful town, capital of the Calvados area and 14km from Cambremer, or one of two campsites (Les Falaises or Lieu Castel) at Gonneville-sur-Mer, north of the Route du Cidre and 14km from Beuvron-en-Auge. For Honfleur, stay at Le Phare.

FIND OUT MORE

Calvados Pierre Huet ⌀ calvados-huet.com

Calvados Tourism ⌀ calvados-tourisme.co.uk

Domaine Dupont ⌀ calvados-dupont.com

Les Jardins du Pays d'Auge
⌀ lesjardinsdupaysdauge.com

Manoir de Grandouet ⌀ manoir-de-grandouet.fr

Route du Cidre ⌀ routeducidre.com

7 COASTING THE ATLANTIC

LOOK OUT FOR THE BEST BEACH
ALONG THE ATLANTIC COAST

WHERE	Normandy & Brittany (Manche, Ille-et-Vilaine, Côtes-d'Armor, Finistère, Morbihan, Loire-Atlantique)
DISTANCE/TIME	658 miles (1,058km)/7 days
START/FINISH	Goury (Cap de la Hague)/Guérande & Côte d'Amour

Isn't it wonderful how a piece of music can remind you of a particular journey? A song played repeatedly on tour – hear it again elsewhere and suddenly you're transported back to 'that' trip. *Lost* was the title of one of the pieces on a trip along the Atlantic coast, an apt title given that I was chief navigator while driving, and I refuse to use satnav.

The thing is, it's often when 'lost' that you find those gems; a pretty road, an almighty view, a magnificent town that – had you stuck to your route – would never have been discovered. That's how it was on this occasion.

Our trip begins as dawn breaks over Cap de la Hague, at the very northwest tip of France, the light rising above the tiny village of **Goury** like a real-life Impressionist painting. I had assumed cliffs but this Cap runs down to the sea. An *aire* provides us with perfect views as we, uncouthly, dip brioche into steaming hot chocolate with the heater on full – unexpected for early summer. A walk to the water's edge is cut short with pea-sized hailstones stinging our faces; on another day the Cap, with its iridescent light, would provide fantastic walking territory.

The light changes as the storm clouds dissolve. Travelling along the D901, nicknamed the Route des Caps, the rugged cliffs further south are tinged with rusty pink. Postage stamp-sized fields, serrated with prickly yellow gorse dominate the headland while pine trees, bleached by the salt air, demonstrate the wind direction, their limbs indicating harsh gusts from the sea.

In this part of the Cotentin Peninsula every village is a -ville and, like a party game, we stick a pin in the map to choose which ones to visit: Auderville, Querqueville, Biville, Flamanville, Surtainville, Barneville, Granville? We choose **Les Pieux** and **Saint-Pair-sur-Mer**! Les Pieux sits on a hilltop slightly inland but overlooking the sea while Saint-Pair, Granville's smaller (and more attractive) neighbour, has a long stretch of sand that separates the two. The old town area of Granville, though, has lots of little streets to explore.

Next stop is **Avranches**, a town with a view from the Jardin des Plantes towards the famous Mont-Saint-Michel that never fails to impress as the River Sée snakes its way to the sea. Avranches has long been a religious centre, particularly for pilgrims on the way to Mont-Saint-Michel. The Église de Nôtre-Dame is worth a look, with its interior showing simplistic beauty.

The 500km^2 **Mont-Saint-Michel Bay**, over which Avranches gazes, has UNESCO World Heritage status; it has one of the highest and widest ranging tides in Europe, with a massive tidal bore. When the tide is out the vastness of the bay makes the tiny monastic island of Mont-Saint-Michel appear all the more diminutive. It appears top-heavy, looking like a large cake topper that's ready to sink into soft icing.

There's plenty of tourist tat to view or bypass in the little village on the island but a steady climb leads us to the monastic abbey, from which there's more peace amid the symmetry of the cloisters than there is in the chaotic streets below; there's also an astonishing view.

We lunch overlooking **Cancale**, on the west coast of the bay, Mont-Saint-Michel by now a speck in the distance. The tractors sliding through the sludge of low tide towards the town's famous oyster beds offer us lunchtime entertainment. It's far from the perception of exotic and romantic cuisine. Thankfully our tour finds other delicacies including the chance to introduce the children to *îles flottantes* in **Dinard**. These little islands of soft, caramelised meringue floating in a sea of *crème anglaise* is a dessert I, too, had discovered as a child in the very same town. Dinard also has a lovely town centre beach, a tick on the children's checklist.

From here we lurch from one white-walled, slate-roofed town to the next along the northern coast of Brittany. I confess, after a while they tend to merge in the memory, each one 'pretty' with its houses clinging to a hillside, a sandy beach and a parade of *crêperies* appearing to be a prerequisite to a traditional Breton town. **Binic** stands out, more because we spot a dead otter in the harbour, as does **Trégastel-Plage** where stone buildings begin to creep in surreptitiously, breaking up the whitewash.

But the beaches along the **Côte de Granit Rose** certainly jolt the reflexes. This small stretch of Breton coastline, from Perros-Guirec to Trébeurden, has sandy coves, inlets

↑ Growing oysters in Cancale (Arndale/Shutterstock)

and curious rock formations carved by nature, the giant boulders of pink granite making excellent equipment for young climbers looking for rock pools. The beach of **Coz-Pors** at Trégastel-Plage is given the thumbs-up with miles of inlets, smoothed rock formations, and sandy coves to explore. A few miles further on at **Trébeurden** we find a pink beach where dozens of beachcombers, looking for shellfish, dig for their supper. Some, buckets and spades in hand, return to campervans parked in the *aire* overlooking the beach, a great location to spend a night.

It's not long, though, before we're on the lookout for treats ourselves. **Roscoff** delivers, with a plentiful supply of *crêperies* serving delicious buckwheat *galettes*, plus seafood restaurants, *boulangeries* and *pâtisseries* selling the Breton speciality *Kouign-amann*. Best described as an unbelievably rich doughy pastry with a sticky top, it's a cross between *tarte tatin* without the apples, and a lardy cake. *Kig ha farz*, a traditional Breton dish of beef stew, provides the main course.

Roscoff becomes our favourite of Breton coastal towns. It has a unique feel with a heart that beats outside the summer season because of its specialist children's hospital, and its marine research laboratory set in ancient granite buildings with sunny courtyards. Tourist facilities are here, too, with a good selection of restaurants and shops, a pleasant harbour area and promenade. An *aire* next to the Chapelle Sainte-Anne allows a very enjoyable 20-minute walk around the harbour to the town centre.

On leaving Roscoff, we pass elderly flat-caps harvesting artichokes in their allotments and young men yielding Samurai-style swords slicing at cabbages and cauliflowers in the fields around **Saint-Pol-de-Léon**; the area is renowned for its vegetable production.

↑ Côte de Granit Rose (Caroline Mills)

We cut a diagonal across the heartland of Brittany to visit **Guimiliau**, a village that has a fine example of a Parish close. These churches are specific to Brittany, enclosed by a wall within which is an elaborate stone archway and incredibly ornate stonemasonry on the church, calvary and ossuary within the grounds.

Approaching the west coast at **Douarnenez**, the estuary appears to have its own ossuary, offering up the skeletal remains of redundant boats. It's a sorry sight so we move on more quickly than planned. At the most westerly point of mainland France, we find the usually devilish and rugged **Pointe du Raz** and **Pointe du Van** (the first French land the sweeping Atlantic finds) are passive, the sandwiched **Baie des Trépassés** making the perfect lunch stop for feasting and fun on the sand; jumping waves becomes an obligation. Close by at **Plogoff** we discover one of the many *biscuiteries* in Brittany stamping out the famous *galettes* and *palets*, snaring passing tourists with samples of freshly made biscuits.

It seems most visitors head to the Pointe du Raz, designated as a Grand Site de France. The Pointe du Van sees fewer sightseers and has fantastic walking opportunities along the cliffs. The scenery is stunning: craggy rocks thunder down to harsh Atlantic seas below, the isolated **Chapelle Saint-They** ministers to passing sailors and clumps of pink sea thrift are dotted like pin cushions among the wild grasses.

In addition to excellent beaches at Guidel-Plages and Larmor-Plage, the southern coast of Brittany first brings beverages as the apple orchards around **Fouesnant** produce AOC Cornouaille cider to rival that of the Normans. Meanwhile **Étel**, a cul-de-sac town forgotten by tourists in favour of the Côte

↑ **Top** Chapelle Saint-They, Pointe du Van **Above** Picking shellfish at Étel (both Caroline Mills)

des Mégalithes, is the place to be at low tide, the locals arriving to dig out teatime *coquillages*. Like neighbouring Carnac, famous for its fields punctuated by ancient stones, Étel offers megaliths too. More 'mega' in size, **Les Géants (the giants) de Kerzerho** make the Alignements de Carnac look like a crèche.

At **Quiberon**, we manage to forego tins of oiled sardines, its gastronomic speciality. The town sits at the end of a promontory that juts into the Atlantic and whose Côte Sauvage (Wild Coast) does indeed look savage. Rocks are shaped according to the crashing waves on the western edge, with the softer eastern side providing for bathers.

A place on our 'must return to' list is the **Golfe du Morbihan**, only just making it into the Atlantic Ocean via a tiny inlet from the Baie du Quiberon. A five-minute boat trip from Port Blanc takes us to the green **Île-aux-Moines**, the largest of the gulf's islands with narrow streets and alleyways to explore, stone cottages and a couple of tiny restaurants hugging a quayside. It's serene, away from the rush of summer traffic, and great for exploration on foot or bike.

Our final stop as we cross into the department of the Loire-Atlantique is **Guérande**. Famous for its salt, the town is separated from the ocean by rectangular pans. These provide a savoury flavour in contrast to the bastioned buildings selling sweet caramels en masse to the tourists flocking over the old drawbridge, long before the salted caramel became ubiquitous.

Lost? Well, only as we closed our eyes, and opened our ears to the sound of the Atlantic surging in that evening on the Côte d'Amour while tucked up in bed; it's quite a lullaby after a busy day of beachcombing.

To continue this tour along the Atlantic Coast, see page 130.

↑ Île-aux-Moines (Pascale Gueret/Shutterstock)

ESSENTIALS

GETTING THERE & AROUND

This is a long road trip and it's impossible to mark up every road; grab yourself a map and, basically, follow the coast and keep it in view as much as you can depending on where you wish to visit. We began along the D901 at Goury, on the Cotentin Peninsula, and drove south to Avranches, where we turn west to cross from Normandy into Brittany. At Roscoff we cut off a proportion of Brittany's northwest coast by driving along the D69 to Landivisiau for nearby Guimiliau, then the D30 to Sizun and D18 to Le Faou, where we picked up coastal routes again to head west, then east along Brittany's southern coast, finishing at Guérande and the Côte d'Amour (ready to continue south along the coast).

For **parking**, there are many overnight motorhome *aires* in Normandy and Brittany and these should also be used for daytime parking as you'll otherwise find signs that forbid motorhomes frequently, particularly in Brittany. Note that motorhomes are not accepted in Dinard; to visit, either park in one of the *aires* in Saint-Malo and use public transport or stay in Dinard's very attractive beachside campsite (see below).

There's a pay car park at Pointe du Van, while it's free to park from November to end of May at Pointe du Raz, with dedicated motorhome parking.

ACCOMMODATION

The west coast of Normandy and the whole of Brittany is one of the most densely populated areas of France with ***aires*** (more than 350 in Brittany alone) and **campsites**, so you will have no trouble finding somewhere to stay.

We stayed at: *aires* in Auderville, Saint-Pair-sur-Mer, Lermot, Roscoff, Étel, Le Pouliguen, and a **France Passion** site at Elliant (Cidrerie Melenig).

Campsites: Camping Municipal du Hâble, Ormonville-la-Rogue; Château de Lez-Eaux, Saint-Pair-sur-Mer; Camping du Port Blanc, Dinard; Bellevue Mer, Hillion; Aux 4 Saisons, Roscoff; Le Cabellou Plage, Concarneau; Camping Municipal Étel; L'Océan, Le Croisic.

FIND OUT MORE

Brittany Tourism ⌀ brittanytourism.com
Guérande/La Baule ⌀ en.labaule-guerande.com
Normandy Tourist Board ⌀ en.normandie-tourisme.fr

Pointe du Raz ⌀ pointeduraz.com
Roscoff Tourist Board ⌀ roscoff-tourisme.com

TOP TIP: OUR PICK OF THE BEACHES

Baie des Trépassés
Binic
Côte d'Amour
Dinard
Étel to the Côte Sauvage

Granville/Saint-Pair-sur-Mer
Guidel-Plages (beach includes
    wheelchair access) to Larmor-Plage
Perros-Guirec
Trégastel-Plage

8 LE JARDIN FRANÇAIS

VISIT THE GARDENS OF ANDRÉ LE NÔTRE, DEEMED THE FATHER OF FRENCH GARDEN STYLE

WHERE	Île de France (Oise, Yvelines, Hauts-de-Seine, Seine-et-Marne)
DISTANCE/TIME	240 miles (386km)/4 days
START/FINISH	Chantilly/Vaux-le-Vicomte

"Too much gold!" That was my 11-year old daughter's initial analysis of the Château de Versailles as we strolled through the glittering front gates. A budding gardener, I fear she would not have gone far up the career ranks with Versailles' 17th-century owner, Louis XIV. Self-styled The Sun King, he loved gold to indicate his wealth, power and self-proclaimed allegorical link with Apollo, the Greek Sun God. My daughter didn't appreciate his opulence.

We'd come to the Île de France to visit some of the compositions of a celebrated landscape gardener, André le Nôtre. Born in 1613, some 100 years before England's Lancelot 'Capability' Brown (arguably the master of the 'English Garden'), le Nôtre is regarded as the French master garden designer. Speak of a French garden or *mode à la Française* and it actually refers to a garden designed in the style of André le Nôtre.

Following in the footsteps of his father and grandfather before him, Le Nôtre was employed by the French king as chief gardener. He remained within Louis XIV's service for almost 40 years, continuing with garden design until his 80th birthday, and was so revered by the king that the pair became good friends.

Royal approval meant that anyone who was anyone also wanted to employ Le Nôtre to design the gardens on their patch of France. And indeed England

↑ Parc de Sceaux (lesart/Shutterstock)

for that matter; le Nôtre had a hand in the designs for the gardens at Greenwich, Hampton Court, St James' Park and Windsor.

His handiwork can be seen within various gardens across France such as the magnificent Château d'Ussé (page 109) and La Bussière in the Loire Valley or the public gardens at Castres in the Languedoc. But it is in and around Paris that Le Nôtre's work is at its most prolific.

We began our tour north of Paris at the **Château de Chantilly**. At first glance, the long, ornate building overlooking the prestigious Hippodrome (racecourse) de Chantilly looks to be a worthy palace to house a nobleman. But no, these are just the Grandes Écuries, the great stables merely fit for a horse! Built by the Prince of Condé in 1719, the stables house the Museum of the Horse, where visitors can see everything from sleek thoroughbreds to the miniscule Shetland pony. There's often a chance to watch the horses schooled and trained for equestrian shows while the museum provides exhibits presenting the relationship between humans and horses since the beginning of civilisation.

It's the gardens around the château where Le Nôtre demonstrates his creativity, in particular the parterres and Grand Canal. His very precise, formal 17th-century style contrasts with the more relaxed 19th-century Jardin Anglais adjacent and the rustic Le Hameau (The Hamlet) sitting within the estate grounds. A picturesque half-timbered farm, Le Hameau is where flowers colour up both the landscape and roof ridges, with florid iris growing atop the buildings. It's also where Lara and I were able to sample the best-ever tasting Crème Chantilly, the famous sweetened

SOUVENIR

What makes a 'Le Nôtre' garden? It doesn't take long to see the resemblances between his charges. Long infinite vistas created using his mathematical training to deduce the contours of the land and the innovative scientific techniques of the day to gauge proportion in relation to perspective. Canals and water features, practical by design, to irrigate the land, drain a marshy area or prevent livestock from reaching the pleasure gardens around the house. Sculptures and statues depicting allegorical classical myths, simple geometric shapes and embroidered tapestries woven from neatly clipped hedges, parterres designed to be seen 'bird's-eye' from terraces above. Extending an estate, large woodland areas necessary for firewood and workshops, a symmetry extending the architectural lines of the house into the garden, topiary figures and exotic plants that kept a patron happy with all-seasons colour and the creation of *bosquets*, private outdoor rooms used for entertaining in woodland clearings. All feature in Le Nôtre's works of art.

whipped cream originally created at the dairy in Le Hameau, before walking (some of) it off along the banks of the 2.5km Grand Canal, one of Le Nôtre's most impressive water features.

Leaving Chantilly behind we circumnavigated Paris anticlockwise to reach the town of **Saint-Germain-en-Laye** bathed in a late afternoon sunlight. Nineteen kilometres west of Paris and perched high on a hill above the River Seine, the town's public gardens – the work of Le Nôtre – show off the incredible façade of the château here and the nearby house within which King Louis XIV was born. More so, the gardens are a popular place to sit out and offer magnificent views over La Défense, the business district of Paris. You can even see the Eiffel Tower poking its head above Mont Valérien.

Le Nôtre was a master of perspective. His former mathematical training was put to good use at Saint-Germain-en-Laye where the 2.4km-long terrace looks even longer than it actually is. And, having seen two gardens, we could notice some of the distinguishing features of the landscape gardener's work.

En route to Versailles, just a matter of minutes south of Saint-Germain-en-Laye, we stopped off at **Marly-le-Roi** where The Sun King built another château with less opulence than Versailles. Le Nôtre at least had some influence over the design of the gardens, though it's thought the architect of the châteaux at Versailles and Marly, architect Jules Hardouin-Mansart laid the final touches.

The buildings are long gone and the formal shape of the garden had long been lost amid the undergrowth. However, in a vast landscaped and wooded park, the gardens are gradually being restored and visitors can wander in and take a look at the work-in-progress, where formal lines and parterres are, once again,

← Le Hameau, The English Garden and the Museum of the Horse, Château de Chantilly (Caroline Mills)

appearing out of the surrounding woods. Close by is also the park of another missing château, that of **Saint Cloud**. We missed out on this occasion, though the Le Nôtre gardens here provide even more impressive views of neighbouring Paris than those of Saint-Germain-en-Laye.

By morning it was time to tackle one of André Le Nôtre's finest masterpieces – the gardens at the **Château de Versailles**. Covering hundreds of hectares, these gardens did not take shape overnight. From 1661 until his retirement at the age of 80, Le Nôtre worked tirelessly with his regular work colleagues: Jean-Baptiste Colbert, Superintendent of the King's Buildings; Charles Le Brun, appointed First Painter of the King; and the architect Jules Hardouin-Mansart who between them, created the stately scenes that we can walk around today.

The views across the estate from the top terrace are special. Understandably so, for Le Nôtre had planned these gardens in the utmost detail. They were laid out on an east to west axis, following the course of the sun, allowing light into the King's bedroom in the morning and setting at the end of the Grand Canal in the evening, with the Water Parterres reflected in the palace's Hall of Mirrors (which alone is worthy of a visit). Individual parterres were created in front of both the King's windows and those of Queen Marie Thérèse, Louis' wife, while Apollo, gilt in gold, graces the central fountain to reflect Louis' own identification with the sun god.

There's more gold flaunted across most of the pools and some are gleaming. Latona's Fountain, for example, one of the most famous at Versailles, was restored in 2015; this and other fountains glisten in the sunlight or brighten up the darkest of thunderclouds.

Most coach-led visitors don't step much beyond Apollo's fountain. Venture further and you'll find places to call your own. While there's the option to hop on the miniature train, hire an electric cart or take a bike ride to explore the estate, we decided to walk to the Grand Trianon, also within the estate grounds. Understated

↑ Views of La Défense, Paris, from Saint-Germain-en-Laye (Caroline Mills)

and gentile by comparison to Versailles, the Grand Trianon is where Louis XIV would escape the pomp of court life. Le Nôtre designed the gardens here too, with his now characteristic avenues, boulevards and garden rooms evident once more.

So it was a refreshing change to find ourselves wandering into the rural space of Queen Marie-Antoinette's world. The wife of King Louis XVI, she escaped court life in the Petit Trianon and the rural Hamlet, a farm that's based upon Le Hameau at Chantilly. With lakes, secret winding paths and a farmyard of animals, this is the antithesis to the ordered world of Le Nôtre's garden of Versailles.

By the time we reached the park at **Sceaux**, Lara was becoming a self-proclaimed expert in French garden style! With much of Le Nôtre's work still visible and the parterres being restored to original plans, this was perhaps more popular with us than Versailles. The château (not the original building) at Sceaux houses a museum dedicated to the Île de France, with a large collection of paintings from the School of Paris. But the park, rather than taken up with global visitors, was thronging with locals out for a jog or an afternoon stroll, avid readers soaking up the sunshine, families picnicking on the lawns or simply enjoying a chat with friends on the terraces.

Of all the Le Nôtre gardens that we visited on this occasion it was **Fontainebleau**, where we visited next, that was the most disappointing. The Grand Parterre has all the hallmarks of the garden designer's hand in its formal structure but, at the time we visited in early spring, it only had the bare bones. We have visited the garden on a previous trip, however, in high summer when the garden has looked a real spectacle, its borders filled with colour to add an alternative depth to the sheer scale of the parterre.

↑ Palace of Versailles (Vivvi Smak/Shutterstock)

Our preference here was, once again, for the neighbouring **Jardin Anglais** where a stream meandered at will through the parkland, late daffodils fought with early camellias for attention and the tight buds of the magnolias were about to erupt into a glorious display amid specimen trees.

If Fontainebleau was the low point of the tour – and, in the greater picture, it wasn't that 'low'! – our final garden, **Vaux-le-Vicomte**, to the east of Paris, was the highlight. The gardens here also happen to be regarded as André le Nôtre's first official engagement and his finest garden. At first glance, it looks very similar to his other gardens – and in some respects it is – but the more we delved and discovered, the more we saw the genius of both the garden and its designer. His mathematician's brain had, once again, been put to masterful use to create perspective and optical illusions so that, by the time we'd walked to the hilltop statue of Hercules far from the château, our brains were truly being put to the test.

It was Louis XIV's Minister of Finance, Nicolas Fouquet that built the opulent château to show his own wealth and power. However, The Sun King grew jealous of the gardens Le Nôtre had designed for Fouquet, which were far more ostentatious and extravagant than anything he owned. So he whipped Fouquet into jail and usurped the services of the gardener, pressing him into designing the gardens at Versailles to make them bigger and better.

Our circumnavigation of Paris had come to an end and we had visited only a small selection of André le Nôtre's gardens. On a previous trip to France we'd admired his Parisian work – the Jardin du Luxembourg, the Palais Royal, the Tuileries in front of the Louvre and, his most famous work, the Champs-Elysées. The fact is, wander around any park or garden in Paris and the Île de France that pre-dates 1700 and the chances are, Le Nôtre had a hand in it.

Today, the gardens, some 350 years on still live and breathe, enjoyed by thousands who enter their Baroque world.

↑ Gardens at Château de Vaux-le-Vicomte (KievVictor/Shuttetstock)

ESSENTIALS

GETTING THERE & AROUND We approached the area on the A16 to Beauvais, the N31/D1016 to Creil and the D44 to the Château de Chantilly. Our route took us west of Paris on the N184 to Saint-Germain-en-Laye followed by the N186 to Marly-le-Roi and Versailles. We took the N12 and A86 to Sceaux before heading south on the A6 for Milly-la-Forêt, whereby we picked up the D837/D409 to Fontainebleau. Finally we took the D606/D636 to Vaux-le-Vicomte. Check the current status of environmental road schemes and their requirements around Paris and the Île de France region before you travel.

For **parking**: Saint-Germain-en-Laye, Sceaux and Fontainebleau is roadside, though there are areas close to each château to park large vehicles. At Saint-Germain-en-Laye the road due north of the château (D284 Avenue des Loges) has wide laybys to pull off the road; at Sceaux there are parking spaces next to each park entrance; and at Fontainebleau there are many on-street parking bays along Rue Dénecourt, adjacent to the château.

There are car parks at Chantilly, Marly (directly off the roundabout on the N186) and Vaux le Vicomte. Note that the last couple of kilometres or so to Vaux-le-Vicomte from Melun are relatively narrow; it's not single-track but extra care should be taken.

For Versailles, the Place d'Armes, right in front of the château, is the nearest place to park but there's a height barrier at 2.5m (and it's outrageously expensive). There are other parking areas without height barriers: large coachbuilts can park within the town at 'Parking Sceaux' and 'Avenue de l'Europe'.

ACCOMMODATION We stayed at *aires* in Chantilly and Milly-la-Forêt and **Camping** Huttopia Versailles, 2km from the château. Satnav or an excellent road atlas is essential to reach this campsite; there are some fairly tight city streets to negotiate close to the site entrance and signposts aren't great. *Aires* are extremely limited in the Île de France though there is one at Saint-Fargeau-Ponthierry, west of Melun.

Other recommended campsites: Le Mont César, Gouvieux (for Chantilly); Camping La Musardière, Milly-la-Forêt; Camping La Belle Étoile, La Rochette (for Vaux-le-Vicomte).

FIND OUT MORE

Château de Fontainebleau ⊘ musee-chateau-fontainebleau.fr
Château et Parc de Chantilly ⊘ domainedechantilly.com
Château Saint Germain ⊘ seine-saintgermain.fr
Château Sceaux ⊘ domaine-de-sceaux.hauts-de-seine.fr

Château de Vaux-le-Vicomte ⊘ vaux-le-vicomte.com
Château de Versailles ⊘ châteauversailles.fr
Marly-le-Roi ⊘ marlyleroi.fr/Domaine-de-Marly

9 ALL CALM IN THE LAND OF FIZZ

VISIT THE CHAMPAGNE REGION DURING HARVEST & DISCOVER RARE FIZZ-FREE WINE

WHERE	Champagne (Grand Est: Marne & Aube)
DISTANCE/TIME	338 miles (543km)/4 days
START/FINISH	Bouzy/Chamery

Red wine is not generally on my menu at breakfast – indeed I cannot think of a time that it has been, least of all chilled. Until now, breaking the morning fast among 14 other visitors – all French – to witness the Champagne grape harvest. Some guests sup bowls full of black coffee; others take a stronger, smaller mix. I sip tea. But we all drink red wine along with our croissants from the village boulangerie, *pâte croute* (best described as a long pork pie) and regional cheeses, the combination making up a Champenois breakfast.

I'm in the village of **Bouzy**, a name (pronounced 'boozy') that's simply perfect for sitting in the heart of Champagne country. It's a village I frequent as often as I can to visit Rémy Galichet, a France Passion site and a small family producer of champagne – and Bouzy Rouge, an anomaly of the Champagne region that's otherwise synonymous with bubbles. Once the favourite tipple of France's Sun

↑ Looking over the vineyards at Bouzy (Marcello Brunetti/Shutterstock)

King, Louis XIV, this still red wine is so scarce that it's rarely available to purchase outside the village and its environs.

With breakfast over it's time to meet the family. Monsieur Galichet bemoans in jest that, when he wanted a male heir to his domain, he produced three daughters and yet, he admits, how useful they are to the family business. For Ingrid and Aurélie are front of house, in charge of sales and export while Carole is slowly taking over the production side from Papa, helping with the vines and creating new *cuvées*. Madame Galichet heads up the accounts.

First up, is a trip to one area of the family's 9ha (20 acres) of vines to fill a bucket with grapes. Says Aurélie, 'We have 3ha of vines in each of the three main champagne-producing areas around the Champagne capital, Épernay: the Montagne de Reims (where Bouzy is located), the Côte des Blancs (where white Chardonnay grapes are grown) and the Vallée de la Marne. So, with three grape varieties – the famous Pinot Noir, Pinot Meunier and Chardonnay – we can make various different champagnes including a blanc de blancs (made purely from the white grapes of the Côte des Blancs) and a rosé. Plus, because Bouzy is certified

as a Grand Cru village, the highest accreditation afforded in the Champagne region, we can also produce vintage and Grand Cru champagne, made from the finest grapes.'

Monsieur Galichet, dressed in his overalls and breaking off from the harvest for a few minutes, takes us to the top of the hill above Bouzy for immaculate views across the Marne valley towards the Côte des Blancs. 'It's difficult for producers such as us,' he says, 'as visitors to the region tend to head to the grand houses and *caves* (cellars) in Épernay, to the big brand names they've heard of. Fewer people visit Bouzy. That's why the France Passion scheme works as it attracts would-be passers-by to stop.'

Yet, as a Grand Cru village, Bouzy makes some of the best champagne in the region under strict regulations – the grape bunches, for example, must be cut off the vine by hand, not machine, during the harvest. Hence, Rémy Galichet's 'neighbours' include one of the *vendangeoirs* (grape harvest buildings) for the famous G H Mumm champagne next door and Moët and Chandon opposite. Renowned champagne house Vranken has its *vendangeoir* in Bouzy too, while Laurent-Perrier is in neighbouring Tours-sur-Marne. Bollinger, the favourite of legendary film character James Bond and considered likewise among the British in general, is a matter of miles away in the village of Ay.

↑ Guests pick grapes at Rémy Galichet on a harvest Matinée du Vigneron visit (Caroline Mills)

Arriving back at the Galichet's HQ, the three sisters explain the process of champagne making as box loads of grapes are tipped into the *pressoir*. The resulting juice already seeps through for us to taste. Aurélie's two young sons, meanwhile, scrape up the squeezed-out skins below. Like so many champagne houses, this really is a family affair and, during the grape harvest, everyone lends a hand – it takes 60 people ten days to bring in the harvest for Rémy Galichet, while 120,000 are employed Champagne-wide for Le Vendange.

You're not expected to buy without tasting and Ingrid always keeps a chilled bottle in the fridge should you arrive in time for dinner. As a France Passion site, stopping overnight provides the perfect opportunity for a glass. And tasting on this occasion involved trying vintage and Grand Cru wines as a part of the Galichet's Matinée du Vigneron tours, laid on during the harvest for guests.

My next stop was **Épernay**, at the very heart of champagne production. Undeniably an industrial town from the outskirts (champagne is a massive industry, after all), Épernay's centre has all the glamour associated with the Belle Époque, when fizz became truly fashionable. The Avenue de Champagne is one of the finest addresses in the world – grand champagne houses on a grand avenue, each building creating a statement of wealth, indicated at every ornamental entrance by the champagne name in gold lettering. Castellane, Perrier-Jouet, Mercier, Moët and Chandon – they're all here and, each with their own tasting rooms and gardens. This is *the* place to be seen sipping fizz.

Many of the champagne houses provide tours of the cellars and I stopped by at Mercier, one of the best tour providers. Like so many of the champagne houses, their underground cellars (or *caves* as the French prefer to call them) go on for miles, toured using a little 'train'. A tasting always comes at the end of a tour but if you don't fancy the whole package, you can head straight to the Mercier shop, where you can look down upon the gargantuan carved champagne barrel, taken by the company to the 1889 World Fair.

I returned to **Bouzy** overnight, with a walk at dusk as fingers of late summer mist seeped through the vines from the hilltop. By morning I ventured across the River Marne to the **Côte des Blancs**, picking up the **Route Touristique**

SOUVENIR

If visiting during the grape harvest, many champagne houses lay on Matinée du Vigneron visits to the vineyards and *pressoir* (grape press). Details are available from the tourist board. Tours of the caves and champagne houses in Épernay are generally available all year round. Most producers sell direct and are open all year round, too. Other notable producers of Bouzy Rouge include Champagne Edmond Barnaut.

du **Champagne**. While I was quite happy creating my own tour, this 400km signposted route takes you through almost every champagne village, highlighting touristic features along the way. Every village along the *côte* has its own character – first Cuis on the hillside, then Cramant, Avize with the *vendangeoir* of Veuve Cliquot, the floral displays of Oger and the beguiling buildings of le Mesnil-sur-Oger, Vertus and Bergères-les-Vertus. And there, suddenly, the vines disappear. I climbed **Mont Aimé**, at the southern foot of the Côte des Blancs, for sweeping views across the Marne valley towards the Montagne de Reims and, west, towards Paris.

Leaving the vines behind, I ventured south across the vast agricultural plain of the **Champagne Seche** – huge fields, giant wind turbines and the occasional farming village like Euvy, Salon and the attractive Arcis-sur-Aube. It's easy touring – I passed one car in 50km.

Skirting the town of **Troyes** (page 141), I climbed into the **Forêt Domaniale de Rumilly** with vast, leafy beech woods that clear the mind of all that you've seen so far. For leaving the forest is like walking through a wardrobe to a completely different landscape – small pastures, hills, cattle, orchards, stone

↑ Champagne Castellane, Épernay (Caroline Mills)

houses and farms notifying passers-by that their milk is used to make Chaource, the famous cheese that was offered at our Champenois breakfast table the previous day. The cheese's namesake town is the first of many undeniably pretty towns and villages within the Aube *département* in this southernmost area of the Champagne region.

I was heading for **Les Riceys**, three conjoined villages almost brushing the border with Burgundy that are arguably some of the prettiest villages you'll find anywhere in France. Far removed from the champagne heartlands around Épernay, the triplets sit along the Côte des Bar, Champagne's 'other' production area. But Les Riceys has an anomaly too. For, like Bouzy, it also produces a still wine, Rosé des Riceys, that's hard to find outside the area.

Indeed, Les Riceys is unique in France, it being the only village in the country to hold three AOC (Appellation d'Origine Contrôlée) classifications, granted to identify specific origins and, in theory, the quality of the wine. Bouzy is the only other village within the Champagne region to hold an AOC for its still wine, Bouzy Rouge.

You can purchase Rosé des Riceys direct from various producers within the villages, each locale a warren of narrow streets all focusing on the River Laignes, a tiny tributary of the Seine. It's difficult to decide which is the prettiest of the three, though Ricey Bas, with its elegant steepled church and sumptuous château beside the Laignes, perhaps trumps its neighbours.

↑ Les Riceys (FreeProd33/Shutterstock)

Dropping down to a very young and youthful River Seine, it's even harder to choose between the Champagne villages along the valley – Courteron, Gyé-, Neuville-sur-Seine and Buxeuil. Each one, with its cluster of stone cottages, is bewitching. Because of its France Passion site, I opted for **Neuville-sur-Seine**, where Pedro Péréa owns Champagne Fleurette.

Parked up in his garden amid the ducks and chickens, he showed me into his cellars where everything is done by hand, including turning – or riddling – the bottles, a process required during champagne production. Naturally, a tasting, of both the fresh grape juice pressed that morning and an aged champagne, followed.

Pedro owns 5ha (11 acres) of vines on the slopes above the village, which he works traditionally using shire horses, Fleurette and Iris. He's passionate about champagne and is keen to pass on his knowledge to visitors. Asked if there's any rivalry between the areas of champagne production, unsurprisingly he argued that the Côte des Bars produces the better champagne, with the top houses buying grapes from the area to blend with those from the Vallée de la Marne. Aside from those he uses to produce his own fizz, Pedro's grapes, he told me, are bought by G H Mumm.

If there is any rivalry between the two champagne areas, the Côte des Bar is arguably more attractive with its undulating, forested landscape and snug-feeling villages. It's also a lovely area to freshen up with a walk after a glass of bubbly – the Circuit des Cadoles links a dozen or so stone hovels, used by ancestral *vignerons* (vine workers) hundreds of years ago while tending the vines. Many are tucked into forests where vines once stood, high above the current vineyards. On your

↑ An ancient *cadole* (Bennekom/Shutterstock)

way back it's worth stopping off at **Nôtre-Dame-des-Vignes**, a tall statue who lovingly looks over the vines above Neuville-sur-Seine. The hilltop provides magnificent views of the Seine valley and beyond.

With that view a passing memory in my campervan mirrors, I returned to the Champagne area around Épernay, the vines reappearing at Jâlons along with a new panorama of both the Côte des Blancs and Montagne de Reims.

At **Hautvillers**, I paid homage to Dom Pérignon, the man who, according to the French tourist signs, invented champagne. Of course, that's not strictly true (the champagne- or traditional-method, upon which sparkling wines are created, was originally invented by an English man from the Cotswold town of Winchcombe). Nonetheless, the landscape of the region owes much to the famous monk, who significantly developed the process of making champagne and whose final resting place is at the abbey church in the very picturesque and popular village.

That evening, as I was tucked up in **Chamery** listening to the hum of a tractor amid the vines on the hillside above, and the rumble of trailers bringing home bunches of sweet grapes, the setting sun glowed through the leafy vineyards. The vines went quiet as the twinkling lights of nearby Reims sparkled like bubbles. It was a fitting end to a magical few days of visiting old friends and meeting new acquaintances – all thanks to the France Passion scheme. Not to mention tasting the occasional glass of bubbly.

ESSENTIALS

GETTING THERE & AROUND From Reims (Junction 23); then the D951 towards Épernay and D9 to Bouzy. Motorhomes will have no problems with any of the roads within the area though it can be narrow through some streets within Les Riceys; simply approach with care. **Parking** is easy everywhere – for Épernay, campervans can park roadside on the eastern end of the Avenue de Champagne, approached directly from the D3, while there is an *aire* on Rue Dom Pérignon, accessed off the D951 from Pierry, which is better for larger motorhomes.

ACCOMMODATION I stayed on **France Passion sites** in Bouzy (Montagne de Reims), at Rémy Galichet Champagne, and in Neuville-sur-Seine (Côte de Bars), at Champagne Fleurette. I also stayed at an *aire* in Chamery, southwest of Reims. **Campsites**: Camping Municipal, Épernay; Les Terres Rouges, Clérey (16km southeast of Troyes).

FIND OUT MORE

Champagne Tourist Board ✍ tourisme-en-champagne.com
Épernay ✍ ot-epernay.fr

Hautvillers ✍ tourisme-hautvillers.com
Rémy Galichet Bouzy ✍ champagne-remy-galichet.fr

10 FREE FRANCE

THERE'S MORE TO CHAMPAGNE THAN FIZZ

WHERE	Champagne (Grand Est: Aube, Marne & Haute-Marne)
DISTANCE/TIME	135 miles (218km)/6 days
START/FINISH	Les Riceys/Bailly-le-Franc

I t seems that having an airport named after you means you've made it on the world's stage as a leader. New York has John F Kennedy Airport, New Delhi has Indira Gandhi International. David Cameron Airport or Ed Miliband International don't have quite the same ring, but Charles de Gaulle? Well, it's one of the most famous airports in Europe.

President de Gaulle cropped up in my history lessons in school days gone by, so I was anxious to refresh my memory as to why it was that France named its number one airport in such a fashion. Besides, Monsieur President's favourite bolt-hole from glitzy state occasions in Paris' Elysée Palace was the golden fields of Champagne country, so who was I to argue where to discover more about the man?

And, what better way to begin than by arriving around *apéritif* time at one of our favourite France Passion sites in the small and beautiful village of **Les Riceys** (page 85), on the Côte des Bar? Jean-Jacques Lamoureux makes a cracking bottle of rosé – appropriately named Rosé des Riceys – in addition to Champagne. Rosé des Riceys is a rare treat, so grab a bottle when you can.

Across the River Seine from Les Riceys is the small village of **Essoyes**. It was once home to Pierre Auguste Renoir (his family lived here until 2012), one of France's greatest painters not least for helping to create the French Impressionist movement. I tend to think of Renoir in the light of glamorous exhibitions and

↑ The cross of Lorraine at Colombey-les-Deux-Églises (David South/Alamy.com)

giant multi-million-dollar paintings that hang in opulent art galleries, with each brush stroke so famous it's undoubtedly 'a Renoir'. Rarely is he thought of at home in a little-known village in the middle of the Champagne countryside, passionately in love with a voluptuously curvy local girl. Aline Victorine Charigot was born in Essoyes; she became Renoir's model and they later married.

Renoir's little art studio at the bottom of his garden, and just a few paces from his final resting place in the village graveyard, is so much the antithesis of grand art galleries. Blink and you'd barely notice it at all – it's not advertised in the way a grand exhibition is either – merely a simple wooden-floored, sunlit room with a few personal belongings gathered together by the family. It's unpretentious, and all the better for it.

In the Place de la Mairie is a relatively new cultural centre with a permanent exhibition about the life of Renoir and his family; tickets to his studio, house and garden are obtained from here. A collection of walks in the local area, with places associated with Renoir and his paintings also leave from here.

From Essoyes, our tour took us slowly east across the *département* of the Aube and into the Haute-Marne, through pretty forests and dormant villages, on to the town of **Chaumont**, on the confluence of the rivers Marne and Suize. From the outskirts, it appears an unremarkable town, but persevere. There's a pretty hilltop old town, together with the excellent National Centre for Graphic Art (Le Signe). Chaumont's finest artwork, though, is its viaduct. At 600m long, with 50 double arches, it is an extraordinary sight.

↑ Essoyes, where artist Pierre Auguste Renoir lived (Novinit/Shutterstock)

At Chaumont we turned northwest to the village of **Colombey-les-Deux-Églises**. Thousands of French pilgrims are attracted to the village every year to visit the home of former President Charles de Gaulle. Avoiding politics, I couldn't imagine the British getting quite so blurry-eyed over leaders from the recent past (with the possible exception of Sir Winston Churchill, who had strong connections with Monsieur CDG) so I was keen to see what made this man special, and why he loved the area so much.

Staying overnight in the village, the morning heralded a fog that had laid its blanket so thick upon the ground we could barely see the Champagne countryside to which de Gaulle became so attached. However, even with a few outlines of field shapes and silhouette-like trees, I could appreciate why the man and his family enjoyed the serenity that the rolling landscape brought him, away from the pomp and pageantry of palatial Paris.

De Gaulle's home – La Boisserie (once a brewery, hence its name) – stands towards the edge of the village, set in its own leafy grounds with views of the open fields that gave the General his literary inspiration. In the fog, we saw little of it, the trio of Tricolores at the entrance appearing intensely coloured with an otherwise white and drizzly background.

The house visit was somewhat disappointing – three downstairs reception rooms filled with what could be described as knick-knacks (gifts from world leaders) from the President's travels and the 2½ha of grounds very much fenced off. But the sight of the pretty, yet very ordinary, house placed the man; being able to see how a general and president of such standing could be more comfortable in these rural surroundings helped to put his life into perspective when we came to visit, latterly, the excellent Mémorial Charles de Gaulle exhibition, 900m from his country house.

The year 2020 marked 130 years since de Gaulle's birth and 50 years since his death (he and his wife are buried in the village graveyard). Perhaps more importantly 2020 marked 90 years since the exiled General made his call to arms to the French nation. It's made all the more compelling for British citizens visiting the exhibition as he made this call, which began the whole movement of the French Resistance, on BBC Radio from London when he was given 'shelter' by Churchill.

Of course, as I discovered from the memorial exhibition (which is in English as well as French and has plenty of interactive material to stimulate children), he was not always revered by the French people, once stripped of his military titles and sentenced to death for treason by the politically motivated Vichy government (the 1970s film *The Day of the Jackal* was based upon real-life assassination attempts on de Gaulle) until the Resistance gained momentum. Now, in honour of the free France that he helped to bring about (from which came the return of the French emblem, *Liberté, Égalité, Fraternité* and the national anthem, the Marseillaise after they were banned by the Vichy government), a giant cross of Lorraine – the symbol of the French Resistance – stands on the hill above his home.

There is no doubt that this cross is imposing, its giant bulk – that had appeared large on the horizon from almost 50km away the day before – now loomed even larger out of the suffocating fog. However, having discovered who Charles de Gaulle was and what he stands for to the French people, this was no longer just a cross on the horizon, its vast wingspan spread over the countryside, but a symbol that means something of immense significance. We drove away knowing so much more about why the French people hold such passion for this man and their country.

With our history lesson over, it was playtime, taking in the sights of the giant **Lac du Der-Chantecoq**, the largest manmade lake in Europe. Big it is, sinking two villages in its making as a flood defence for Paris. But, with the exception of a large dam-like levee, it is naturalised within the environment.

There are watersports a-plenty on the lake, mainly based at the gateway village of **Giffaumont-Champaubert**, with strolls and cycle rides along the lakeside path.

ESSENTIALS

GETTING THERE & AROUND Follow the D70 from Les Riceys to Essoyes. You can take any number of routes through the forest to Chaumont; we followed the River Ource on the D13, then D65 to Chaumont and D619 to Colombey-les-Deux-Églises. The D619 continues to Bar-sur-Aube (also worth a stop) and then the D384/D12 to Giffaumont-Champaubert.

We found no problem finding free **parking** anywhere. There is no official parking near Renoir's studio/grave in Essoyes, though the roads are quiet enough to park nearby. There's free parking at the Mémorial Charles de Gaulle, but better for motorhomes is the *aire* in the Rue du General de Gaulle – follow directions to La Boisserie.

ACCOMMODATION We stayed on **France Passion** sites at: Champagne Lamoureux, Les Riceys; Champagne Christian Peligri, Colombey-les-Deux-Eglises; Champagne Brisson Jonchère, Bar-sur-Aube, and *aires* at Chaumont and Giffaumont-Champaubert.

Other *aires* in the area include Les Riceys, Colombey-les-Deux-Églises, Essoyes, Bar-sur-Aube, Sainte-Marie-du-Lac-Nuisement.

Campsites: Camping Municipal, Chaumont; La Plage, Giffaumont-Champaubert; Le Clos du Vieux Moulin, Châtillon-sur-Broué; Camping les Rives du Lac, Geraudot (for Lac d'Orient). There are many campsites around the Lac du Der and Les Grands Lacs, but nothing within the Côte des Bar.

There's a good little museum, too, the Village Musée du Der – on the north side in the village of **Sainte-Marie-du-Lac-Nuisement** – that has preserved the traditional way of life from the area before the lake was built. It includes some of the old, relocated buildings that would otherwise have been lost beneath countless cubic metres of water.

Close by is the **Route des Églises à pans de bois** (Route of timber-framed churches), which takes you through idyllic villages and countryside in search of some rustically appealing 16th-century churches. A vaguely circular route, it officially begins in **Montier-en-Der** (also known as La Porte du Der), 7km south of the lake. We deemed the churches in the villages of **Outines**, **Châtillon-sur-Broué** and **Bailly-le-Franc** the most beautiful and the most notable to look at.

We've toured the length and breadth of France over many years and I felt that I knew what makes the country tick. Having 'met' Charles de Gaulle in an area of the country that he called home, I feel I know it just that little bit better. And the next time I walk down the Rue Charles de Gaulle (whichever street of hundreds in the country named after him), or pass by the famous airport, I'll understand.

FIND OUT MORE

Aube Tourist Board ☌ aube-champagne.com

Charles de Gaulle Memorial
☌ memorial-charlesdegaulle.fr

Du côté des Renoir ☌ Renoir-essoyes.fr

Haute-Marne Tourism ☌ tourisme-hautemarne.com

Lac du Der ☌ lacduder.com

Marne Tourist Board ☌ tourisme-en-champagne.com

Village Musée du Der
☌ villagemuseeduder.com

TOP TIP: EXTEND YOUR TRIP
The Lac du Der is one of many large lakes in Champagne. To extend this tour, and create a circular route, continue south to the **Parc Naturel Régional de la Forêt d'Orient**.

This protected area includes Les Grands Lacs – three large manmade lakes that also help to regulate the water flow of the Seine and Aube rivers. The Lac d'Orient and Lac du Temple, are also part of a national nature reserve; they are the quieter of the trio, reserved for sailing and rowing boats, canoeing, fishing and bathing. Lac Amance allows motorboats, jet skis and waterskiing from the *base de loisirs* at Port Dienville.

Brienne-le-Château, a small town to the north of the lakes, is a worthwhile entry point, with a delightful château and former military school; Napoleon Bonaparte is its most famous pupil. The Museum of Napoleon I is housed in the former school, with displays about school life and exhibitions on Napoleon's military campaigns.

11 FROM WATER TO WINE

AN ODYSSEY OF RIVERS, MOUNTAINS & VINEYARDS IN FRANCE'S FAR EAST

WHERE   Alsace (Grand Est: Meurthe-et-Moselle, Vosges, Haut-Rhin, Bas-Rhin)
DISTANCE/TIME   315 miles (507km)/4 days
START/FINISH   Toul/Rodern

Catering for our hungry family is like feeding the five thousand. Places where something as simple as devouring a couple of baguettes can hold off statements of starvation, for a few hours at least, are vital. A slow meander along one of France's most enticing rivers, the Moselle, and a gastronomic jamboree of biblical proportions in Alsace helped.

The Moselle River is perhaps best known for its passage through Germany coupled with its idyllic Weinstrasse (wine route) but, to place this 340-mile long river on a European scale, the Moselle breathes life on the western slopes of the Ballon d'Alsace, one of the highest peaks in the Vosges mountain range. It picks up pace to flow north through Épinal, Toul and Metz before flowing towards the Luxembourg border, dividing the sovereign state from Germany, and then snakes its way to Koblenz where it joins the Rhine.

We chose to take an up-river exploration of the lesser-known French section. The river is wide enough to carry serious-sized cargo from Neuves-Maisons, southwest of Nancy, and is therefore quite industrial on its route north to Luxembourg, so we joined the Moselle at the fortified town of **Toul**.

Our first sight of the river, shimmering in the sunlight between overgrown banks, created a rush of excitement, to be short-lived. A wrong turn meant that we

↑ The Vosges mountain range in Alsace (Alexander Sorokopud/Shutterstock)

crossed over it four times before we could get anywhere close to its watery channel. Our attempts were thwarted further by a road diversion at Pierre-la-Treiche so we could not, in fact, join the river until **Pont-St-Vincent**, a tumbledown town of unexciting character. It was here that we wished we'd brought bikes with us; signs indicating a riverside bike route would have enabled better river sightings.

Catching mere glimpses of the Moselle was to become the story of our encounter with it. Frustratingly, we could see the river every so often, usually when we crossed over, but we just couldn't get close enough. Indeed, at first we saw more of the Canal de l'Est, which runs parallel with the Moselle, than we did the river.

Undeterred, we pressed our eyes to the windows while the river gave us occasional flirting glances until we came across one of its prettiest sections, at **Velle-sur-Moselle**. To reach this tiniest of communes, the river is crossed by a grey-painted, steel-riveted trellis bridge, industrial in nature yet curiously appealing. We found a grassy riverside spot on the left bank just below the bridge where the children could admire the water's flow but, with gushing currents evident, not paddle. However, there was the opportunity for a pleasant riverside walk.

While the Moselle is extremely pretty – when you can see it! – there's no denying that the route along the river we took from Toul to Épinal doesn't have the architectural beauty of the Loire Valley or other notable rivers. Though the Moselle is too narrow for much industrial traffic here, sightings of gravel pits and signs of an area lacking in prosperity detract from the scenery.

Nonetheless we came across some beguiling treasures en route, such as **Neuviller-sur-Moselle**. It's a ribbon village with run-down yet rustic charms that period design magazines would award prizes for. Peeling paint and wooden shutters just about clinging on to their hinges were fashioned against crumbling render mottled with age. Ancient advertisements, faded over time, for out-of-fashion drinks adorned the walls.

At **Bayon**, we found the Moselle again, backdropped by the unusual spire of the town church and beside a series of lakes where we could stop and take in the river's aspects. The town square sports an extraordinarily Gallic round-turreted neo-Renaissance château of graceful proportions, too. At **Bainville-aux-Miroirs**, cow-filled water meadows offered a more rural perspective of the river, with the occasional place available for big toe dipping as the water gradually decreases in width and depth, moving closer to its source.

Crossing into the *département* of the Vosges, the landscape became instantly more appealing. Small and verdant mountain-foot hummocks sprout from the river valley and there are engaging villages such as **Socourt**, which provided opportunities to climb and view the Moselle, and its ribbon of lakes, from a distance. Our final meeting with the river came at the charismatic town of **Châtel-sur-Moselle**, whose flower-decked bridge prettifies the flowing waters beneath and a riverside *aire* provides a suitably picturesque place to stop.

The tree-covered Vosges mountain range, home to the Moselle's source, was drawing near and looked too inviting to ignore. Moving away from the river valley, we began the gradual ascent, east of Épinal, towards Gérardmer. Low-lying grazed hillsides made way for deep and dark pine forests, creased by occasional river valleys.

A short detour down a steep and narrow (but accessible) road took us to the foot of the **Grande Cascade de Tendon**, a 72m waterfall that crashes over rocks and boulders deep among the trees. Therapeutic and captivating, it's a great place for foot-sure children to play and there are plenty of paths among the trees for woodland walks. We were all too keen to join the guests sunning themselves on the terrace of a small *auberge* overlooking the waterfall but time was pressing on and we needed to find a place to stay.

The further east we travelled the less populated and the more remote the landscape became. Just as you're lulled into a sense of isolation suddenly, from nowhere, appears the **Lac de Gérardmer**, overflowing with rowing boats, pedalos and anything else with entertainment value that floats.

At the eastern end of this mountain lake, surrounded by hills on all sides, is **Gérardmer**. The town, popular both as a summer lakeside retreat and as a winter ski resort, buzzes with activity, and is filled with hotels, restaurants and cafés. Lively as it was, we were looking for a quieter place to stay – and we found it, high

SOUVENIR

Alsace is best known for its wines; it grows more grape varieties than any other region in France so if you go for a wine tasting, don't be surprised to find numerous bottles to try. Most of the wines produced in Alsace are white – Sylvaner and Pinot Blanc are the driest, Riesling and Gewurtztraminer slightly sweeter. Muscat is the sweetest, and best served with cold desserts. Alsace also grows the Tokay Pinot Gris grape, which produces a wine with its own characteristics that's different to all the others. Less common, though equally as good as the whites is the Alsace Pinot Noir, a light red wine that's served chilled. Grand Cru status is considered the best, while if you come across Edelswicker, it is a blend made from the poorer quality grapes. Many *viticulteurs* also produce a Crémant d'Alsace, a sparkling white wine made using the *méthode traditionelle*.

Mirabelle plums are a speciality of Alsace. There are many orchards both in Alsace and throughout the Vosges that grow these little fruits and you will often see them sold from people's gardens. Quetsches, a type of larger, purple plum, is specifically from Alsace.

The Kougelhopf is an Alsatian speciality that's baked in a ring. It's like a brioche with raisins that can be eaten at breakfast or used as a basis for tastings. It can be made with or without added butter or fat.

The Alsace Wine Route (Pawel Kazmierczak/Shutterstock)

in the hills, at the ski station above town. We believe we chose well. Far quieter than the boisterous town, our *aire* had restful views of the surrounding hills and overlooked the lake.

A late evening walk at dusk took us across the ski slope and into the woods for beautiful views over the town and a desire to get up early for a longer walk to explore further. The higher we climbed, the greater the wildflowers became, joined by soft mosses, wet ferns and miniature, self-seeded Christmas trees. We had the hills to ourselves, with numerous waymarked trails through the woods allowing any number of walks. It was hard to imagine how bustling the place must be during the ski season but it had an unpretentious feel, without the airs and graces put on by top alpine resorts.

We toured ever deeper into the Vosges hills by road, first past the dark, glassy and mysterious **Lac de Longemer**, much quieter than the lake at Gérardmer, before climbing into the **Réserve Naturelle du Massif du Ventron**, which forms part of the Parc Naturel Régional des Ballons des Vosges.

For those anticipating soaring mountains of jagged rock, the Vosges may disappoint. Renowned for their dense lining of trees (and immaculate autumnal colours), there are few sky-high viewpoints, with each hairpin bend barely visible from the next through the woods. It's an entirely different beauty from mountain landscapes like the Alps or Pyrenees.

↑ Lac de Longemer (Caroline Mills)

Passing through the villages of Wildenstein, Kruth and Oderen, brightly coloured houses of the Alsatian style began to creep in, made all the more vivid by the silhouette-like backdrop of the surrounding hills. The hairpins had stopped, the valley widened and, crossing the Vosges quicker than we had imagined, we realised what a narrow ridge the mountains are.

Joining the main road to Thann, we were heading towards the narrow strip of Alsace between the Vosges and the German border. It's an area we've been to several times before but never seem to tire of. Hardly surprising given the scenery: extraordinarily pretty villages of half-timbered houses bejewelled with window boxes of vibrant geraniums; the ridge of Vosges mountains creating a panoramic scene behind, castellated with numerous ruins of medieval fortifications. Below is a sea of vines, through which runs the Route des vins d'Alsace.

In the valley of the Rhine, with the Vosges mountains to the west and the river to the east, the region's wine route links Thann in the south with the town of Marlenheim, 170km to the north. Sozzled at the very thought of following a wine route that far in one trip, we joined the route at **Gueberschwihr**, a delightful and restful village of powder-pink houses, archways and shuttered windows, spreading out from a cobbled square. Lunch that day could not have been more heavenly – simple bread and cheese with local fruit, eaten among the vines with views of the hills from whence we'd come.

↑ Brightly coloured houses and vibrant floral window boxes, typical of Alsace, in Gueberschwihr (Caroline Mills)

Our journey following the route took us north towards the region's main town, **Colmar**, through the tiny village of **Obermorschwihr**, where I would recommend the wine of Laurent Bannwarth.

It being the season for tiny, golden yellow Mirabelle plums, we stopped at **La Pommeraie**, a self-pick fruit farm on the D10 between Niedermorschwihr and Sigolsheim. There's plenty of ready picked fruit for sale in the farm shop, but on a day of sun-drenching heat, we couldn't resist heading for the orchards, armed with a bucket to fill with these irresistibly sweet fruits that were dripping from the trees. The shop sells other seasonal fruits throughout the year, particularly apples. With varieties not seen in the UK, and samples on offer to try in the shop, the children were more than happy to spend some time there. It's possible to cycle or walk through the orchards, too, for an alternative view of Alsace.

It's hard to pick one Alsatian village out as being prettier than another but **Riquewihr** is the one that the tourist trade has latched on to. It is preposterously

↑ The orchards at La Pommeraie (Caroline Mills)

pretty with cobbled streets of colourful medieval houses encased by fortified walls and surrounded by hillsides of leafy vines. The main street is lined with restaurants and cafés (and a fair amount of tourist tat, too). It was here that we opted to stay, after a wine tasting, at a France Passion site, and dining at one of our favourite restaurants in the area, Restaurant au Dolder, to devour delicious *tarte flambée*. It's a regional speciality that can best be described as a very thin and crisp pizza topped with crème fraîche, onions and lardons.

Continuing along the wine route north, we pottered from one village to the next, each one dotted about as if it has been purposefully dropped into the landscape, and each one littered with *viticulteurs* ready to offer numerous wines to taste. Driving, we opted for the safer option of visiting **Bergheim**, another fortified village with considerably quieter streets than its close neighbour, Riquewihr. Equally charming, it has the odd restaurant but has limited tourist shops, so it tends to be delightfully crowd-free.

Perched on the edge of the hillside above us, overnighting in **Rodern**, we could see the ancient remnants of Château du Haut-Koenigsbourg, defending the Vosges mountains from attack. To the east, in the distance, were Germany's Black Mountains, like lurking shadows through the haze. Time and these hills were beckoning; by mid-morning, Alsace would be but a memory.

ESSENTIALS

GETTING THERE & AROUND
Toul is easily accessible via the N4 from the west, A31 from the north/south. The Vosges mountains are moderate rather than steep and we found all the roads crossing and exploring the area to be perfectly accessible. However, if you are concerned about travelling on mountain roads you can reach Alsace using the N159 tunnel between Saint-Dié-des-Vosges and Sainte-Marie-aux-Mines. While we didn't visit Château du Haut-Koenigsbourg on this occasion, the road is accessible to'vans. As for **parking:** Alsace is well adapted to motorhomes, with plenty of dedicated parking throughout the region.

ACCOMMODATION
We used *aires* at Gérardmer Station du Ski (very quiet and scenic, with mountain views) and **France Passion** sites at Riquewihr (idyllic site at Famille Hueber) and Rodern (Kress-Bleger and Fils). **Campsites:** Camping Les Sapins, Gérardmer; Camping de Riquewihr, Riquewihr; Camping Municipal, Ribeauvillé; Camping Les Trois Châteaux, Eguisheim.

FIND OUT MORE
Alsace Tourist Board ⊘ visit.alsace   **Vosges Tourist Board** ⊘ tourisme-vosges.fr
Alsace Wine Route ⊘ wineroute.alsace

12 GARDENS GALOIRE

A GREEN-FINGERED TOUR OF THE LOIRE'S BEST GARDENS IN THE VALLEY OF THE KINGS

WHERE	Loire Valley (Pays de la Loire/ Centre-Val de Loire: Sarthe, Loir-et-Cher, Maine-et-Loire, Indre-et-Loire, Loiret)
DISTANCE/TIME	426 miles (686 km)/12 days
START/FINISH	Saint-Biez-en-Belin/Gien

Have you ever wondered how Leonardo da Vinci's *Mona Lisa* comes to hang in Paris' Louvre museum? Well, no, it wasn't through a sale at some prestigious global auction house, or even a dusty attic find. Some 500 years ago, Leonardo came to live in France at the invitation of the French king, François I, who had a passion for Italian art. Amboise, a royal town spanning the River Loire, was to be Leonardo's home. As 'first painter' to François, the artist was offered a residence close to the royal château, the Manoir du Cloux now known as the Château du Clos Lucé. There Leonardo stored three paintings that he had brought with him from Italy: *The Virgin and Child with St Anne; St John the Baptist* and the mysterious *Mona Lisa*. All three masterpieces now hang in the Louvre.

Da Vinci, whose talents as an engineer were put to good use during his three years living beside the Loire (he reputedly designed the helix staircase in the Château de Chambord), is just one of the many people that have helped to shape the Loire Valley over the centuries. The valley's incredible concentration of feudal castles, grand palaces and pleasure houses has not sprung up alongside the river naturally, though it would sometimes appear that way such is the affinity of the architecture with the landscape.

Like any family home, the Loire's châteaux are about people. Royal kings, queens, counts, dukes – and a 15th-century teenage heroine that had a particular dislike of the English – have played a part in creating a landscape that is today one of the largest UNESCO World Heritage Sites. At 280km long (between the towns of Sully-sur-Loire and Chalonnes-sur-Loire) and 800km^2, the heritage site covers a significant chunk of the Loire Valley, incorporating 164 towns and villages and almost as many châteaux.

Little wonder then that the valley, once the chosen pleasure grounds of Renaissance royalty, has become the landscape of choice for tourists who venture from one château to another to gain a glimpse of art treasures, sumptuous interior decoration and a classic river view of regal towns like Amboise or Blois, or indeed, one of the Loire's scenic tributaries – including the Cher, Indre, Vienne, Sarthe, Loir (via the Sarthe) and Loiret.

The Loire Valley is not a place to be hurried. Couple culture cramming with a quiet sojourn beneath the mistletoe-drenched poplar trees on the banks of the peaceful Indre, a gentle drift downstream on one of the Loire's traditional flat-bottomed boats or a pause at the gate of a local fruit grower to purchase pungently ripe peaches.

← Château du Rivau (Superstock)

Châteaux, yes, there are many. Chambord, Chenonceau, Chinon – all familiar names on the visitor's list of this architecturally rich landscape. While I love a bit of interior design, royally opulent or not, family interests lie outdoors. And with the cries from my son of, 'Not another château!', a garden tour was a palatable option. After all, to a young boy, when you've seen one royal bed, you've seen them all!

So we picked our route, selected lots of gardens with varying characteristics and spent a short-fortnight slowly meandering from one patch to the next. To say it was a success would be understating; by the end of the trip, I had three budding garden designers feverishly re-landscaping the Loire Valley on the motorhome's dinette table with all they had seen.

Our tour begins 23km south of Le Mans, at the **Jardin d'Atmosphère Petit Bordeaux** in **Saint-Biez-en-Belin**. Created in 1987 in a clearing of deciduous woodland, the English-style garden has won several awards and is considered to be a Jardin Remarquable, a government-attributed symbol of excellence. Secret paths, garden rooms made from hornbeam and beech hedges that are low enough to peer over and entice the visitor on, water features and borders bursting with bamboos, hydrangeas and hostas all mingle under the canopy of an arboretum. It's extremely peaceful.

We continue to the nearby town of **La Flèche** with its 300-year-old military academy in the town centre. Visitors are only allowed into the formal gardens where immaculately mown squares of grass are bordered by brightly coloured

↑ Jardin d'Atmosphère Petit Bordeaux (Caroline Mills)

annuals. Symmetrical paths match the military style but we're more excited by the march of the new recruits and the serenity of the River Loir on the other side of the road than the sparseness of the garden and it doesn't make it on to our 'return to' list. Our next garden, however, is an old favourite that we return to time and again.

As grand as the Loire is, sometimes the river feels too large and unwieldy. By contrast, its tributaries and affluents, offer a more manageable, pastoral simplicity, none more so than the Loir. We follow the river from La Flèche to where it meets the Sarthe before crossing the pair on our way to the **Château du Plessis-Bourré** near Cheffes. The château is everything one imagines a Loire Vallcy castle to be, made from creamy stone with round turrets at each of the four corners topped by a 'pointy hat'. What's more, the castle is handsomely moated. There are no gardens here per se, it's merely parkland. But the land is vast, providing youngsters the opportunity to let off steam without disturbing other visitors. And picnics are permitted in July and August.

We head south, crossing the Loire for the first time at Angers, to **Brissac Loire Aubance** where we visit the **Château de Brissac**. Here, like Plessis-Bourré, it's not

↑ River and lakeside walks in parkland at the Château de Brissac (Oleg Bakhirev/Shutterstock)

so much about the gardens, but a stomp around the mature parkland, which offers excellent views of the château (reputedly the tallest in France) and plenty of scenic river- and lakeside walks. Our evening overlooking the vines around Brissac is made all the more notable for the flurry of hot air balloons that ascend from the grounds of the château, apparently a regular sight.

The sun has risen long before us by the time we make our way to **Doué-en-Anjou**, which we find to be a good thing for the heat has allowed the perfume of the town to already pervade the air. As we approach, we find ourselves among stripes of colour, field after field of prickly rows.

The town of Doué, southwest of Saumur, is famous for its rose cultivation; the surrounding fields grow more than seven million rose bushes, representing more than 45% of the national production. There are also several rose gardens. One of the largest is **Chemins de La Rose**, a landscaped garden with several thousand rose bushes, grouped by variety, and interspersed with companion plants and roaming peacocks. In town, **Roseraie Foullon**, a formal rose garden, is the town's public park. More than 250, often heavily scented, varieties are displayed here, many of them from historic French rose breeders. I draw near to 'Belle de Lourdes', a chiffon pink flower that turns translucent as the sun warms the petals. For such delicate beauty, its fragrance is extreme and I find myself giddy with its scent.

We gain our first full glimpse of the Loire from the ramparts of the **Château de Saumur**; it's a prodigious view that undoubtedly marks the river as one of the grandest in Europe. Our route follows the left bank east to **Montsoreau** and **Candes-Saint-Martin**, two '*plus beaux*' villages that sit at the confluence with the

↑ Doué-en-Anjou is the centre of rose cultivation in France (Superstock)

Vienne. Like Saumur, the buildings here are made of blocks of Tufa stone, a pale white limestone that glows and changes tint with the cycle of the sun.

We follow the Vienne to the **Château du Rivau** at **Le Coudray**, southeast of Chinon.

Here, beside the fairytale château, are 14 imaginative gardens dotted with contemporary art depicting children's stories. We deem the Gargantuan Potager to be the best of the collection, encircled by the courtyard walls though, despite the gardens being aimed at families in particular, it's not deemed a favourite with the children; it's also the most expensive of the gardens we visit on our trip.

Passing the **Château de Chinon** as we backtrack across the Vienne and head north, we stop overnight in **Rigny-Ussé** beside the River Indre, one of the smaller tributaries, and arguably one of the prettiest, of the Loire. **Château d'Ussé**, which became the inspiration for Charles Perrault's fairytale *Sleeping Beauty,* offers terraced formal gardens that were created by France's most prestigious garden designer, André le Nôtre (see page 72). The terraces are little sun traps that slope down to the peaceful River Indre and it's, perhaps, the setting rather than the garden that is particularly alluring. It's our least preferred garden but it's, conveniently, a handsome short walk through the village from Camping de la Blardière where we sit in the evening sun and listen to the therapeutic shivering of the lean and lofty poplar trees that line the Indre.

↑ Château d'Ussé (Kate_gps/Shutterstock)

We're up early to arrive before the coachloads at nearby **Château de Villandry**, one of the most famous of all gardens. Everything is on a grand scale and the sheer size inspires the children more than any other garden we visit: the clipped box hedges (all 52km of them) of the ornamental garden, the length of the herb garden, the quantity of vegetables (approximately 115,000 plants) in the world's largest kitchen garden. We find it's worth making the effort to climb through the woods to the New Belvedere for views across the garden and, latterly, we determine that Villandry offers the best value for money.

Just like the first garden that we visited, the **Château de Valmer** at **Chançay**, northeast of Tours, is also considered a Jardin Remarquable. It's the formally designed *potager* that is of most significance, where the owner identified and planted thousands of forgotten seeds, vegetables and fruits from yesteryear, grown for flavour rather than commercial purposes. Many are old varieties from the Loire region, making the garden an important historical record. The formal layout is exceptional though we also particularly liked the huge wisteria that hangs over the castle moat that we deem to be have been growing at least a century.

If old regional varieties of fruit and veg are the passion at Valmer, it's tomatoes that are what might be called an obsession at the **Château de la Bourdaisière**, on

↑ Château de Villandry (Gaspar Janos/Shutterstock)

the other side of the Loire and due south of the Chateau de Valmer. The gardens at Bourdaisière, near **Montlouis-sur-Loire**, display more than 700 varieties of the fruit in many guises: red, yellow, green and black; stripy or plain; long, thin, miniature, fat or bizarrely shaped. Unsurprisingly, the garden holds the National Collection, imaginatively planted with other vegetables, herbs and flowers while a tomato festival is held every September.

The talk is of growing tomatoes as we move east, following the River Cher, to one of the Loire's 'biggies', the **Château de Chenonceau**. Thank goodness we're not visiting the royal bedrooms for I'd have some explaining to do; either side of the château, which ceremoniously spans the River Cher, are the formal gardens of Diane de Poitiers and Catherine de Medici, mistress and wife of King Henri II respectively; they each had a patch!

Box balls, swirly patterns in the grass and long pathways along which to swish a flouncy skirt above a French Farthingale are *de rigeur*, though our favourite is the more rustic Potager des Fleurs, the farm kitchen garden where cut flowers for displays within the château and some of the vegetables for the restaurants are grown. With giant blocks of colours, it's an impressive and practical garden, where we're able to watch the florists at work creating bouquets.

Our route takes us northeast to **Chaumont-sur-Loire** where there are prime views of the Loire from the château's parkland high above the river. Held in the grounds, the annual Festival International des Jardins (International Garden Festival) takes on a different, usually thought-provoking, theme each year. Famous gardeners, communities, schoolchildren and horticulture students are involved in designing the many gardens, all based on the chosen annual theme. As we wander from space to space, we find plenty to contemplate, even challenge and reason the perception of what a garden is.

Through the royal town of **Blois**, we move away from the Loire's riverbank and, instead, follow the River Cosson into the **Forêt Domaniale de Boulogne** to visit the **Château de Chambord**. This is the other commercial 'biggie' of the Loire Valley and it's the one château the children are really keen to look in – something to do with it having no bedrooms! Inside, it's Leonardo da Vinci's helix staircase that amuses and puzzles most, before we venture out into Chambord's domain of 5,400ha. Surrounded by a 32km-long wall, it is the largest enclosed forest in Europe and we walk for the remainder of the day on some of the 23km of paths, enjoying the oak woods and wildlife in the nature reserve. A shorter walk is a 4km circuit around Chambord's canal and formal French gardens; bike hire is also available to cycle within the grounds.

We're gradually making our way upstream but the Loire still seems imposingly wide when we cross it again to reach the **Château de Talcy**, on the north side of the river from Chambord. With sweeping views over the Beauce Plain, between Blois

and Orléans, the Talcy estate features a large farm complex that was renowned for its fruit production in the 18th century. Restoration of the garden and orchards began 25 years ago to create a conservation collection and there are now hundreds of heritage varieties of apples, pears and plums. Fruit is ripening well on the neat rows of espaliered, cordoned and fanned trees so we eye up the ones we think look particularly tasty; with names of apples like Rouge de Noël (Christmas Red), Royale d'Angleterre (Royal England) and Reine des Reinettes (Queen of Queens), we come to the conclusion we're unlikely to ever find them on British supermarket shelves.

The Loire is becoming a familiar sight when we cross it for the second time in the day at **Beaugency**. The town has a fabulous *aire* on the banks of the river that determines a scenic stop for lunch before we make our way to our next garden, the **Parc Floral de la Source** on the outskirts of Orléans. A welcome retreat from the city centre, the landscaped park houses a rose garden around a 'mirror pool', shady woodland walks and a garden surrounding the source of the Loiret, the Loire's shortest tributary. There are stunning displays of irises in spring though it's the collection of vibrant dahlias, some the size of dinner plates, that take our summer gaze. We also come across a tropical butterfly house and aviary, in true public park style.

We move away from the river for a while when we head northeast of Orléans, to the **Château de Chamerolles** at **Chilleurs-aux-Bois**. Here, a restored Renaissance garden has been developed based upon old garden plans with six parterres bordered by pergolas covered with hops, vines and roses. The parterres are made up with a small maze, knot garden, vegetable gardens, rose garden and exotic plant plot. For visitors interested in garden history, there's plenty to see but it's not given top spot by the children, who preferred the little lakeside walk that gives good views of the château, which houses a perfume museum.

For our final 'garden' we choose to visit something completely different, the **L'Arboretum National des Barres** at **Nogent-sur-Vernisson** northeast of Gien.

France's National Arboretum is home to one of the most important collections in the world with 9,200 trees and 2,600 species. It's so large we are unable to cover it all but we enjoy the themed trails to visit geographic, systematic and ornamental collections, and there's lots of exploration and quizzes for children. With carpets of cyclamen in late summer, it's a pretty place to while away a few hours.

On our final evening, we come to terms with the enormity of the Loire when, from our campsite, we can sit right beside it. Dusk makes the river's silty sandbanks and the town of **Gien** glow rose pink in the fading light. We count the arches on the town's graceful bridge that crosses the Loire. There are twelve.

← **Top** Espaliered fruit trees at Château de Talcy **Below** Château de Chamerolles (both Caroline Mills)

ESSENTIALS

GETTING THERE & AROUND We began our tour at Jardin d'Atmosphère du Petit Bordeaux in Saint-Biez-en-Belin, on the D32 south of Le Mans, 8km from J25 of A28. I took D32/D323 to La Flèche and from there D323/D74/D768 to Feneu. Brissac-Loire-Aubance is on D748 southeast of Angers. From Angers follow D748/D84 to Doué and D960 to Saumur. Thereafter the route runs east along the Loire, then south on D749 to Château le Rivau, backtracking north through Chinon to the banks of the Indre and continuing east on D7. Château de Valmer is northeast of Tours, off D46. From there backtrack to cross the Loire and take D140 to Bourdaisière, and D40 to Chenonceaux, east of Tours. At Montrichard-Val-de-Cher, the route turns north to Chaumont-sur-Loire. Stay on the left bank (heading east) for the best views approaching Blois. From Blois/Vineuil, Chambord is on the D33, then cross the Loire to Mer and take D15 for Talcy. Head north cross-country to D917 and then west to Beaugency and follow the D951/D14 for Parc Floral de la Source, south of Orléans. Chamerolles is on D109, off D2152 northeast of Orléans. Head east cross-country to D44 south to Lorris/Montereau, then D41 to L'Arboretum des Barres, from where D2007 and D940 take you to Gien. There's easy access to and from all the gardens. There's ample **parking** suitable for motorhomes at all gardens, with the exception of Petit Bordeaux, where motorhomes over 6m would struggle at peak times. Roadside parking only for Villandry and Chaumont-sur-Loire.

ACCOMMODATION Campers are spoilt for choice in the Loire Valley with a huge selection of *aires*, France Passion sites plus campsites of all grades. We stayed at **France Passion** sites in Brissac-Quincé, Vouvray, Huisson-sur-Cosson and Sandillon, and **campsites:** Camping Les Vaugeons, Écommoy; Camping Les Rives du Douet, Doué-en-Anjou; Camping de la Blardière, Rigny-Ussé; Camping Touristique, Gien.

Other sites to stay: Le Bec de Cisse, Vouvray; Huttopia Les Châteaux, Bracieux; Camping d'Olivet, Orléans. Chemins de la Rose is part of the France Passion

scheme. The area is awash with **aires**, many within walking distance of the many châteaux/gardens, including Villandry.

FIND OUT MORE

L'Arboretum National des Barres
⌀ arboretumdesbarres.fr
Château de la Bourdaisière
⌀ labourdaisiere.com/en/portfolio/
the-national-tomato-conservatory
Château de Brissac ⌀ chateau-
brissac.fr
Château de Chambord
⌀ chambord.org/en
Château de Chamerolles
⌀ chateauchamerolles.fr
Château de Chenonceau
⌀ chenonceau.com/en
Château de Montriou
⌀ jardinspaysdelaloire.fr/parc-et-
jardins-du-chateau-de-montriou-
feneu-maine-et-loire
Château du Rivau
⌀ chateaudurivau.com
Château de Talcy ⌀ chateau-talcy.
fr/en

Château d'Ussé ⌀ chateaudusse.fr
Château de Valmer
⌀ chateaudevalmer.com/en
Château de Villandry
⌀ chateauvillandry.fr/en
Chemins de la Rose
⌀ lescheminsdelarose.com
Festival International des Jardins
⌀ domaine-chaumont.fr/en/
international-garden-festival
Jardin d'Atmosphère
 Petit Bordeaux
 ⌀ jardindupetitbordeaux.fr
Loire Valley ⌀ valdeloire-france.
com
Parc Floral de la Source
⌀ parcfloraldelasource.com/les-
jardins
Pays de la Loire ⌀ atlantic-loire-
valley.com
Touraine ⌀ touraineloirevalley.co.uk

TOP TIP: VISIT TERRA BOTANICA
For an amusement park-style attraction, Terra Botanica, 7.5km north of Angers, is aimed towards families. The 30ha site is devoted to a botanical theme but it has a very different, commercial vibe to the centuries-old parkland of the châteaux, the gardens and passionate private collections seen elsewhere in the Loire Valley.

Fields of rose bushes cultivated at Doué-en-Anjou (Caroline Mills)

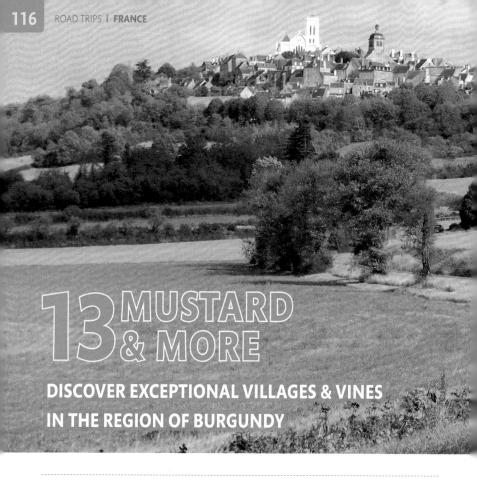

13 MUSTARD & MORE

DISCOVER EXCEPTIONAL VILLAGES & VINES IN THE REGION OF BURGUNDY

WHERE	Bourgogne-Franche-Comté (Yonne, Nièvre, Côte d'Or)
DISTANCE/TIME	373 miles (600km)/6 days
START/FINISH	Rogny-les-Sept-Écluses/Joigny

There's a major problem with Burgundy. It's too good. As I tour through the region, from the quiet and unassuming area of the Puisaye, bordering the Loire, to the famous wine growing district of the Côte d'Or and beyond, I pass through village after village. Each is so seemingly perfect and surrounded by such satisfying countryside that I find myself pleading to see an anomalous architectural faux-pas merely to draw breath. Burgundy's grand-scale beauty is nigh-on impossible to grasp.

I begin in **Rogny-les-Sept-Écluses**, a village set on the Briare Canal, the oldest canal in French history. The canal links the rivers Loire and Seine and, built in the early 17th century, was a part of King Henri IV's plan to build sufficient canals to 'join' the Mediterranean Sea with the English Channel. In the village, as its name tells, there are seven locks in staircase fashion. A modern-day lock

↑ Vézelay (Caroline Mills)

system is now in place but the historic flight remains and, spanning a 24m height difference over some 238m showcases a major advancement in civil engineering. Thank goodness the locks were built – it carried copious numbers of wine barges!

The route to Saint-Fargeau provides a precursor for what's to come with a couple of agreeable villages, **Bléneau** and **Saint-Privé**. **Saint-Fargeau** is one of those towns that is attractive and interesting enough to warrant closer inspection but isn't so overwhelmingly beautiful to have the numbers of tourists to match. There's a plentiful supply of half-timbered buildings, lots of bistros and a timber-framed market hall that's pleasant for a picnic.

The town's château is huge; unusual for the area, it's built of brick and is pentagon-shaped with two giant round towers like fat porters at the entrance. Its plain, once moated, exterior walls hide an ornamented courtyard and there's plenty of 'English' parkland in which to go for a wander.

I move on, taking a detour to **Moutiers-en-Puisaye**. It's a tiny village of yellow-ochre buildings, typical of the area, pastel-blue shutters, and a handsome church that's filled with historic murals, a feature of many churches in the Puisaye. Crab

apples dot the undulating pastures surrounded by oak woodland while carmine geraniums clash prettily with the *mairie* to complete the trio of primary colours. The little lanes are just right for ambling, either on foot or by bike and there are various walks (recommended on an information panel) that begin beside the village church; utterly tranquil, this is not the place for a wild life, though there's lots of wildlife to enjoy.

One of the recommended walks is along the 2km 'back road', a stately beech tree avenue, to Saint-Sauveur-en-Puisaye. The village is a cultural centre based around the village *château* that now houses the Musée Colette. The 19th/20th-century writer and actress Colette, best known for her novel, *Gigi*, was born in the village; her birthplace close by is also a small museum. The hilltop parkland beside the *château* has rewarding views of the Puisaye's wooded countryside.

↑ Rogny-les-Sept-Écluses (Caroline Mills)

From woodlands to open agricultural plains, I take minor roads from **Lain** to **Druyes-les-Belles-Fontaines**, one of four villages in the Yonne that are listed as Cités de Caractère – understandably so. Its beauty nears perfection. With upper and lower parts, Druyes is best-viewed initially on the road from Lain, where only the 'haut' village can be seen. Then, as you approach the 'basse' village, its full beauty is revealed – or most of it. I take a wander through the lower village to see its historic connections; its Roman church, its faultlessly arched viaduct, the *lavoir* and the tiny Druyes River before a strenuous climb reveals, within the fortifications of its 12th-century *château*, the *haut* village. It is giddily sublime!

Across the arable plains broken by beech and oak copses, every village thereafter is noticeably striking, built from honeyed stone beneath terracotta tiles: **Villepot**, **Courson-les-Carrières**, **Fouronnes**, **Fontenay-sous-Fouronnes** are all becoming. And then I reach **Mailly-le-Château**. It renders speech useless!

Like Druyes, the village is on two levels. The *château* and a collection of pale cream-coloured, shuttered houses reflect the sunlight on limestone cliffs above the River Yonne, with superlative river views. At the foot, a second group of houses mingle along the banks of the Yonne, reeded yet fast-paced beneath a 15th-century toll bridge and pocket-sized chapel dedicated to the patron saint of sailors. The two parts are accessed on foot via steps on the cliff-face, passing the intriguing Wolf Fountain, with reference to an old tale about child-eating wolves.

But, there's more to Mailly-le-Château. Parallel to the river is the Canal du Nivernais, which – like the Briare – links the Loire and the Seine (via the Yonne). It was developed in the 19th century to float wood from the Morvan to Paris, but is now the second-most used canal in France (after the Canal du Midi). The setting at Mailly is so serene that I have to spend time here in the soporific heat of the afternoon. More so, the entire length of the 174km-long canal from Saint-Léger-les-Vignes to Auxerre has a foot/cycle path that runs alongside it so you can appreciate its attractiveness slowly.

My route runs south for several kilometres alongside the canal and river; as I drive south it becomes even more exceptional at **Merry-sur-Yonne**, where giant moulded crags, the **Rochers du Saussois**, tower above the sleepy riverside village. The gorge-like cliffs continue until **Châtel-Censoir** where I peel off away from the river, somewhat reluctantly, and climb into the **Parc Naturel Régional du Morvan**. My desire to continue riverside soon fades as the beech, oak and pine woods begin, passing working farms and piles of long, slender logs, an indication of the Morvan's main industry. When **Vézelay** comes into distant view hugging a wooded hilltop, the Yonne is a mere recollection, for now.

Vézelay is regarded as a gateway to Morvan. Its stature, though, offers more than that, including designation as a UNESCO World Heritage Site and Un Plus Beaux Villages de France (page 204). Its main street is 700m long, with quite

↑ Mailly-le-Château (Traveller70/Shutterstock)

a climb to reach the highest point, where the enormous white Basilica Saint Mary Magdalene stands, its belltower offering similarities with the campanile in Florence. There are lots of places to eat and, much like many *plus beaux villages*, Vézelay seems to attract artist studios and galleries in number. Noted, too, is the Zervos Museum, a remarkable modern art collection that includes work by Picasso, Kandinsky, Chagall and Miró.

I desert the main street to explore the web of side streets around the basilica, once a Benedictine abbey, to discover wonderful views to the north, south and east. While I gaze at the view, a mellifluous voice breaks the silence as a wall brown butterfly attempts to camouflage itself against the gingery lichens on the ramparts. The note is held, soaring in a crescendo above the rooftops and I establish that I am standing beside the Cité de la Voix, Burgundy's Centre of Vocal Art.

Vézelay gives its name to a small white wine appellation – views from the village include vineyards for the first time on my route. But at neighbouring **Saint-Père**, alongside the River Cure and in sight of the basilica, visitors can visit the Brasserie de Vézelay, a modern brewery that creates excellent organic craft beers using grains produced by local farmers and spring water from the Morvan. I particularly recommend the gluten-free Blonde!

My head is whirling, not from the beer, but the sheer beauty of the countryside, the open space and every single village. The Morvan here, on the road to **Bazoches** and Lormes, is 'wild' with pastures grazed by beige Charolais cattle interspersed

↑ Rochers du Saussois (Caroline Mills)

with the, by now, ubiquitous oak and beech woods. Hedgerows provide a parkland setting and it reminds me very much of the landscape of the Cotswolds. I take a short detour to **Domecy-sur-Cure** and descend to a small settlement simply named, 'Cure', beside the river. The river carves its way along sharp, steep wooded cliffs; the picturesque scene doesn't help my reeling head.

At **Lormes**, a busy market town, I head cross country towards the Lac des Settons. The twisty lanes through the beechwoods are empty. Every now and then comes a vista and, having recently rained, the sun's low rays create a misty, mystical vision. Thank goodness for **Montsauche-les-Settons**, the first village that isn't picture perfect; my overexcited brain has a chance to calm down and I arrive at the lake ready to relax.

The **Lac des Settons**, through which the Cure flows, is one of the Morvan's 'great lakes', actually a reservoir originally created to help the transport of wood to Paris. It's very much a leisure lake now, with the offer of watersports. There's a hazy start to the morning and mist rises from the lake and seeps through the surrounding woods that offer abundant walks. My brisk ramble along the lake shore is thoroughly peaceful but for birdsong and the crunch of acorns.

↑ Sunset over the Morvan Regional Nature Park (Svetlana Bondareva/Shutterstock)

I continue on to explore more of the Morvan, whose hills get progressively higher and more wooded further south. It's a deliberately contorted route that I take south of **Château-Chinon**, up and over the **Col de la Gravelle**, towards the source of the River Yonne, hidden in the trees, before I eventually head east away from the park. On my way I come across a tiny memorial dedication to the French Resistance; the Morvan was a major area within which the French Resistance operated during World War II.

Leaving the Morvan, the landscape changes as I head east into the **Côte d'Or** *département*. The wild and sparsely populated Morvan had given me time to reflect on all the comely villages I'd already seen; now I'm immediately thrust back in a plethora of extraordinary villages again, this time as I pick up the **Route des Grands Crus de Bourgogne** at **Saint-Aubin**.

Created in 1937 the 60km-long signposted route begins (or ends) in Santenay and passes through 37 legendary wine villages of the Côte d'Or and includes the towns of Beaune, Burgundy's capital of wine and Dijon, the regional capital of Burgundy. It's a bucolic industrial landscape of gentle slopes smothered in vines above which are wooded hilltops and some of the smartest, well-dressed villages in pale limestone.

At **Gamay** I set out on foot to saunter around the tiny hamlet that neatly tucks itself into a crevice in the *côte* with sharp slopes of forest behind. It's a nice thought that such a miniscule place, little more than a dozen or so cottages and an unassertive *château*, may have given its name to one of the world's most famous grapes. If it did, it was a short-lived 15 minutes of fame, for the Dukes of Burgundy banned the grape's use from Burgundy wine in the 14th-century. The Gamay now makes a regular appearance in one of Burgundy's most southerly wine regions, the Mâconnais, and is the staple grape of Beaujolais.

The little parcels of vines, terraced and locked in by stone walls, become ever smaller as I approach **Puligny-Montrachet**. Each is announced by a grand archway as if entering a stately home. The season's grapes are already harvested, but the vineyards are, nonetheless, buzzing with activity as slender tractors on stilts tidy up the rows.

Passing by the imposing Château de Meursault I walk into the village and sit in the central square to write in my notebook, 'Does it get any more beautiful than this?!' There isn't a street or building that lets the village down, least of all the *mairie*, housed in a 14th-century *château* with a characteristic Burgundian glazed-tile roof.

Potentially Burgundy does get more refined – the neighbouring village of **Pommard** is certainly no less attractive and where, for a change of scene amid

↑ Make time to see more than Beaune's Hôtel Dieu (Superstock)

the endless stream of *viticulteurs* and wine merchants, I watch chocolates, homemade macaroons and marshmallows being made in Appellation Chocolat, an artisan chocolatier.

By the time I reach **Beaune**, I could really do with some smelling salts at the Hôtel Dieu, the historic town's remarkably preserved medieval hospice. Its architectural aesthetics inside and out, coupled with a fascinating exhibition on its history, makes it the town's most visited attraction. But there's much more to the town, including a wander along the ramparts for a rooftop view. Also in Beaune is the Fallot mustard museum and factory, where visitors can find out about mustard, a product that is more synonymous with nearby Dijon where the Dukes of Burgundy enjoyed the condiment but which, now as a regional product – Burgundy Mustard – has Protected Geographical Indication status.

By evening, vines envelope my parking spot when I pitch up in a vineyard at **Marey-lès-Fussey**. The sea of undulating green waves is soothing, while every now and then a plop as a pear from the over-productive tree beside me falls and thuds to the ground. It's well beyond dusk when the last tractors trundle home from the vineyard.

Rolling Payne's Grey clouds overshadow the damp morning as I descend the hillside to **Nuits-Saint-Georges** with the whole of the Côte de Nuits before me. I pick up the Route des Grands Crus de Bourgogne to **Chambolle-Musigny**, whose limestone houses climb into a gorge. If I was fastidious, I'd say that the vineyard villages in the Côte de Beaune are prettier than those of the Côte de Nuits, but that's relative. When every village in Burgundy is 'beautiful', one has to select a different scale.

↑ Vineyards at Marey-lès-Fussey (Caroline Mills)

My visit to **Dijon** on this occasion doesn't involve dipping in and out of the multitude of museums and art galleries. Instead I choose to 'follow the owl' recessed in the pavement for a self-guided circuit of the traffic-free city, noseying into courtyards and gardens, ogling at grand mansions and the architectural legacy of the Dukes of Burgundy. The Parcours de la Chouette (Owl Route) takes in all the main sights with 22 points of interest, including the grand Palais des Ducs de Bourgogne.

Dijon may be Burgundy's sightseeing crown in the former ducal kingdom, but it doesn't have the monopoly on urban splendour in the region. Back on the road, I follow the River Ouche west then climb and twist through trees to drive along the **Brenne valley**. It's wide with smooth moulded hills on either side, meadows and an infinite number of Charolais cattle. Oak trees arrive again, too.

At **Pont Royal**, I cross another of Burgundy's limestone cliff rivers, the **Armançon**, which carves its way in a sweeping loop around **Semur-en-Auxois**. The town is my favourite in Burgundy for its slightly aging, crumbling magnificence and ordinary daily life; when I arrive the main cobbled street, Rue Buffon, is deserted as owners shut-up-shop for lunch while I dodge the teacher bellowing instructions to his class of students utilising the wide and elegant chestnut-tree boulevard for their PE lesson. Beside the town's ramparts, the nursery school empties in a noisy cacophony as parents, baguettes under arm, collect their children for lunch. Seconds later, as if nothing has occurred, the street is silent again.

On the hillside, Semur's grand but slightly ragged townhouses come together with its pair of medieval round towers that perch precariously on the edge of the steep ramparts. At the foot, the town becomes a village with the prettiest cottages that quietly peruse the river as it bumbles along.

Thereafter, I follow the Armançon as it sweeps from bend to bend northwest and pick up the parallel Canal du Bourgogne all the way to Tonnerre, with a brief stop in **Ancy-le-Franc** to admire the strikingly angular Renaissance palace.

Tonnerre continues to make the tourist guidebooks and, frankly, I'm not sure why. Tourists come to take a quick snap of the Fosse Dionne – an ancient pool with mysterious depths and no-known source – and then leave. The hallmarks of a once fine town are all here but it has gone beyond the shabby chic stage and has lost its crumbling charm with some remarkably ugly suburbs; now the centre looks depressingly run down, and slightly insalubrious. Until the town tidies itself up, shows some pride in its buildings and gets rid of the over-run rubbish sacks littering the streets, I would recommend visits to Chablis, where I venture next, and Joigny, in the north of the region.

SOUVENIR

There are more than 110 appellations in Burgundy, with four major regions: Chablis, Côtes d'Or (made up of Côte de Beaune and Côte de Nuits), Côte Chalonnaise and the Mâconnais.

Wine was introduced to the area by the Gallo-Romans, though it was the Cistercian monks that really brought wine production to the fore during the Middle Ages. They established the differences in terroir, even in the smallest plots of land and it is they that created the Clos, the famous parcels of vines surrounded by walls most notably in the Côte d'Or. Since 2015, this area has been recognised as a UNESCO World Heritage Site for its unique characteristics.

Today there are 33 Grands Crus, 561 Premier Crus and 44 village appellations. The Grands and Premier Crus of Burgundy that relate to a specific vineyard, which may only be a couple of hectares, are not classified in the same way that a Grand or Premier Cru is in Bordeaux, where it relates to a specific *château* or estate. Pinot Noir and Chardonnay are the dominant grape varieties.

Most wine producers sell direct, though be careful which producers you visit – you can pick up a bottle anywhere between €5 and 20,000! Great places to find out more about Burgundy wine are the Musée du Vin de Bourgogne in Beaune or the L'Imaginarium wine experience, at Nuits-Saint-Georges, which particularly focuses on sparkling Crémant de Bourgogne.

Chablis gives its name to some of the grandest Burgundian white wines and there are plenty of places within the village in which to buy or try some. Its good looks and appeal draw more tourists than many in Burgundy, with wine, naturally, the centre of attention; it's possible to hire ebikes and take a tour of the Chablis vineyards.

The River Serein flows through the village and I follow it northwest as, together with the Armançon, it joins the Yonne. Unlike the youthful Yonne I saw in Mailly-le-Château, the river is wide and fully grown when I meet it in **Joigny** as I cross the floral Pont Saint-Nicolas in town. Joigny is regarded as 'one of the best detours in France', a town that's not on the routine tourist trail, but ought to be. Like Tonnerre, it too is crumbling, but it has more presence and personality. The town was once divided into parishes, and each quarter still bears its distinctive

ESSENTIALS

GETTING THERE & AROUND Rogny-les-Sept-Écluses is on the D90, in the northwest corner of Burgundy. Take D90 to Saint-Fargeau, then D85 to Saint-Sauveur-en-Puisaye (with a detour to Moutiers-en-Puisaye and a mooch around the little, wooded lanes of the Puisaye), then cross-country (I go via the villages of Lain and Fougilet) southeast to Druyes-les-Belles-Fontaines. D104/D950 to Mailly-le-Château and D100 to Vézelay. D958/D42 to Lormes then D17/D977bis to Lac des Settons. D37 to Château-Chinon then D27, cross-country roads to Glux-en-Glenne and a detour to Haut-Folin (the highest point in Burgundy), D18/D3 to Saint-Léger-sous-Beuvray/Autun. D973 to Nolay, then D906 to Saint-Aubin to pick up the Route des Grands Crus de Bourgogne. From Dijon, D10F to Sombernon, D905/D70/D970 to Semur-en-Auxois. D980 to Montbard/D905 to Tonnerre, then D965 to Chablis (and Auxerre). N6/D606 to Joigny (and Saint-Julien-du-Sault).

Some of the wine villages along the Côte d'Or have exceptionally narrow streets, which prove awkward to drive down with a coachbuilt motorhome if a car or delivery van is parked. My recommendation is to park on the outskirts (most have parking areas) and walk or cycle around the villages – and, indeed, in between them.

There are no problems **parking** anywhere except, possibly Beaune. There is a dedicated motorhome *aire* but it's very popular and very small (only six spaces). There are roadside parking possibilities around the ring-road (with a 5-minute walk into the centre; for longer vehicles, I recommend parking up at one of the many *aires* in the outlying villages and using public transport). For Mailly-le-Château, park beside the Canal du Nivernais; access and parking around the *château* and upper part of the village is difficult; there is also an *aire*.

Dijon's centre is entirely traffic-free. Motorhomes can park at the *aire* next to the campsite in Talant (on the outskirts) and catch the L3 bus (20 minutes), or park at the *aire* in Marsannay-la-Côte and catch bus L4 (30 minutes).

character. The western area of the right bank, for example, was occupied by wood carvers in the Middle Ages and the artistry is still on show in the carvings on the numerous timber-framed buildings. What's more, the wood carvings, though aged and bearing the scars of several hundred years, are exquisite. On the hillside behind are vines used for the lesser-known Côte Saint-Jacques appellation, the most northerly of all Burgundy appellations.

I step into the Église Saint-Jean-Baptiste, whose giant dome dominates the town skyline. Calming Gregorian chants fill the acoustic void while gusts outside make the stonework and stained glass creak. For a shrill wind has whipped up and shrieks along the river valley. It bangs shutters and tears leaves from the vines; the church door slams hard creating echoes along the street when I leave. I sense it is time to move on.

At Sémur-en-Auxois, aside from the *aire*, there's plenty of roadside parking on Rue de la Liberté or park in the large parking area down Rue des Vaux (signposted Pont Pinard).

ACCOMMODATION I stayed on *aires* at Rogny-les-Sept-Écluses, Mailly-le-Château, Lac des Settons, Dijon and Saint-Julien-du-Sault, plus a **France Passion** site at Marey-lès-Fussey. There are many other excellent *aires* (and France Passion sites) along the route, including at Blénau, Saint-Privé, Saint-Fargeau, Marsannay-la-Côte, and Brienon-sur-Armançon.

Campsites: Camping des Lancières, Rogny-les-Sept-Écluses; Camping Municipal Le Pré du Roy, Mailly-le-Château; Camping Merry-sur-Yonne; Camping et Chalets Plage des Settons, Lac des Settons; Camping Huttopia, Meursault; Camping Municipal, Beaune; Camping du Lac Kir, Dijon; Camping du Serein, Chablis; Camping Municipal, Joigny.

FIND OUT MORE

Burgundy Tourism burgundy-tourism. com

Cote d'Or Tourism cotedor-tourisme. com

Morvan Regional Nature Park parcdumorvan.org

Puisaye Tourism puisaye-tourisme.fr

Yonne Tourism tourisme-yonne.com

TOP TIP: EXTEND THE TRIP For an interesting detour, visit Auxerre, one of Burgundy's other great cities, situated on the River Yonne. Besides the huge Cathédrale Saint-Étienne, the medieval quarter is a delight, while the town reputedly has the oldest wine domain in France, the Clos de la Chaînette, established in the 7th century.

To extend this trip, the Pays d'Othe, northeast of Joigny offers gorgeous, gentle countryside that crosses into the Champagne region. The area is noted for its apple orchards and cider production, so often overshadowed by Burgundy's wine industry.

14 CHASING WAVES: TO BAYONNE & BEYOND

TOUR THE ATLANTIC COAST IN SEARCH OF THE BEST BEACHES & REGIONAL FOOD

WHERE   Pays de la Loire/Nouvelle-Aquitaine (Loire-Atlantique, Vendée, Charente-Maritime, Gironde, Landes, Pyrénées-Atlantiques)

DISTANCE/TIME   780 miles (1,256km)/6 days

START/FINISH   Saint-Nazaire/Saint-Pée-sur-Nivelle

We've already been following the Atlantic coastline for a week (page 64) when we switch regions from Brittany to the Pays de la Loire. We've also crossed the colossal **Pont de Saint-Nazaire** that spans the River Loire as it reaches the Atlantic. And I'm sure I've kept my eyes open all the way. But as we cross over a second bridge, to **Île de Noirmoutier**, things are not as they seem.

For we appear to be not on the Atlantic coast but in the Mediterranean. Whitewashed houses with terracotta pantiles and turquoise shutters transport us to some other region. In between are plots of potatoes, row-upon-row seemingly grown to complement the surrounding salt beds; with a pretty harbour and pleasant beach **l'Herbaudière**, at the northwest tip of the island, is the perfect place for fish and ready-salted frites.

The island is verdant and fertile, and has a lusciousness about it by contrast to the mainland where the rough meadows, dykes and salt marshes of the Marais

↑ The Atlantic Ocean at Bretignolles-sur-Mer (Superstock)

Breton remind us of the reclaimed plains of northwest Holland. The bl
the marsh, speckled by cows tearing the tough grass, is no less endearing
than the cheerfulness of Noirmoutier.

Further down the coast we stop at small towns like **Sion-sur-l'Océan**, holding an
organic farmers' market next to the beach, **Saint-Gilles-Croix-de-Vie** and **Jard-sur-
Mer** with its backdrop of holm oaks and pine forests. Each has its own character
and local events.

We much prefer these smaller seaside towns, together with **Saint-Hilaire-de-Riez**
and its low-lying rocky Corniche Vendéenne, and the rough surf of **Bretignolles-
sur-Mer** preparing for a round of the World Surfing Championships, than the
larger, more cosmopolitan resorts of Les Sables-d'Olonne and La Rochelle. These
both seem to cater solely for tourists than residents. And, as a change from coastal
scenery, we relish our slow travels through the **Forêt Domaniale d'Olonne**, with
its luminous green new leaves, and the **L'Île d'Olonne**, where white egrets add to
the mysterious beauty of the salt marshes.

I feel that we really need to overcome our apathy towards oysters and, famous
for its pearls from the sea, **L'Aiguillon-sur-Mer** would be an appropriate place to
do it. The tiny market huts that sit yards from the boats are doing a brisk trade

↑ Selling oysters at L'Aiguillon-sur-Mer (Caroline Mills)

early on a Sunday morning, vivid lemons accompanying the graded oysters. But the drizzling rain and overcast sky have turned the muddy sludge of the oyster beds spied from the market huts even more grey and the sight means we still can't find them appealing. **Fouras**, south of La Rochelle, also has a plethora of oyster restaurants and from then on every few yards of coastline produces another oyster bed, a makeshift retail outlet (oysters the only option on sale) or a precariously perched hut on stilts, its large boom nets dangling over the muddy waters.

Some of the most strangely beautiful countryside that we encounter are the **marshes** between Moëze and Marennes, a narrow road cutting a swathe across the 3,000ha of grassy swamp. The unexpected gem in the middle is a peaceful star-shaped citadel at **Brouage**, built by Cardinal Richelieu in the 17th-century as a Catholic bastion. The tiny village, sitting snugly inside the walls, was once an inland port for salt. Now stranded by the extensive marsh, it is perfectly preserved.

Oysters are here too, as they are in **Marennes** and on the **Île d'Oléron**. But we are now approaching vineyard country, and the island's spine is taken over by rows of vines producing Cognac and its associated apéritif, Pineau des Charentes. We suddenly come across a surprising cage of hops, and discover that Maxime Pinard, producer of Cognac and Pineau is also brewing a beer mixed with Cognac, a strong yet refreshing drink that tastes similar to the hoppy, wheat beers produced in Belgium.

Within a few miles we're bordering the gigantic Gironde along its east bank, the white grapes of the Charente turning red as we approach the UNESCO city of **Bordeaux**. Here ornate iron balconies grace cream-coloured stone buildings dressed in architectural finery. This elegant city of columns, colonnades and curvy balustrades – and the capital of the Bordeaux wine region – is a fine place for a riverside walk along the Garonne, a stroll in the many parks, and an arty picture of the Miroir d'Eau in the Place de la Bourse.

We eat a simple lunch among the stumpy vines in the vineyards of the **Haut-Médoc**, the area that covers the spit of land between the ocean and the estuary. Touring from village to village (Arsac, Margaux-Cantenac, Moulis-en-Médoc, St-Julien-Beycheville) and around the châteaux is like visiting the homes of the stars, putting a face to A-list celebrities: Cantenac-Brown, Palmer, Lafite Rothschild, Latour, Margaux, Mouton Rothschild and, possibly the prettiest wine *château* of them all, Cos d'Estournel with its turrets and towers. The disappointment, though, is **Pauillac**; a glorified estuarial town that places a damper on the image of some of the most exclusive and exceptional wines in the world.

A few kilometres west and we hit the beach again – one long, continuous stretch from the **Pointe de Grave** at the top of the Médoc down to Biarritz. We toy with the coast, dipping in and out of the tall, spindly pines splattered with yellow broom and gorse like some Pointillist masterpiece, the undulating dunes held in place by manmade forests.

We find a great *aire* to stay at **Le Huga**, near Lacanau-Océan. It's set up like a campsite with pitches under the cool of the pine trees and a cycle track from the

↑ Place de la Bourse, Bordeaux (Alexander Demyanenko/Shutterstock)

site takes us the 2km to the busy but compact seaside town and beaches. In fact, there are cycle tracks throughout the forests of **Les Landes** and we find it far more picturesque than I had envisaged.

The scent of the pine is powerful, hitting the back of the throat, but the trees make a welcome retreat from the sun-drenched beaches and the hot climb up the **Dune du Pilat**, Europe's biggest sand dune and the children's ultimate 'beach' along the Atlantic they decide – at last they've found a favourite 'newly discovered' (they can't recall a visit years earlier).

The roads are long, straight and quiet through the forests. Sometimes the pines are tall and as straight as the roads, others bushy and squat, creating a clearing for the sun to shine brilliantly before returning to mottled light. Interspersed among the trees and fluorescent broom, we discover lovely villages and tiny towns like **Biscarrosse**, capital of sea-planes, **Pontenx-les-Forges**, with buildings built – as its name alludes to – of the darkest brown ironstone, and the tiddly village of **Uza** and its logging yards, pungent with pine.

So large an area is Les Landes that we are under the cover of the forests for some while. When we emerge, we catch our first glimpse of the snow-tipped Pyrenees and we know we are nearing the end of our journey. First we have to visit **Bayonne**, for I love the dry-cured ham that the town is famous for. In fact, the only 'ham' we find is made of chocolate.

We discover that the Basque town has been the 'capital of chocolate for four centuries', as it proudly states on road signs. The narrow streets, with half-timbered pencil-thin terraced houses accompanying the twin-spired cathedral, also have

↑ Houses in Bayonne (Boris Stroujko/Shutterstock)

enough chocolate shops to rival any Belgian town; even the fresh pasta bought in the covered market includes chocolate. The local speciality Touron, a colourful marzipan wrapped in pastry, looks good too, but we choose Gâteau Basque, a cherry pie.

We feel inappropriately dressed for glitzy **Biarritz**, for we are wearing neither designer clothes for the casino or wetsuits that enrobe the surfers congregated at the other end of town, it supposedly having the best surf in Europe. So, gazing in passing admiration at the extravagance of the Hotel du Palais (regarded as one of the finest hotels in France) we move on to **Saint-Jean-de-Luz** and its twin on the left bank of the River Nivelle, **Ciboure**.

Brimming with a juxtaposition of Italianate-style villas and half-timbered houses in rusty red, the towns' medley of architectural styles gives an exciting feel to the Basque twins. The restaurants serve tapas, indicating how close we are to the Spanish border; relaxed al-fresco diners soak up the sunshine beneath the plane trees in the main square.

Driving along the corniche of the **Côte d'Argent**, past slivers of gleaming silver rock shimmying into the sea, we stop briefly at **Hendaye**, with the entire length of France's Atlantic coast completed. But we've grown weary, tired of the crowds that the Atlantic heat and beaches have lured, and we escape to the cool of the Pyrenees, spending our final night at **Saint-Pée-sur-Nivelle**, in the lush green meadows of the foothills.

Our beachcombing days over, we're glad to retreat to the mountains but are thankful for the soporific sound of the ocean that remains in our cognizance for days to come.

↑ Don't miss the corniche of the Côte d'Argent (Caroline Mills)

ESSENTIALS

GETTING THERE & AROUND Like its predecessor, *Coasting the Atlantic* (page 64), this is a long road trip and it's impossible to mark up every road; basically, follow the coast and keep it in view as much as you can depending on where you wish to visit. We began on the D213, crossing the Pont de Saint-Nazaire, then the D758 through the Marais Breton and the D38 to Noirmoutier.

The D38 continues south to Les Sables d'Olonne; peel off on to the D6A for the Corniche Vendéenne. Unless visiting the Île de Ré and La Rochelle (we did neither on this occasion), the N237 and N137 helps bypass the town. Further south, I really recommend a visit to Brouage, on the D3 between Rochefort and Marennes, where there's access to the Île d'Oléron. Then continue to follow the right bank of the Gironde estuary to Bordeaux.

Our route out of Bordeaux to the Haut-Médoc, was on the D1 via Eysines. The towns on the southern edge of the Bassin d'Arcachon are busy and not particularly attractive, so using the A660/N250 is a useful bypass to reach the Dune de Pilat, or cut across to the dune using the D256 further south.

If, having completed this road trip, you don't want to drive to the UK back through France, consider taking the ferry from Bilbao or Santander in Spain; both cities are within a 3-hour drive of the Spanish border at Hendaye/Irun.

For **parking**, there are *aires* all the way along the coast; we had no problems parking anywhere with the exception of Biarritz. In Bordeaux, the parking of motorhomes is allowed in the Parc des Allées de Chartres, near the Esplanade des Quinconces, between 08.00 and 20.00. In Biarritz, on-street parking of

motorhomes is banned throughout the town and the busy streets are nerve-wracking to negotiate with a wide 'van. There are two *aires*; both are on the south of the town towards Bidart, between 2–3km from the centre.

ACCOMMODATION We stayed in *aires* at: Jard-sur-Mer, Meschers-sur-Gironde, Le Huga (near Lacanau-Océan), Capbreton and Saint-Pée-sur-Nivelle.

Campsites: La Pomme de Pin, Jard-sur-Mer; La Plage, Meschers-sur-Gironde; Les Grands Pins, Lacanau-Océan; Camping Municipal La Civelle, Capbreton; Merko Lacarra, Saint-Jean-de-Luz; Camping Ibarron, Saint-Pée-sur-Nivelle.

FIND OUT MORE

Bayonne Tourism ⊘ bayonne-tourisme.com

Bordeaux Tourism ⊘ Bordeaux-tourism.co.uk

Cognac Country Tourist Board ⊘ atlantic-cognac.com

Île de Noirmoutier ⊘ ile-noirmoutier.com

Saint Jean-de-Luz ⊘ saint-jean-de-luz.com

Vendée Tourism ⊘ vendee-tourism.co.uk

TOP TIP: PICK OF THE BEACHES

Biarritz
Fouras
Gascogne
Île d'Oléron (La Grande Plage)

Jard-sur-Mer
Les Sables-d'Olonne
Pointe de Grave to Golfe de Saint-Jean-de-Luz

Dune du Pilat (Otortarolo/Shutterstock)

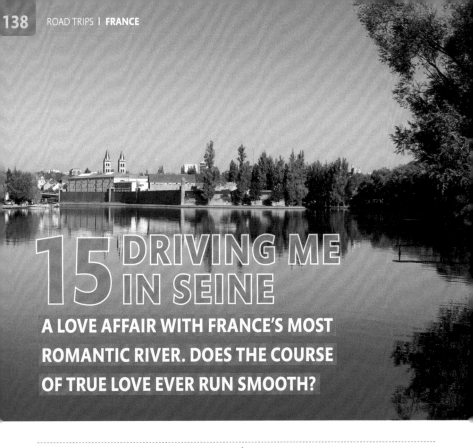

15 DRIVING ME IN SEINE

A LOVE AFFAIR WITH FRANCE'S MOST ROMANTIC RIVER. DOES THE COURSE OF TRUE LOVE EVER RUN SMOOTH?

WHERE	Burgundy, Champagne & Île de France (Côte d'Or/Aube/Seine-et-Marne)
DISTANCE/TIME	193 miles (310km)/3 days
START/FINISH	Saint Seine-l'Abbaye/Vaux-le-Vicomte (Melun)

The Seine is the second-longest river in France and, owing to its special relationship with Paris, one of the most famous rivers in the world. It's also meant to be one of the most romantic. So the children and I chose to attempt a love affair with it, following the river from its source, journeying alongside and over it, sometimes on it, and even in it.

The Seine rises in the Côte-d'Or *département*, in Burgundy, 29km northwest of Dijon and among the trees of the Forêt Domaniale d'Is-sur-Tille. Our starting point began a few kilometres southeast of the source, at the aptly named **Saint-Seine-l'Abbaye**, a true pilgrim's stop with a 13th-century church and a cluster of pretty dwellings. The village nuzzles in a bowl with steep, twisting climbs either side along the D971.

The road, which runs across the **Plateau de Langres**, is important geographically as it marks the watershed; on its eastern side, water runs south into the Rhône-

↑ River Seine at Melun (Superstock)

Saône basin while streams on the west head north towards the mouth of the Seine. Confusingly, the tiny commune named Saint-Germain-Source-Seine is not at the river's source. Neither does the river run through it; our first example of being driven half-mad as we looked for the source.

In among the woods, it's easy to accidentally pass by and be oblivious to the humble beginnings of this most famous of French rivers. We arrived at its source, quite appropriately, in spring when wild violets, wood anemones and hellebores burst forth on its 'banks'. Secluded and alone, we heard nothing but sweet birdsong and the trickle of water. Our romance had definitely begun. We were already in love with the river.

France worships the Seine. The main spring is deified as Goddess Sequana (Latin-Gaulish for 'sacred' (*sanctus*) from which comes *seine*. At the end of the first century a Gallic temple was built close to the source and in the 19th-century the city of Paris paid homage to 'its' river by building a grotto to protect the Nymph of the Seine. She can be found lying next to the source, keeping a watchful gaze over it. Checking feet were clean to avoid polluting the pure water, the children paddled.

↑ Measuring the width of the Seine at its source (Caroline Mills)

Away from the motorist, the river trickles through open fields. We caught up with it at **Courceau**, the first hamlet through which it flows. Our route along the D971 then followed the river for some miles, through the unimaginative **Saint-Marc-sur-Seine** and past the turreted **Château de Rocheprise** at Brémur-et-Vaurois.

A string of pretty villages then appear, each one accepting the swelling water: **Aisey-sur-Seine** with its higgledy-piggledy rooflines and **Nod-sur-Seine** sitting guard on a hill above. On to **Châtillon-sur-Seine**, it twists and meanders consistently for one so young, through open countryside with shallow banks just too wide to jump. Youthful, this is the river at its prettiest, though it hurries through the next few villages and towns as if not wishing to stay. It passes directly alongside the forlorn looking ribbon village of **Gomméville** before encircling the little town of **Mussy-sur-Seine** where the population is aging, the buildings crumbling, the shops abandoned and the *hôtel de ville* appears sorrowfully grand. As a walled village once commercially rich and important, it is, however, a pretty spot that's worth a look around.

The river begins to swirl as we change *département* to the Aube, named after the Seine's tributary. As the river comes of age, it tastes its first champagne through the villages of **Courteron** and **Gyé-sur-Seine** where cream-coloured stone houses overlook the copper-blue waters. It's more than a bubbling stream now; a full-grown river with natural weirs, waterfalls and backwaters. Wild cowslips and primroses decorate the banks.

It's not until we reach **Troyes** that we see anything of big-town life on this particular journey. We refresh ourselves wandering the narrow half-timbered streets that make up the champagne-cork shaped town centre while the Seine flows around the head of the cork. We find plenty to see, sampling the many pavement cafés serving crêpes (unpretentious Crêperie La Tourelle on Rue Champeaux was our preference) and catching multi-coloured sunbeams through the rose window of the Gothic Cathédrale Saint-Pierre-et-Saint-Paul, before mingling with shoppers in the covered market.

Catching up with our river again on the outskirts, we drive along its banks as it makes a right-angled turn west. From **Romilly-sur-Seine**, the river slows its pace, the Aube joining it before the industrial backdrop of the electricity generating station at **Nogent-sur-Seine**.

Here's a riddle for you? When is a river not a river? When it becomes an old river? Yes, the river was indeed beginning to send us barmy. Downstream from Nogent we were never quite sure whether we were following La Seine or La Vieille Seine, a combination of the old course of the river and a canal that allows boats to reach Nogent. To avoid confusion we renamed the real river La Nouvelle

↑ Troyes (Leonid Andronow/Shutterstock)

Seine, which runs through a succession of lakes like beads on a string. Hence, Châtenay-sur-Seine isn't actually on the river at all; it's on La Vieille Seine. Even more puzzling, geographically, the Seine is really a tributary of the Yonne, but the river's romantic tones seem to disappear at the prospect of strolling hand-in-hand along the Parisian banks of a river named Yonne.

Château de la Motte-Tilly does, however, sit on the Seine, or by it at least. It's an 18th-century house of great symmetrical proportions and has magnificent views of the river. We wandered through quiet and pretty villages – **Courceroy** and **Grisy-sur-Seine** on the river and **Villiers- and Noyen-sur-Seine**, both situated away from it. All were unassuming; houses with mottled tiled roofs and painted window shutters, old stone barns and poplar trees with mistletoe hanging like giant baubles. At **Bray-** and **Mouy-sur-Seine** the river divides the two settlements, with an anachronistic juxtaposition of modern industry and medieval houses.

We fell out of love with the river at **Montereau-Fault-Yonne** and **Moret-Loing-et-Orvanne**; the towns seem heavily industrial and unappealing. Our final sojourn with the Seine before the river runs its course through the southern suburbs of Paris was at **Fontainebleau** (page 77) where the river skirts the edge of the forest, and at **Château Vaux-le-Vicomte** (page 78) northeast of Melun, through which the Seine flows. A grand finale to the first part of our pilgrimage, the châteaux and their surroundings restored our conviction in the romance of the river; we were in love with it once more.

To follow the complete length of the river from source to the sea, continue with road trip *Romance of a River* (page 144).

ESSENTIALS

GETTING THERE & AROUND The **Source de la Seine** is 29km northwest of Dijon, 2km west of the D971. We followed the Seine along the D971, D671, D78, D20, D619 and D411 together with a series of minor back roads. Parking is generally not an issue throughout this trip, with the exception of Troyes, where it is a nightmare for large coachbuilt motorhomes. We parked roadside on the Quai la Fontaine; otherwise, Parking Victor Hugo (Delestraint) is a possibility, or stay/park at the *aire*/campsite in Nogent-sur-Seine and take the train to Troyes.

ACCOMMODATION We stayed at: Camping Municipal, Saint Seine l'Abbaye and *aires* at Buxeuil and Bray-sur-Seine. Other suggested **campsites** are: Camping Les Terres Rouges, Clérey; La Peupleraie, Bray-sur-Seine; Camping Municipal, Samoreau.

FIND OUT MORE

Aube Champagne Tourist Board
⌀ aube-champagne.com
Burgundy Tourism ⌀ burgundy-tourism.com
Château de Fontainebleau
⌀ chateaudefontainebleau.fr
Château de la Mottle-Tilly ⌀ chateau-la-motte-tilly.fr

Château de Vaux-le-Vicomte ⌀ vaux-le-vicomte.com
Nogentais/Valley of the Seine Tourist Board ⌀ tourisme-nogentais.fr
Troyes Tourist Board
⌀ troyeslachampagne.com

↑ Aisey-sur-Seine (Caroline Mills)

16 ROMANCE OF A RIVER

ON A JOURNEY FOLLOWING THE RIVER SEINE FROM SOURCE TO SEA, THIS ROUTE PICKS UP IN PARIS

WHERE Île de France & Normandy (Ville de Paris, Hauts-de-Seine, Yvelines, Eure, Calvados)

DISTANCE/TIME 175 miles (279km)/5 days

START/FINISH Paris/Honfleur

B eginning with *Driving me in Seine* (page 138) the children and I had set off on a pilgrimage following the course of the River Seine from source to sea. The story paused as we reached the southern suburbs of **Paris**. Here the journey continues, watching an ever-widening river swallow up many a lover's heart.

Romantic couples the world over choose Paris to congregate and it's the river that seems to be a part of the draw; even Swedish pop-group ABBA have sung about lovers walking the banks of the Seine.

Both the left and right banks, from the Pont Sully and Île Saint-Louis to the Trocadero Gardens and Eiffel Tower, are designated as a UNESCO World Heritage Site. We found it so easy to enjoy the river in Paris. With every angle it appears different, from the gardens of the Louvre, the steps of Nôtre-Dame, the heights of the Eiffel Tower, the seat of a sightseeing boat, or from the Pont Alexandre III, 'the most romantic bridge in Paris' according to the boat's guide. However much of a cliché it is, however many lovers we have followed in the footsteps of, it is still a magical river.

↑ View of the Seine from Pont Alexandre III, 'the most romantic bridge in Paris' (FadiBarghouthy/Shutterstock)

Past the *péripherique* (ring road) heading west the river starts to meander on a grand scale. Eager to stay by 'our' river, we stayed at the riverside campsite in the **Bois de Boulogne** allowing easy access into the centre of Paris or a quick exit west moving, slowly, downstream. Like a slithering serpent, the river curls so much that, exiting town through La Défense, we crossed the river three times to reach our next destination, **Saint-Germain-en-Laye** (page 75), an attractive village-like suburb of Paris where the château's gardens, high on a hill, offer fine views of the river below and towards Paris. It is also the first open space, including the **Forêt Domaniale de Saint-Germain** ringed by the Seine, since leaving Paris.

Our drive following the river sped up for a short while passing the industrial areas of Les Mureaux and Mantes-La-Jolie to reach the gardens of Impressionist painter Claude Monet at **Giverny**; it's the current favourite place 'in the whole of France' for six-year-old son Dominic, who loves the water garden with its Japanese bridge. The lily pond is made from a diversion in the Ru, a tiny stream that flows into the River Epte, itself a tributary of the Seine.

↑ Monet's Garden at Giverny (Caroline Mills)

Despite the number of tourists that visit Giverny, the nearby town of **Vernon**, on the river, is quiet in comparison. An appealing town that's worth visiting, it has quiet streets with old timber-framed houses, a pretty church, ramparts and a beautiful old mill precariously perched above the river that seems ready to topple into the water. The mill once sat on the original bridge, which was destroyed during World War II. **Château de Bizy**, a grand palace on the edge of town, is also worth some time.

With the river wider and more ponderous, the pace of our trail slowed navigating the graceful twists and turns towards the sea. Taking the little D313 back road along the northern right bank, we climbed up to overlook the river valley, itself carving a path through wooded, chalky cliffs, to the ruined remains of **Château Gaillard** at les Andelys. The castle was built in 1197 by King of England, Richard the Lionheart, to defend nearby Rouen from the French. The views of the river and the old part of les Andelys are dramatic from the fortifications, with the white chalky cliffs rising high above the riverbed.

Well within Normandy now, **Rouen** is the next and last big conurbation on the Seine's route, although its compact historic centre belies the fact that it is a large city. Our visit included a trip to the Cathédrale Nôtre-Dame, so often painted

↑ Château Gaillard (Leonid Andronov/Shutterstock)

↑ Gros Horloge, Rouen (artem evdokimov/Shutterstock)

in changing lights by Monet, through the Norman streets to the bizarre shaped Église Sainte-Jeanne d'Arc, named in memory of the place where she was burned at the stake in 1431. A plaque commemorates the spot and trying to explain to young children in reassuring tones proved difficult; there were several gruesome questions to be answered. We returned via the Gros Horloge (Great Clock) to the 'sanctuary' of the river, still bombarded with questions about burning women. In an attempt to divert the conversation, we followed the river west swiftly.

After Rouen there are just three main crossing points over the Seine: the **Pont de Brotonne** is the first, followed by the **Pont de Tancarville** and latterly the **Pont de Normandie**. We curled along the left bank through the **Forêt Domaniale de Brotonne** and the **Parc Naturel Régional des Boucles de la Seine Normande**. We lunched on the banks at **La Mailleraye-sur-Seine**, a tiny village on a bend in the river, which prevents you from seeing too far either left or right. By the water's edge we couldn't even see the Pont de Brotonne, first spotted some distance away when approaching the village. Crossing over the bridge to the right bank later, the only toll-free bridge of the three, we could see the beautiful village of **Caudebec-en-Caux**, a must-stop spot.

Our pilgrimage came to an end at **Honfleur**, arguably the more attractive of the two towns that sit either side of the river's estuary; Le Havre has a rich architectural heritage and an industrial beauty about its vast port along the riverbanks.

↑ Paddling at the Baie de la Seine, Honfleur (Caroline Mills)

We sat overlooking the Vieux Bassin in Honfleur, watching the yachts come in from the estuary and the river cruisers who had perhaps navigated the river in the way it was intended. We celebrated our adventure with *galettes* (savoury pancakes) in La Trinquette on Quai Sainte-Catherine, toasting the Seine with a glass of Normandy cider. And, just as they did at the source, the children paddled in the Baie de la Seine as if to draw to a close the final chapter of our journey.

Crossing over the Pont de Normandie on our return home, we looked to the right, upstream, at the long trip completed, then left, out to the Baie de la Seine. We had come along way together, the Seine and us; our pilgrimage had come to an end, our love affair with the river had not. We certainly hadn't been driven insane, only mad with longing to visit parts of the river again.

ESSENTIALS

GETTING THERE & AROUND From Melun (where the first part of the Seine tour left off), take the D372 and A6, then the inner ring road (*le périphérique*) west around Paris to the Bois de Boulogne (exit Porte Maillot/Bois de Boulogne). We left Paris via the D7 and D186 from the Bois de Boulogne to Saint-Germain-en-Laye. If you wish to avoid the Parisian suburbs, leave Paris on the A13 Autoroute de Normandie. In Rouen, motorhomes can **park** (including overnight) on the Quai de la Seine. In Honfleur, motorhomes should park at the dedicated *aire*.

ACCOMMODATION We stayed at *aires* in Giverny, Rouen and Honfleur and, initially, **Huttopia Camping de Paris**, with spaces for tents, caravans and motorhomes. A shuttle bus takes guests into the city centre (Porte Maillot). At the time of writing (2020) a Vignette Crit'Air certificate is not necessary for reaching the campsite via the *périphérique*; check before you travel.

Other recommended **campsites:** Camping Les Fosses Rouges, St Marcel (for Giverny); L'Île des Trois Rois, Les Andelys; Camping du Phare, Honfleur.

FIND OUT MORE

Bateaux Parisiens ⌔ bateauxparisiens. com

Honfleur Tourist Board ⌔ honfleur-tourism.co.uk

Monet's Garden, Giverny ⌔ foundation-monet.com

Normandy Tourism ⌔ Normandie-tourisme.fr

Nouvelle-Normandie Tourist Board (area around Giverny) ⌔ cape-tourisme.fr

Paris Tourist Board ⌔ parisinfo.com

Rouen Tourist Board ⌔ rouentourisme. com

17 SEEING RED

CELEBRATE A LOVE OF STRAWBERRIES IN THE DORDOGNE

WHERE	Nouvelle-Aquitaine (Corrèze & Dordogne)
DISTANCE/TIME	100 miles (161km)/6 days
START/FINISH	Beaulieu-sur-Dordogne/Brantôme

It's quarter to nine on a Sunday morning in early May. The bells from the Église Abbatiale peal, their tone resonating through the hills and sending ripples along the River Dordogne. However, the peals are not calling a congregation to church this particular Sunday, they are inviting us instead to pay homage to a nation's favourite summer fruit – the strawberry – and, in particular, the Gariguette.

Every second Sunday in May, the small town of **Beaulieu-sur-Dordogne** stages La Fête de la Fraise, a festival that celebrates the produce from the surrounding fields, all cultivated with *les fraisiers* (strawberry plants). Despite a population of just 1,300 inhabitants, Beaulieu is responsible for 1% of the country's overall Gariguette production, equating to 400 tonnes of fruit.

By 9am a dozen strawberry growers, commuting from neighbouring fields and villages, are ready to trade at the Marché aux Fraises (Strawberry Market), their decorated stalls a sea of red, lined with the glossiest, most perfectly red strawberries ever likely to be seen. No bruised or mouldy specimens that have

↑ Punnets of highly scented Gariguette strawberries (Caroline Mills)

travelled across Europe in a refrigerated container, no hard bullets, no white tips; these juicy fruits were on the plants hours before. Behind the stallholders, boxed supplies stand 2m high – by 4pm all the strawberries are sold.

The warmth of the spring sunshine picks up a soft breeze and the sweetest scent tickles the nose, the lips begin to quiver, the throat suddenly feels dry, longing to be reacquainted with the mouth-watering juice that follows the bite of each delicate berry. For the Gariguette is a sensual fruit, its flavour and scent the sweetest and most pungent of strawberry varieties.

Characterised by an elongated, brilliant red appearance, it is made all the more special because of the availability for only three to four weeks of the year in May to early June – no flavourless extended seasons. And, because the fruits don't travel well, they are virtually unobtainable in the UK. So, as in days gone by, you have to wait and look forward to their seasonal arrival.

We move from one stall to the next, the temptation to taste becoming more unbearable with each passing collection. The final stall sells *les fraisiers* for those who wish to cultivate at home, a worthwhile investment.

With a competition for the best decorated stall and best fruit, there's a friendly rivalry among growers. I speak to Yves Sembille, a producer whose entire crop is grown in polytunnels. On the next stall, Alain Roche is selling produce from his one-hectare plot. I ask if he too grows everything undercover. A look of surprise

↑ Beaulieu-sur-Dordogne (Superstock)

(or disgust) falls on his face. 'Not at all,' he replies, 'while I do use polytunnels for some of the fruit, many of our strawberries are cultivated in the open air. It's more natural than polytunnels and there's more sunshine. We are up in the hills where the air is fresh. The fruit is better when it's grown outside.'

My family seem to agree with him after a taste test. Buying a punnet of both the polytunnel and open-air strawberries, which look identical in their red jackets, we perform a blind-tasting experiment and the verdict is unanimous. The fruits grown outside appear to have significantly more flavour – a taste that explodes in the mouth and which requires a return visit to his stall to buy a complete box.

By mid-morning the bells have called the festival congregation from around the hills and beyond; strawberry purchasing by the tray is intense, together with anything else strawberry related. Visitors can be seen devouring while ambling the streets or sitting in doorways, the fruit too delicious to wait until later.

The whole town joins in: shop windows are decorated, the pâtisseries sell strawberry tarts and pink meringues, syrups and jams packed with fruit; market stalls offer other local specialities like *vin paillé* (straw wine), a sweet wine made with the grapes dried on a bedding of straw before pressing in December. It's a speciality of Corrèze, localised around Beaulieu and neighbouring Queyssac-les-Vignes and Meyssac.

The crowds are entertained by a medley of tunes from Brazilian Sambas to brass band numbers, all participants costumed in red, of course. But the showstopper is a giant tart! Eight metres in diameter and containing 800kg of strawberries, the enormous pastry fills the market place, a sea of red that is shared among the visitors at the end of the festival. No wonder the celebrations attract 20,000 visitors. *Vive la Gariguette!*

Beaulieu, as its name explains, sits by the River Dordogne, one of France's most loved rivers for its beauty. The little village is exquisite in its rustic charm, tucked among oak trees that line the river's banks.

After the festival, we venture out into the countryside for a short tour of the Dordogne. The valley throngs with tourists – arguably, too many – during the

SOUVENIR

The Gariguette is one of the earliest ripening strawberries, with fruits ready to pick from April. Gariguette strawberry plants can be purchased at the market during the Fête de la Fraise in Beaulieu. You will also find plants to purchase in early spring in garden centres throughout France. Gariguette plants can be purchased in the UK by mail order from ⬧ kenmuir.co.uk.

← The strawberry market, decorations and giant strawberry tart at Fête de la Fraise
(top: Caroline Mills; bottom: © Dordogne Valley)

height of summer but late spring, which already has the feel of summer in the Dordogne's southerly location, feels just right.

We follow the river west as it meanders relentlessly, as if trying to wriggle free amid the tamed countryside through which it flows. At **Domme**, a bastide village that demonstrates perfection in its imperfections of erratic rooflines, honeyed façades and rambling roses, we climb through the medieval web of streets for views. Perched on the edge of a bluff 150m above the Dordogne the village offers one of the finest expansive panoramas of the river.

We continue on, first to **La Roque-Gageac** and then to **Beynac-et-Cazenac**. Each village sits hemmed in between river and cliff. Each appears to personify perfection more than the last with a respective assemblage of cottages and castles reflecting in the river's water.

The Dordogne is well known for its canoeing and kayaking opportunities. At La Roque-Gageac, it's possible to enjoy a leisurely boat trip on a *gabare*, a traditional 18th-century flat-bottomed barge that was once used for carrying wine, truffles, chestnuts and all manner of other cargo for which the Périgord region is known.

There's only so much beauty one can consume continuously and by the time we reach **Sarlat-la-Canéda**, its concentration of historic buildings (the highest number of any town in France and all protected by law), becomes all too much. We are grateful to find an excuse to sit down and enjoy delicious Périgord cuisine. Or so I thought; without thinking I order a steak medium-rare.

↑ View of the River Dordogne from the village of Domme (RossHelen/Shutterstock)

I'd forgotten that in France I need to order *bien cuit* (well cooked) to my liking; when it arrived my medium-rare cow was all but still running in the field. Even more grateful than to find an excuse to sit down was I for the heavens to open, my al-fresco plate to be drenched by the rainwater flooding off the restaurant's sun canopy and to find an excuse to leave and sightsee Sarlat's rich collection of buildings once more.

From Sarlat, we drift northwards away from the river, to **Périgueux**, the Périgord's regional capital. It's the largest town in the area and, like Sarlat, has a healthy contribution to historic architecture, including Gallo-Roman remains. It's impossible not to notice the dominant white Romanesque cathedral, with its puffed-up domes and whimsical rooftop embellishments. And if the structure looks familiar, the cathedral's architect modelled his later Sacré Coeur, in Paris, on it.

We're in time to visit **Brantôme en Périgord**, where the Friday market is regarded as one of the finest gastronomic experiences in the Dordogne/Périgord region. The food perhaps tastes all the finer for the town's attractiveness; a clustered circle of stone dwellings beneath uniform brown tile roofs, all enveloped by a ring of the River Dronne.

We buy pork from local pigs that snuffle on truffles – the queue of nattering neighbours waiting to buy is so long that you know the pork must be something special. We buy cheese and a kilo of early cherries that vanish by the end of the day. And, yes, we buy Gariguette strawberries.

↑ A *gabare* barge on the Dordogne at La Roque-Gageac (beboy/Shutterstock)

ESSENTIALS

GETTING THERE & AROUND
Beaulieu-sur-Dordogne is on the D940 from Tulle to St Céré and half an hour's drive from Junction 52 of the A20 south of Brive-la-Gaillarde. From Beaulieu, we followed the river west on the D41/D803 to Souillac, the D703 to Domme and Beynac-et-Cazenac. Head northeast on D703 to Sarlat, the D47/D710/N221 to Périgueux followed by the D939 to Brantôme en Périgord. There are dedicated motorhome *aires* to **park** in all the main tourist villages and towns mentioned here, including Beaulieu-sur-Dordogne.

ACCOMMODATION
We stayed at **campsites**: Huttopia Beaulieu sur Dordogne (formerly known as Camping des Îles) beside the River Dordogne in Beaulieu-sur-Dordogne and Camping Peyrelevade, Brantôme en Périgord, plus *aires* at Domme, Sarlat-la-Canéda and Périgueux.

There are campsites every few metres along the River Dordogne, sometimes next to one another; it's one of the most popular areas of France for camping: Le Capeyrou, Beynac-et-Cazenac; Le Perpetuum, Domme; Le Grand Dague, Atur (for Périgueux). Like campsites, the area is filled with *aires* and it is also an excellent area for **France Passion** sites.

FIND OUT MORE

Dordogne Périgord Tourism
⊘ dordogne-perigord-tourisme.fr

Périgord Dronne Bell Tourist Board ⊘ perigord-dronne-belle.fr/en/home

Sarlat-la-Canéda ⊘ en.sarlat-tourisme.com

Vallée de la Dordogne Tourism
⊘ vallee-dordogne.com

Sarlat-la-Canéda (rui vale sousa/Shutterstock)

18 FRANCE'S GRAND CANYON

A PROVENÇAL TOUR THAT CIRCUMNAVIGATES THE GORGES DU VERDON IN A CAMPERVAN, ON FOOT & BY CANOE

WHERE	Provence (Alpes-de-Haute Provence & Vars)
DISTANCE/TIME	143 miles (230km)/3 days
START/FINISH	Castellane/Comps-sur-Artuby

Lit only by streetlamps, the façade of La Petite Auberge doesn't appear to have changed in centuries. Faded frescoed lettering advertises its name across the softened walls and its pigeon-blue shutters are half-closed to keep out the evening's soporific warmth. Diagonally opposite is La Taverne and numerous other quintessentially Gallic bistros. They all help to bolster the collection of ageless buildings that fit snugly around Castellane's central square, the Place Marché.

The inner sanctum of the square is decorated by stunted plane trees with silver-smooth trunks, laced together by La Tricolore bunting. The central water fountain, embellished by geraniums so carmine they glow luminous in the dark, continues to deliver crystal-cool mountain water, its constant trickle like a backing vocal harmonising with the performing jazz band.

In the half-moonlight, the silhouettes of forested hillsides shape the ethereal backdrop to the square. Around its edges, elderly residents sit straight-backed on benches to digest their Mediterranean meal while young innocents, no more than the height of their elders' seats, dance and twirl, naively the centre of attention as they leap. Others are lulled to slumber in comforting arms as their parents twitch, mesmerised by the music. A little boy, eager for bed, sucks his thumb and

↑ Gorges du Verdon (JFFotografie/Shutterstock)

takes his pew to look on, his summer culottes displaying muddy knees beneath and the signs of an active day beside the river.

Carefree couples shimmy amid the parked mopeds under the plane trees while the shy huddle around the peripheries, shielded from notice by shrubs. Unbeknown to us, the musicians, dressed in linen white had been supping at the table beside us in La Taverne, thimble-sized coffee cups the remnants of their meal. Now they sway across the makeshift stage, the soft and silky song gliding over the village rooftops into the hills.

Braver souls begin to toe-tap over the gravel square, the very same that, hours earlier, in the merciless heat of the midday sun had held the sights and scents of the *mercredi* market. Then, sheltering beneath the canopied shade of stalls, we had sampled cured hams, soaked up the scent of herbs and the perfume of giant peaches. We'd tasted the sweetest of Provençal melons, sampled any number of honeys delicately flavoured with lavender and mountain pine, and bought the smelliest of cheese to accompany a fresh baguette for a lunchtime spread. Our reason for being here was to explore France's Grand Canyon, the Gorges du Verdon.

An hour or so from the Côte d'Azur and the Med, the Verdon is one of Provence's best-loved rivers. It's also one of the most dramatic in France, it's emerald green colour (hence its name) a thing of beauty.

Rising in the southwestern Alps, south of Barcelonnette and flowing into the River Durance 166km west, it is the section of the Verdon between the villages of Castellane and Riez that are regarded as the most impressive, when the river gouges a path through the Jurassic limestone to form a vast canyon that, in places, is almost 305m deep.

We began our exploration of the river at **Castellane**, an ancient trading post where many mountain roads meet. The loveable village, with its harmonious combination of captivating buildings, bistros, riverside setting and backdrop of mountains, is full of character and is popular as a centre for tourism. It's a great base from which to begin a multitude of walks – either along the riverside or climbing into the hills, with or without a guide – and there are many signposted walking trails within the area. Numerous outdoor activity companies also base themselves here, offering activities including rafting, canoeing and canyoning.

And so, returning to our riverside *aire* with a shopping bag groaning from our market purchases fit for a feast, we set about exploring the river. While I took to the footpaths to follow the river upstream, the three children spent a leisurely afternoon in it. For the river is suitably shallow at Castellane and it proves a popular bathing spot with families. That said, caution is always required: the Lac de Castillon, upstream of Castellane, has a hydroelectric dam, so the depth of the river may rise at any time, even when the summer weather dictates shallow water.

Our first sightings of imposing scenery appeared on a walk not long after we left Castellane to follow the right bank of the river. Rocky crags seemed to pierce the sky before us as the stripy limestone rose and fell like a soundwave. With every footstep through parched grassland, the ground erupted with the flutter of cobalt blue and copper, each butterfly ascending mere inches before landing on the electric-blue globe thistles that peppered the landscape. The wild scent of brilliant pink sweet peas was enough to ensure we became intoxicated with Provence and we were only a few miles into our exploration of the gorge!

Breathing in as we passed through narrow passages and wound our way along the river in the motorhome, sometimes 'ducking' for overhanging rocks, we began to climb sharply towards the **Point Sublime**. The Point acts as the entrance to the narrowest section of the canyon and offers eagle-eyed views of the ravine below. Beyond is a seeming desert landscape, high above the gorge with ironed-out mountains shimmering silver, scattered with stunted trees.

Our motorhome too cumbersome for the 24km, one-way Route des Crêtes – a road that shaves the dizzying canyon sides on the north bank but offers some of the finest views of the gorge – we continued to **La Palud-sur-Verdon**. Here the slimline streets end abruptly in tiny courtyards paved with flowerpots while the château and church stand out like giants. Past the village are lavender fields, the plants left uncut to leave the faintest tinge of mauve and welcome nectar for the resident bees.

Our route doubled back, briefly, in a hairpin to climb once more, delivering supreme views of the river at plummeting depths below. The Verdon is now deep enough to have turned from a glacial green to emerald and, plying the waters were dozens of microscopic boats, canoes, pedalos and rafts. They pre-empt a view, for one more corner in the road and the aquamarine **Lac de Sainte-Croix** appeared.

At first glance the lake seems moderately sized before it disappears from view when we climb through the oaks and heavily scented pines of the **Forêt Domaniale de Montdenier**. Another bend or two in the road and the vastness of the lake – all 2,185ha of it – is clearly apparent.

Being the height of summer, the lake was teeming with tourists enjoying the cooling water. The heat was savage but we managed to find a quiet smooth-pebble beach with shady lakeside woodland for a spa-like swim.

Just north of the lake is **Moustiers-Sainte-Marie**, one of the most beautiful of all Provençal villages – indeed it is affiliated to Les Plus Beaux Villages de France (The most beautiful villages of France). Perched on the side of a terracotta hill brushed with almonds and cypress trees, we found pale pink houses with powder blue and olive green shutters and a tiny chapel that appears to grow from the rock. The village is renowned for its pottery and the narrow, cobbled streets are thronging with pottery studios and artists.

← **Top** Castellane **Below** Bathing in the Verdon at Castellane (both Caroline Mills)

As the sun sank and paragliders drifted back to earth, the colossal crags behind the village glowed salmon pink and Moustiers' famous star, dangling between two peaks, continued to shine long into the evening.

Full morning sun sent us on our climb from the village to the **Valensole plateau**, a vast agricultural plain that, in summer, is adorned with purple stripes amid patches of golden yellow. The area is the largest lavender (or, on a commercial scale, the hybrid lavandin) growing area in Provence, interspersed with crops of durum wheat. While most of the lavender heads had long been harvested when we were there, we still came across mauve blushes that continued most of the way to our destination, **Quinson**.

↑ Moustiers-Sainte-Marie (Caroline Mills)

West of the Lac de Sainte-Croix, Quinson lies beside the River Verdon. Here the children hired kayaks to explore the gorge downstream towards **Lac d'Esparron** while I took, once again, to the footpaths. Trekking west, it's a notable walk. At times the path rambles along the clifftops before descending riverside.

We returned to Moustiers-Sainte-Marie along the eastern side of the Lac de Sainte-Croix via **Aups**, a village that lies at the centre of olive production. Despite the brutal afternoon sun, players of *pétanque*, dressed in team kit and who were deep in serious concentration, swamped the village square to outwit opponents.

Moustiers disappeared from view before sunrise as we set out to drive the left bank of the gorge. The Lac de Sainte-Croix appeared a still, pallid blue, the entrance to the gorge resplendently verdant in its silence as we crossed over the **Pont de Galetas**. Climbing towards the perched village of **Aiguines**, the sun rose with us, and the lake became laced with a pink ribbon of sand.

Our route was quiet with a long, slow climb to **Étroit des Cavaliers** and its snake-like cliffs that all but touch at the rim. The descent took us over the **Pont de l'Artuby** but not before we stopped to gaze open-mouthed at adventurers taking an early-morning dip in the Artuby River via bungee rope. The bridge is a work of art and the gorge extraordinarily deep! A little further on and another climb, it was as much as we could do to precariously peek over the edge of the **Balcons de la Mescla** to appreciate the terrifying views and watch the waters of the Rivers Verdon and Artuby swirl together in a giant bend.

↑ Quinson, a scenic village and a good place from which to hire kayaks to explore the Basses Gorges
(Juan Carlos Munoz/Shutterstock)

We'd reached the highest point east of the Pont de l'Artuby and the closest to the Verdon that we'd get on the left bank. From here on, the road descends and moves away from the gorge into open ranch-like plains dotted with transhumant herds of sheep.

Whether using footpath, river or road, we'd seen some of the most superlative scenery in Provence and, now our jar of lavender honey has long since been devoured, we won't hesitate to return.

↑ Pont de l'Artuby (kavram/Shutterstock)

ESSENTIALS

GETTING THERE & AROUND We approached the town of Castellane from the north on the N85. An alternative entrance to the Gorges du Verdon, from the west, is at Riez, useful if arriving from the A51 motorway.

The route along both the right and left banks is narrow, winding and precipitous in places but is perfectly acceptable for motorhomes taking it slowly (as everyone is); we drove at little more than 20mph for the entire route. There are places to pull-off the road every few metres.

It is not recommended for motorhomes to travel along the Route des Crêtes. Verdon e-bike, based in La Palud-sur-Verdon, offers e-bike tours along the route, a much less nerve-wracking experience than negotiating the road in a large vehicle.

For those who would prefer to leave the motorhome in a campsite and explore the canyon 'van-free, the Navette des Gorges shuttle bus operates daily throughout July and August and every weekend and public holiday between 1 April and 30 June, and 1 to 15 September.

Petrol stations are scarce along the route. Fill up at the Super U supermarket in Castellane or Régusse. We came across one other petrol station at les Salles-sur-Verdon but it is very expensive – use for emergencies only.

The lakeside road from Moustiers-Sainte-Marie to les Salles-sur-Verdon is wide and there are many huge parking areas along the left bank of the Lac de Sainte-Croix. There is the occasional height barrier but motorhomes will have no problem parking.

ACCOMMODATION We stayed on *aires* in Castellane and Moustiers-Sainte-Marie. There are also *aires* at: Riez, les Salles-sur-Verdon, Trigance (though beside a busy road), Comps-sur-Artuby and Quinson. Quinson is particularly useful for canoeing or hiring an electric boat on the Verdon, being just 200m from two hire centres. There is also a private *aire* directly opposite the most popular part of the Lac de Sainte-Croix, where the boat hire kiosks operate.

The Gorges du Verdon is a popular tourist area and there are many campsites along the route including 15 around Castellane, many in the area near Rougon, and also around the Lac de Sainte-Croix. Recommended: Huttopia Gorges du Verdon, Castellane; Terra Verdon, Castellane; Camping Municipal, Rougon.

FIND OUT MORE

Alpes de Haute-Provence *⌗* alpes-haute-provence.com
Castellane *⌗* castellane.org
Location-Nautic (canoe & electric boat hire) *⌗* locationnautic.fr

Maison du Parc naturel régional du Verdon *⌗* parcduverdon.fr
Moustiers-Sainte-Marie *⌗* moustiers.fr
Verdon e-bike *⌗* verdonebike. pagesperso-orange.fr

19 PROVENDER IN PROVENCE

GATHER SUMMER PRODUCE IN SPRING

WHERE	Provence (Provence-Alpes-Côte-D'Azur: Vaucluse; Bouches-du-Rhône; Gard)
DISTANCE/TIME	160 miles (258km)/4 days
START/FINISH	Apt/Aigues-Mortes

Silvery green olive trees are baked in parched soil, their stunted snake-like trunks blackened with age. Opening the door of the motorhome as we pull up beside argentine slivered rocks drenched in sunlight at the summit of Les Alpilles, a wave of scent hits me with such potency, it's like a beguiling linctus. Rosemary, thyme, lavender, marjoram, pine, all mingle together in a heady concoction that explodes among the senses. Earlier, riotous coloured cloths in customary Provençal patterns had covered the tables of open-air cafés in Saint-Rémy-de-Provence, each groaning with a plentiful supply of mouth-watering platters.

We were on a 'where-shall-we-go-next?' tour of France and had spent a few days drifting south-ish. Parked up under the gaze of Mont Blanc, with skiers arriving for a last-minute end-of-season charge down the slopes, 'Where next?' came the question. Hands clasped tightly around my hot chocolate, the heater

↑ Bunches of dried lavender for sale in a Provençal market (Alon Farago/Shutterstock)

on full and a harsh frost decorating the windscreen, an image of sun-baked olive groves began to appear. 'The market is on in Apt tomorrow.' We were suddenly on a schedule; to reach Apt by nightfall.

Leaving Chamonix, early April, in fleece-lined trousers and extra jumpers beneath a clear winter sky, we moved into spring around lunchtime while driving through the lime-green Chartreuse Natural Park (famed for its liqueur that is as green as its fields), cowslips smothering the fields and the roadsides. The scenery ever changing, the famous walnut trees around Grenoble still bare, we hit summer as we turned south following the River Rhône, and the winter layers were peeled off. First came blossoming almond trees and vineyards, then the odd patch of lavender, too early for its purple hue, passing the names of well-known Côtes-du-Rhône wine villages. We arrived in Apt at dusk.

Apt is a small town in the centre of the Vaucluse *département* of Provence, but its Saturday market is considered one of the most important – and largest – in the region. It's weekend entertainment: we watched as a pavement piano was wheeled into place ready for the weekly festivities. It's also huge; when you think you've come to the end, another alleyway filled with stalls appears.

Everything you expect from a Provençal market selling local produce is here: olives, oils, charcuterie, fish, bread, meats, cheeses, wine, herbs, delicious lavender honey, plus of course, lavender. We were just in time for the first of the season's strawberries from Carpentras, a nearby town renowned for its fruit, and the first asparagus. Supper that evening was an easy find.

↑ **Left** Charcuterie for sale in the market at Apt **Right** Apt is renowned for its production of glacé fruit, made with locally grown produce (both Caroline Mills)

Apt is also the self-proclaimed capital of the world for glacé fruits. It's rare to find these on the town's market stalls due to the heat, but there are plenty of producers who have air-conditioned shops about town. We bought ours from Confiserie Le Coulon Denis Ceccon on Quai de la Liberté (the main road through Apt). Talking to the assistant, she explained that all the fruit is sourced locally, using specific varieties for colour and flavour to avoid using artificial enhancers. The glacé apricots and baby figs are heavenly!

We chose a grassy spot out of town for lunch, among the blossoming cherry trees and the vineyards of the Côtes du Luberon. The Montagne du Luberon was on one side of us and the soothingly pink hilltop town of **Gordes** perched high above on the other. It was the most unpretentious, yet, as panoramas go, the grandest of picnic spots to munch on a baguette before we ventured to visit the **l'Abbaye de Sénanque**.

Hidden deep in the hills, the 12th-century abbey is a retreat for Cistercian monks who, amid prayers, grow and sell lavender (actually the commercial variety, lavandin). The abbey's peace and serenity is breathtaking; silence must be observed at all times. Spring is by no means the best time to view the lavender in its purple finery but the scent within the valley still creates a rewarding visit.

Through **Cavaillon**, France's main melon-growing centre and also home to an important market (on Mondays), we headed for **Saint-Rémy-de-Provence**, a touristy but civilised town filled with characteristic plane trees, an imposing *hôtel de ville* and plenty of pavement cafés. Our only outdoor eating was an ice cream in the summer heat; naturally it had to be flavoured with lavender.

↑ We visited L'Abbaye de Sénanque in spring, before the lavender was in flower, but summer is the time to see it at its best (ventdusud/Shutterstock)

Saint Rémy is also famous for its association with artist Vincent Van Gogh, who, as a sick patient, stayed at Saint-Paul de Mausole for 12 months. The gardens and grounds of the former monastery are open to the public (it remains a hospital and therefore quiet must be observed), where it's possible to see the views the artist painted locally during one of his most prolific phases of artwork. The more recently opened Musée Estrine is also one to visit for fans of Van Gogh art.

We pottered cross-country to **Les Alpilles**, a chain of small, rocky mountains just south of Saint-Rémy, that are fantastic for walking. At the top, Le Caume,

↑ Saint-Rémy-de-Provence (trabantos/Shutterstock)

there is plenty of parking, and being Easter Sunday, many people were enjoying the sunshine, walking and picnicking under the holm oak and pine trees. The fresh scent of wild rosemary, thyme, rock roses and privet covered the ground. This was the perfect place for our Easter egg treasure hunt with chocolate treats bought earlier in Saint Rémy, something that took onlookers by surprise!

South of Les Alpilles, more vineyards and olive groves vie for position while deep purple irises, just like those that Van Gogh painted, filled the villages of Maussane-les-Alpilles and Fontvieille.

We were on our way to the **Camargue**, a regional natural park of unique character that covers much of the Rhône delta. Don't judge the Camargue from the main thoroughfares, though. It's on the tiny roads and while walking that you see the beauty of the area, its marshland and wildlife. We saw rice paddies glinting in the sunlight, then huge white mountains, the saltpans of the Camargue stretching for miles and numerous flamingos, pale pink, their huge bills slurping up the marine landscape.

Past **Salin de Giraud**, a tiny, but passable, road between flamingo lakes leads to the sea and a beach, miles long, where scores of motorhomes park on the sand for remote windswept activities. It's a wild place.

Crossing the Camargue from east to west, slowly exploring this unique salty marsh, we began to see the indigenous white 'wild' horses for which the area is famous, along with black bulls bred for bullfighting in the nearby town of **Arles**. Small sheds appeared every few miles on the roadside offering regional produce. Each sold a selection of Camargue rice, salt and olive oils, Vins des Sables (Wine of the Sands) and Saucisson Taureau, a charcuterie sausage made from Camargue bulls.

Lured in by the prospect of buying more Provençal strawberries, one stall thrust a sample thimble of chilled Muscat de Frontignan, a sweet *apéritif* wine made in the nearby village of Les Paluns, into my hand as I arrived. The sweetness in the late afternoon sunshine against the salty air tasted delicious and I succumbed to their sales tactics.

We arrived early evening in **Aigues-Mortes**. The medieval walled town, built at the time of the Crusades, was buzzing. Its network of criss-crossed streets are lined with some pretty tawdry knick-knacks but there's a wealth of eateries, too. We opted to pick over the remnants of our Provençal provender for dinner in the 'van, peaceful and out of the way from the town centre bustle.

Later that evening, with the children fast asleep, the remains of a glass of red in hand, I sat outdoors under a lamp where we were staying, close to the Étang de la Ville. Early April, in shirtsleeves, I could gaze up at the illuminated town's ramparts, smell the salty sea air and listen to little boats arriving back from a day at sea. For us, this is what touring is all about.

← **Top** Traditional horses of the Camargue (GUDKOV ANDREY/Shutterstock) **Below** Flamingos are a regular sight in the Camargue (pixelshop/Shutterstock)

ESSENTIALS

GETTING THERE & AROUND Apt is 44km east of the A7 (junction 24), on the D900. Cross Les Alpilles on D5 south of Saint-Rémy-de-Provence. As the D36D from Salin de Giraud to the beach road is narrow with lakes either side, it's worth making sure that you are not arriving at the seafront as the exodus of vehicles back to dry land occurs. **Parking** motorhomes is very difficult in the heart of Saint-Rémy-de-Provence – it's always busy and a one-way system is unforgiving in searching for a large enough space. But there are five campsites within walking distance of the town, including one on the road from Cavaillon and we had no trouble with off-road parking just near this, a few hundred metres from the centre.

ACCOMMODATION
We stayed at: **Le Camping des Cèdres**, Apt (in the centre of town, just a few minutes' walk to the market) and *aires* in Gordes, Les Saintes Marie de la Mer and Aigues-Mortes. Campsites: Le Clos du Rhone, Saintes-Marie-de-la-Mer; La Petites Camargue, Aigues-Mortes).

FIND OUT MORE

Arles Tourist Board (for the Camargue) ⌂ arles-tourisme.com
Luberon Pays d'Apt Tourist Board ⌂ luberon-apt.fr

Saint-Rémy-de-Provence & Alpilles ⌂ alpillesenprovence.com

Aigues-Mortes (Pascale Gueret/Shutterstock)

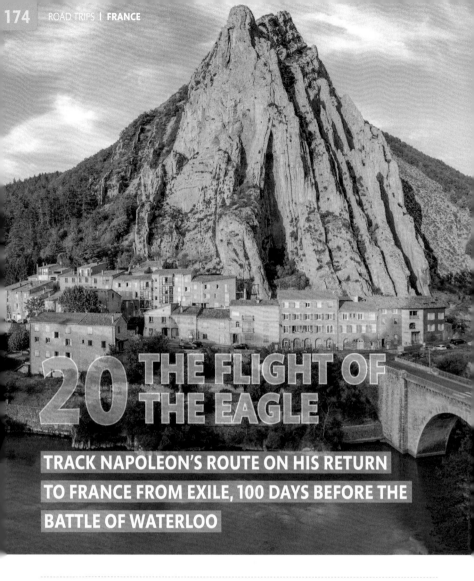

20 THE FLIGHT OF THE EAGLE

TRACK NAPOLEON'S ROUTE ON HIS RETURN TO FRANCE FROM EXILE, 100 DAYS BEFORE THE BATTLE OF WATERLOO

WHERE	Provence-Alpes-Côte-d'Azur (Alpes-Maritimes, Alpes-de-Haute-Provence, Hautes-Alpes) & Auvergne Rhône-Alpes (Isère)
DISTANCE/TIME	265 miles (427km)/4 days
START/FINISH	Saint-Laurent-du-Var/Grenoble

A s history lessons go, lying on a beach in sun-blessed Cannes and climbing mountains perfumed with lavender beats a stuffy classroom and an even more tiresome textbook.

On 18 June 1815, the British General, the Duke of Wellington, aided by Prussian forces, defeated the French Emperor Napoleon I a handful of kilometres south of

↑ Sisteron (Tatiana Popova/Shutterstock)

Brussels to bring an end to a turbulent period of history across Europe. Napoleon abdicated and was exiled to the Atlantic island of Saint Helena but it was not the first time he'd had to flee.

Just four months earlier, Napoleon returned from his first stint as an exiled emperor, on the Italian isle of Elba, to land on French soil and reclaim his throne. His trek though the Alps was treacherous in both the terrain and the potential hostilities from Royalist soldiers towards he and his congregating army. 'The Flight of the Eagle', as his journey became known, from the south coast to Grenoble (and on to Paris), is considered not only daring but also, today, one of the most beautiful tourist routes in France. The Route Napoléon, France's first-ever signposted tourist route created in 1932, is as popular today as it was then; history aside, with the countryside on offer, one can appreciate why.

My tour begins with a fabulous sun-drenching, soul-lifting drive *au bord de la mer* from **Saint-Laurent-du-Var**, through Antibes to **Golfe Juan**. This is where, returning from exile, Napoleon landed from his boat trip across the Mediterranean.

There's an air of glamour that lines the **Côte d'Azur**, with gleaming yachts the size of mansions, but Golfe Juan is quieter than neighbouring Antibes or Cannes. With a very attractive sandy beach and a handful of coastal cafés, it's right on the promenade that the plaque announcing Napoleon's arrival – and the start of the Route Napoléon – sits. Town centre parking is awkward (on-street only) and the first few metres of the route incorporate a 2.6m underpass so many motorhomes need to continue along the seafront to Cannes and pick up the D6185. It's an appealing drive and, historically, more accurate.

There's no doubt about it, **Cannes** really does have elegance in abundance. The wedding cake hotels, a glistening sea with boat trips to neighbouring islands, and multiple eateries both in the centre of town or refined dining at beachside restaurants, make a special day out. Unfortunately, Cannes does *not* like motorhomes so visits to the town require some forethought; see *Essentials*, page 180.

Napoleon stopped in **Grasse**, and so do I. The capital of perfume, 60% of the world's production originates from the town. Many of the 65 perfumeries welcome visitors, of which none have especially famous names. Though, as my tour guide at **Galimard** perfumery explains, 'While you'll have heard of Christian Dior or Chanel, you won't have heard of the "noses" that create their perfumes. You pay more for the posh bottle and the name than you do for the actual perfume.'

Galimard is the oldest perfumery in Grasse, dating back to the 18th century. The company has 150,000 formulae for scents and a tour around the labs allows you to smell (and buy) the latest perfume trends. Popular among tourists is the opportunity to visit the bottling room and create your very own scent, departing with a 100ml bottle of Parfum Whoever.

As I climb out of Grasse, stopping for lunch at **Le Chêne de l'Empereur** – a picnic spot with magnificent views of the coast – the soft, warm air is indeed perfumed as it rises above the wild thyme and the fragile, crumpled pink paper Cistus. The picnic area is a great place from which to begin a walk among the skipping butterflies, including one to **Saint-Vallier-de-Thiey**, where I was heading next.

Sheltered by a horseshoe wall of rock, the pretty town of Saint-Vallier is pleasing on the eye. Place de l'Apié is the Napoleonic landmark but venture a little further and you'll find charming alleyways and courtyards to poke around. And while there's an assortment of open-air cafés, the vast green in the centre of town is a focal point.

From here on, the Route Napoléon really does become one of the best and most scenic tourist routes in Europe. Initially, with long, winding hairpins, there are incredible views over the Côte d'Azur and the wooded hills of **Esterel** as the sun loungers become microscopic dots. Indeed, with every kilometre through the Préalpes the scene changes, the mood alters and there's something new to look at, from a plateau of hills and rocks around **Escragnolles** to terraced 'parkland' and wide grass valleys at **Séranon**. With footpaths through the pine woods and the vociferous song of the cicadas, it's tempting to stay put and bask in the 'silence' of the secluded landscape.

By the time I descend into **Castellane**, I've crossed three administrative *départements* and entered the Gorges du Verdon Forest. At an ancient crossroads that made Castellane a prosperous trading point eons ago, the town is arguably the most beautiful on the route. Like St Vallier, it too has narrow cobbled streets

↑ Perfume museum at Galimard perfumery (EQRoy/Shutterstock)

and alleyways to navigate on foot and the joy is not to head straight for the tourist information centre for a map, but simply to see where each turn leads.

Climbing high above the rooftops provides magnificent views of the surrounding hills, and of the gargantuan rock that precariously resides over the town. There are views also of the superlative Gorges du Verdon; Castellane is a focal point for kayaking and white-water rafting along the river (page 158). It's also the perfect place from which to set out for a walk.

By evening, the decorative town centre comes alive with attractive restaurants serving an array of regional dishes. I wait until morning for my sustenance, to take pleasure in a stroll around the Wednesday market. There's no more than a dozen stalls but each one sells local produce – homemade sausage, goats cheese from a nearby farm, the delectable scent of Provençal strawberries and nougat – enough to create a lunchtime feast with a visit to the neighbouring boulangerie.

Such is the beauty of the countryside along the Route Napoléon that it's tempting to dive off and explore side roads. But I know now that I wouldn't miss one inch of the route. From Castellane, Napoleon went north across the mountains to **Saint-André-les-Alpes** while today's tourist route continues along the N85. I take a quick detour off the Route (towards St-André) to venture as far as the swimming-pool-blue **Lac de Castillon**, and watch the swifts enjoy the warmth emanating from the mountain-high concrete dam. But the map's contours are foretelling me not to deviate from the signposted route and I soon realise why.

Returning to Castellane and climbing northwest on the Route Napoléon, I come across the first lavender fields along the way, lake views followed by enormous

↑ Spring in Castellane (Caroline Mills)

slabs of rock. A geologist's dream, the scenery is more than dramatic as the road winds around and between the **Clue de la Roche Percée** and the **Clue de Taulanne** to Senez. For those brave enough to peer over the roadside, below is the crashing water of the River l'Asse as it hides in canyons. On the horizon, the dominant snowy peaks of the Alps are beyond.

I descend to the valley floor, where the drive from a rather disappointing Barrême, little more than a ribbon of rundown warehouses, to **Digne-les-Bains** continues to follow the l'Asse initially; it's picturesque but nothing like as dramatic as the section from Grasse to Senez. Beyond, Napoleon spent the night at the château in Malijai – a plaque on the pink walls tell you so, while his soldiers dozed in the park behind. On this occasion, the park throngs with troops of pétanque playing locals.

I pass olive groves and views of folded rock formations, with a short detour to **Les Mées**. Prettier still, having turned north into the great Durance valley, is the tiny village of Volonne. On the banks of the Durance, and with a lovely riverside recreation area, it's the kind of ancient village you'd expect to see in a set for an old French movie. I'd have liked to stay longer but I'm keen to get to **Sisteron**, a town with numerous National Heritage sites, including an impressive citadel.

Perched high above the town, the citadel was disarmed while Napoleon ate lunch in Volonne. I limber up with a wildflower-strewn walk to this mammoth fortress from the motorhome *aire*, which sits directly beneath. It's worth the climb, for the views over the Durance valley to the craggy peaks in the distance are something special. By late evening the setting sun laces the peaks with an orange ribbon.

↑ Clue de Taulanne on the Route Napoléon (Caroline Mills)

With the Durance a brilliant emerald and the citadel iridescent in the morning splendour, I leave Sisteron anticipating that the initial drive along the side of a motorway is likely to be rather dull. How wrong I am! Fruit orchards, perched villages and the whitest of mountains so dazzling with beauty they are hard to ignore. One appears higher, whiter and greater than them all, a beacon symbolising my proximity to the **Massif des Écrins**. Abruptly, my eyes focus on a flock of parachutes gracefully playing with the air. It is, indeed, a perfect day for flying.

The tandem skydivers had taken off from the alpine airfield at **Tallard**, reputedly Europe's busiest leisure flying centre. I watch as they land and no sooner has one bunch touched the ground others take off, ready to make the jump of a lifetime. The mountains beckon and I find myself requesting a flight in a light aircraft from the Aéroclub Alpin. Within half an hour, headset on, my pilot and I are speeding along the runway in our four-seater plane. What a view!

Flying over the château at Tallard, I follow the Route Napoléon in a way I hadn't imagined just an hour earlier. Eye-level with the mountain tops, it is 30 minutes well spent. How quickly Napoleon would have reached Paris!

If I'm honest, I would probably have ended my tour at **Gap**, some 21km north of the airfield. Despite the external urban sprawl, the town centre is a gorgeous cluster of painted houses, colourful shutters and suntrap squares perfect for al-fresco dining; all with a panoramic backdrop of snow-tipped mountains. It, I discover latterly, is the last of the excessively pretty towns; each town beyond becomes ever so slightly more down-trodden, crumbling and lacking sparkle.

That's not to say that the countryside and villages just north of Gap – the **Champsaur** – doesn't warrant stepping into a pair of boots for a mooch around the mountains, with wonderful scenes of the Massif des Écrins. These are pretty villages, in particular Saint-Bonnet-en-Champsaur, as the route picks up the stumbling River Drac.

↑ Take a flight in a light aircraft from Gap-Tallard for aerial views of the region (Caroline Mills)

ESSENTIALS

GETTING THERE & AROUND I picked up the Route Napoléon, which is signposted the entire way, at its starting point in **Golfe Juan** on the Côte d'Azur (having stayed overnight at Saint-Laurent-du-Var west of Nice and travelled along the coast via the D6007 to Golfe Juan). The route finishes in the centre of Grenoble though, and – as a large city – traffic and parking are difficult, particularly for motorhomes (Crit'Air sticker required). I didn't stop in Grenoble; for those that wish to, your best option is to stay at the nearby campsite (see below) and take the tram into the city centre.

Extreme care should be taken on the 8km section of road between Laffrey and Vizille (Rampe de Laffrey). The descent is more than 274m, with no stopping places or emergency escape lanes. Vehicles over 3.5m high are banned.

I had few problems **parking** along the Route Napoléon – there are places to pull off and admire the view every few metres. Parking is, however, tricky for 'vans on the Côte d'Azur. Motorhomes are not tolerated in Cannes, with signs that your vehicle will be towed away if it's left parked. Best options are to park further north, in Le Cannet and take the bus, or stay at one of the many campsites within the vicinity.

For Grasse, motorhomes should park during the day in the railway station car park and use the free bus to the town centre, or there are two dedicated motorhome spaces at Parking La Roque. In Gap, there's a motorhome *aire* on the road to Grenoble, within five minutes' walk of the town centre.

ACCOMMODATION I stayed on *aires* in Saint-Laurent-du-Var, Castellane and Sisteron. All three have a motorhome service point, felt safe and secure though none have hook-ups. There are many other *aires* along the route, including at Digne-les-Bains, Tallard and Gap. France Passion sites are limited, but there is a particularly useful one in Grasse, at Espace Terroirs, a shop that sells regional produce.

↑ Gap (Alastair Wallace/Shutterstock)

Laffrey, 25km south of Grenoble, is one of the most important settlements in Napoleon's return. Here, he advanced alone, unarmed, to face Royalist troops. He won them over making the path clear to arrive in Grenoble. A grand statue of the Emperor on horseback is at the Prairie de la Rencontre, where he met the troops.

Napoleon arrived in Grenoble to a siege, requiring a battering ram to break down the city gate. Upon my arrival I find myself under siege from the evening rush hour and I too would require a battering ram to make much headway through the traffic. So I sidle quietly away and, while Napoleon tracked on to Paris for his second bite in power, I begin a drive to Waterloo, in Belgium, where the Emperor lost his crown.

Regrettably, I did not have the 100 days that Napoleon had in France. Though I'd happily tour *his* route again.

There are more than 20 **campsites** along the Route Napoléon, with many more in the vicinity: Camping Le Rossignol, Antibes; Parc Bellevue, Cannes; La Paoute, Grasse; Les Framboiselles, Castellane; Camping des Prés Hauts, Sisteron; Le Bois de Cornage, Vizille.

FIND OUT MORE

Aéroclub Alpin ⌀ aeroclubalpin.fr
Castellane ⌀ castellane.verdontourisme.com
Gap-Tallard Airfield ⌀ gap-tallard.com
Grasse ⌀ tourisme.paysdegrasse.fr
Grenoble ⌀ grenoble-tourisme.com/en

Parfumerie Galimard ⌀ galimard.com
Provence-Alpes-Cote-d'Azir Tourism ⌀ provence-alpes-cotedazur.com/en
Route Napoléon ⌀ route-napoleon.com
Sisteron ⌀ sisteron-buech.fr

↑ Prairie de la Rencontre at Laffrey (Superstock)

21 BASQUE IN THE PIC OF THE PYRENEES

FROM BASQUE RED TO LAKE BLUE, ENJOY THE COLOURFUL PYRENEES

WHERE   Pyrenees: Nouvelle-Aquitaine & Occitanie (Pyrénées-Atlantiques, Hautes-Pyrénées & Haute-Garonne)
DISTANCE/TIME 314 miles (505km)/6 days
START/FINISH Saint-Jean-de-Luz/Tilhouse

The mountains are purple humps when I first meet them in early morning light. The sky is a pallid blue with tangerine-tinged clouds as the sun rises. Lingering mist seeps through the damp grass and valleys, and I note a hint of autumn in the air.

Clutching the hillside, little white cottages laced with Basque red light up the morning in a tell-tale sign I'm approaching the western foothills of the Pyrenees. I'm about to begin an in-depth tour of the mountains, initially in the Pays Basque before heading southeast towards the Hautes-Pyrénées and the Ariège.

The introduction to autumn doesn't last long. By the time I'm wandering around the harbour in **Saint-Jean-de-Luz**, the start of my tour, summer has regained momentum. Early-rising swimmers make the most of the sunshine as glistening white horses from the Atlantic lap on the beach, where yoga devotees also welcome the morning. Elsewhere in the historic town, cafés come to life with

↑ Vignemale, Hautes-Pyrénées (Caroline Mills)

le petit déjeuner and the first coffee of the day. Fresh figs, strawberries, layers of baguettes sculpted like a Jenga game and a huge frying pan of browning chicken thighs colour the stalls of the outdoor market.

The coastal town of Saint-Jean-de-Luz, 14km from the Spanish border, is a delight. Basque architecture is elegantly on show around the harbour, on the villa frontages along the beachside promenade and lining the streets of the old town centre. Art galleries are in abundance, painters attracted by the incandescent light of the Côte d'Argent (Silver Coast). In earlier years, Louis XIV was also attracted to the town – the French king married Maria Theresa of Spain here. There's a small museum in the house where the monarch stayed, though take a look in the church where the nuptials took place, too – and be sure to look up; the ceiling is quite a sight.

While Saint-Jean-de-Luz is at sea level, the mountains of the Pyrenees appear within touching distance. The **Montagne de Ciboure** and **La Rhune**, a popular mountain that endears itself to the folklore of the area, are visible from the town. I follow the River Nivelle from the town harbour on a very pleasant short drive into the foothills, through the radiantly pretty village of Ascain, to **Sare**. This village is so outstanding it makes 'radiantly pretty' Ascain suddenly look quite ordinary!

I feel as though I've walked into a film set as I approach Sare's tiny village square. My enthusiasm for the place was already overflowing not long after I arrived at the *aire* and sat to relish the lusciously verdant gentle mountains that surround the village. Now, late morning in the square and life is abundant. Wedding revellers, many dressed in traditional Basque attire, throng the Café de la Post for pre-ceremony drinks before dancing in file into church. The bells chime as spectators sit on terraces to watch a Basque speciality, a weekend *pelota* match. Both the boulangerie and tiny market stall on the opposite side of the square are accomplishing excellent trade selling traditional Gâteau Basque (choice of a filling of *crème pâtissière* or fresh cherries). And, all the while, the green mountains are seen from every direction.

Sare is a fabulous village for wandering and from which to set off hiking or cycling. While the main square sits on a hill, the village is made up of seven or so fragmented communes dotted across the countryside. There are little lanes and footpaths in abundance, including the national GR10 footpath, which traverses the Pyrenees from the Atlantic to Mediterranean coasts, and which is also used by pilgrims heading over the Pyrenees to Spain's Santiago de Compostela.

I follow a hearty lunch in Akoka, a seven-table restaurant serving a traditional Basque menu of local produce, with hours of ambling, first on the GR10 to visit some of Sare's communes and then a steep climb to La Rhune and the Col des Trois Fontaines. What a walk! Chestnut and oak trees keep the heat of the afternoon sun away before arriving at a clearing for immense views of wooded hills and a trio of slivered rocky outcrops.

Sare is affiliated to and recognised as one of Les Plus Beaux Villages de France (The Most Beautiful Villages of France) – and it is. So, too, is its near neighbour, **Ainhoa**, where I visit next – a long one-street village lined with big Basque residences and alluring views of the hills. Likewise, my next stop, Saint-Jean-Pied-de-Port, a historic crossing point and hostelry stop for pilgrims on the Saint James' Way to Santiago, is also within the scheme.

I have the choice of reaching Saint-Jean from Ainhoa via Spain or remaining in France. I choose the latter because the route, via **Espelette** (renowned as the centre of pimento cultivation) and **Cambo-les-Bains**, is sublimely beautiful. The road follows the valley of the bubbling River Nive; it's a well-used river for rafting with the village of **Bidarray** the focus for such activities.

I arrive in **Saint-Jean-Pied-de-Port** early morning, something that's worth considering in high season (though I recommend a stay at the very attractive riverside municipal campsite) as the town becomes extremely busy by 11am. The town retains its four ports, including one at either end of the main street, the Rue de la Citadelle. It's an ancient, cobbled thoroughfare that has seen thousands of pilgrims over the centuries and where it's possible to buy anything, so long as you want espadrilles, stripy Basque fabrics, cured hams and cheese.

← **Top** Magnificent walking at Sare, including along the ancient GR10 pilgrims' footpath **Below** Saint-Jean-de-Luz and Ciboure (both Caroline Mills)

Climb to the citadelle for excellent views over the town, the surrounding hills and the Roncesvalles Pass (route to Spain). Otherwise, head along the riverside and within five minutes there are pretty walks along country lanes.

If the bustle of town becomes too much, make the 3km journey to **Saint-Jean-le-Vieux**, a neighbouring village with old Basque houses and an attractive village square with a pleasant restaurant. Or grab a baguette and head off into the hills on the signposted **Route des Cols**, as I do. The views are immediate and worthy, including the first *pic* (peak) of my trip (the **Pic de Behorleguy**), with a run along the valley to **Bassaburua** before beginning the ascent of the **Col d'Iraty**.

The Pyrenees feel so different to the Alps. There aren't the lush meadows one finds in the Alpine valleys. The Pyrenees appear more rugged and wild, even on the lower slopes, and more remote, too. For views west, the **Aire d'Iraty** is a good place to stop, though continue a little further uphill to the Saint Sauveur Chapel, and the panorama extends towards the wild Forêt d'Iraty and Sommet d'Occabe.

A gentle descent enters into the charming **Iraty River valley**. It's merely a bumbling stream that creates a very popular picnic and paddling spot for families, and a place to begin a walk in the Iraty Forest. I press on by road, through the beech forest (reputedly the largest in Europe at 170km²), until I reach **les Chalets d'Iraty**. A short walk here is rewarded with 360°-degree views of the forest, of distant peaks, of smooth, moulded moors and north, beyond the foothills, to the plain and the Gave d'Oloron.

The **Col d'Orgambidesca** is my first big road descent, with the Ossau valley hundreds of metres below. The scenery changes with every turn and It feels a

↑ Road to the Col d'Iraty (Caroline Mills)

very long time before I reach the tiny hamlet of **Larrau**, passing wild Basque pottock ponies along the way. If the landscape didn't feel wild and remote enough before, it becomes even more so as I turn off towards Sainte-Engrâce. The route is pleasantly level for ten or so kilometres – a chance to catch one's breath after the mammoth descent of the Orgambidesca – running alongside a small stream and with views of the chalky-rocked **Gorges de Kakouetta**. Then the road climbs again, past the even more remote **Sainte-Engrâce** – little more than a church, a couple of farms and a *pelota* court – until arriving at the tremendous karst landscape around **Arette-la-Pierre-Saint-Martin** ski resort, just a couple of kilometres from the Spanish border.

I arrive as mist swirls in to generate the belief that anywhere other than my immediate surroundings exist. A very agreeable, raucous cacophony of mountain bells sound out as a thousand-strong herd of sheep, each with a bell around its neck, nibble down the ski slopes beneath the resort's chairlift. That evening, as dusk falls, and the sonorous clang of the munching sheep go quiet, the mist clears in dramatic fashion to reveal the highest mountain in the western Pyrenees – the resplendent **Pic d'Anie**, poking up from behind the limestone pavements. So compelling, I do nothing else but watch until it goes dark. Very, very dark.

You don't need to walk far from the ski resort to view the limestone landscape. It's all around. Walk a little further, though, and you'll find a panorama that draws you in. I walk towards the **Pescamou plateau**, where I discover a giant circular wall of rock. Having passed half-a-dozen roaming cattle and a mountain hut making

↑ Karst landscape at Arette-La-Pierre-Saint-Martin (Caroline Mills)

and selling *fromage du brebis* (sheep's cheese) I have no company – except for the silence of a golden eagle that soars above, and a marmot that appears from a crevice in the limestone pavement.

Heading north to Arette, east, crossing the **Vallée d'Aspe** to Arudy, and running south along the valley of the **Gave d'Ossau**, I arrive in the small town of **Laruns**. It's a scenic spot for a town at the crossroads of two valleys, the Ossau and the Valentin, with a wall of mountains separating this focal hub of activity from the Aspe valley. As seems to be quite frequent in the Pyrenees, one moment you're in the remotest of locations, wild, rugged and absent of people, and suddenly a focal hub such as Laruns appears.

I take the road along the Valentin valley, with a climb up to **Eaux-Bonnes**. It's a crumbling spa town that has a charm about its tattered chic, with architectural relics from a beautiful past life and excellent views of the Gave d'Ossau River.

I always find it rather unsettling to see a shrine to the Madonna and child just before beginning the ascent to a mountain pass. Perhaps it's to remind one to treat the road and its hairpin bends cautiously, and to enjoy the views once stopped rather than while approaching a bend. Madonna greets travellers at the ski resort of **Gourette**, amid steep, steep jagged peaks as the ascent appears ever higher to the 1,709m **Col d'Aubisque**. The road climbs on to wide open moorland and the views from the summit of serrated rocks and fertile valleys can't fail to inspire. This, combined with the **Col du Soulor** (the two peaks proceed one another), is a popular mountain climb for robust cyclists, with the just reward to have a photograph taken beside a collection of colossal Le Tour bicycles.

Of the two, my preference is for the Col du Soulor. Here, the views to the Val d'Azun below, together with far-reaching peaks – including the Pic du Midi de

Bigorre in the distance – need some time to take in. The descent is rewarded with views over the pretty village of **Arrens-Marsous**, with smart houses, painted shutters and floral arrangements, and the vast Chapelle Notre-Dame de Pouey-Laün. Both offer a worthwhile stop.

After all the mountain passes, the Azun valley offers a welcome change, with wide, open pastures and the smell of fresh cut grass. I rename it the 'valley of the stone barns' for the numerous centuries-old barns along the way.

As I drive along the 'neighbouring' **Vallée de Saint-Savin** towards Cauterets later, early evening, it feels as though I'm facing an onslaught of traffic coming towards me. I understand why by mid-morning the following day, but not before I take an evening stroll around one of the most popular towns in the Hautes-Pyrénées.

Cauterets is a little like Eaux-Bonnes. It's a historic town that has become a fading relic of its Belle Époque. The architecture is all here, with coloured lacy balconies and spindly pinnacles that adorn rooflines. But once-grand spa buildings now house garish amusement arcades, the grand casino looks more like a seedy nightclub, back streets look tired and forlorn with boarded up windows and an all-too-frequent number of *À Louer* ('to rent') signs. But there's also something rather atmospheric about aging beauty, and the immediate centre, through which flows the glacial green Gave Gaube River, looks smart with plenty of places to eat.

I leave Cauterets early the following morning for the short drive to the **Parc National des Pyrénées** protected zone. The road terminates at a large car park, upon which one either sets out on foot, or chairlift to avoid a steady climb. There are a variety of paths, but I'm keen to take the one to the **Lac de Gaube**, a lake high in the mountains. It's a one-hour healthy climb (allow anywhere between 45 minutes and 1½ hours) along a rocky path, but the walk in the early shade amid trees, the constant trickle of gushing rivers and waterfalls, and wafts of mountain scent is glorious. When I arrive at the lake, it's in shade although some of the

↑ Tour de France bikes on the Col d'Aubisque (Caroline Mills)

mountain tops are already glowing. A rocky walk along the left bank to the far end is rewarding with level open ground and masses of rivulets amid stunted pine trees trickling towards the lake.

I'm not especially interested in bagging mountain summits, but I'll bag the **Vignemale**, the highest mountain of the French Pyrenees. Though I didn't climb it, as I return lakeside along the left bank, the sun rises up from behind a line of mountains and the Vignemale falls into the lake. It's a magical sight that's worth getting up early for.

It's a gentle wander on level ground to return from the lake via the chairlift, from which I can spy a long queue along the road into the car park. By the time I reach the famous **Pont d'Espagne** that spans a formidable waterfall plunging at full volume, it's busy with selfie-takers and I no longer have the peace of the mountain.

I follow the road back to Cauterets and the Saint-Savin valley to latterly drive along the parallel valley of the Gave de Pau, to Gavarnie. The village is famous for the nearby Cirque de Gavarnie, a vast circle of rock that is a UNESCO World Heritage Site – the top of the rock is the Spanish border. Most visitors head direct to Gavarnie but a few turn off the valley road at the village of **Gèdre**, as I do. The reason? To visit the Cirque de Troumouse.

The approach is dramatic, the scenery on an ever-larger scale. The road climbs over a 4km sharp ascent from **Héas** until it reaches the lone **Auberge de Maillet**. From there, unless you step out on foot, a tractor and road-train takes you the

↑ Cauterets (Caroline Mills)

remaining couple of kilometres to **Cirque de Troumouse**, a vast amphitheatre of mountains that is, reputedly, 11km wide. Its enormity is incomprehensible – far larger than the Cirque de Gavarnie – and you can easily spend a day here, walking, taking a picnic to sit beneath the walls of the circle or on the moorland plateau that's sheltered by Troumouse's mountain sides. I take the train up, and return on foot, basking in the heat of the day, appreciating the monkshood wildflowers and the large skipper butterflies that never seem to settle.

By the time I reach the village of **Gavarnie** in early evening, there are biblical scenes of walkers returning from their visit to the UNESCO site. From the village, the views of the cirque, despite a vivacious moon, are still drenched in sunlight.

There's only one way to reach the **Cirque de Gavarnie**; it's on foot, through the village and on one path alongside the Gave de Pau. That path is, naturally, lined with shops and eateries to catch the returning walker eager to stock up on cheap souvenirs or line the belly. For an evening 'stroll', I peel off on to a parallel stony path, past the church. It is the Saint James route to Santiago and the views of the river valley slopes and tiny fields, as I climb, are just right. It turns out to be less of a stroll, more of an energetic hike to a Bellevue, and I return to a quieter village. The stars that night! How they glisten *en masse* without the pollution of streetlights, tucked deep into the river valley.

I set out on foot as it's getting light the next morning to walk the hour or so to the Cirque. The cool air is invigorating and I find myself marching at pace for some reason. Perhaps it's the rhythm of the fast-flowing Gave de Pau beside me – like walking against the forward motion of an elevator – but the wall of rock

↑ Lac de Gaube (Caroline Mills)

and prospect of the Grande Cascade, reputedly the highest and longest waterfall in Europe, pull me along. I'm deliciously alone except for one family that set out at the same time.

If short on time, a 30-minute walk with the most level of ascents will get you to the vast bowl that's filled with pine trees and footpaths. But imagine, if you will, a Venn diagram. The cirque 'proper' is like a circle within a circle and you don't see this until you get there, which is another 45 minutes' walk of, initially, level walking then climbing through trees. The views of the cirque are arguably more impressive from the village than up close, but you do see the waterfall with greater intimacy as it nosedives towards the valley floor, and greater focus on the 1,500m sheer cliffs that, in places, are so ironed, they look as if the rock has been quarried.

As with the Lac de Gaube, I witness the sun rise over the mountains while walking in the shade but by 9am, as I return to the village, there's a continuous trail of walkers heading out towards the cirque.

From Atlantic to Mediterranean coasts via the Route des Cols, the overall ridge of the Pyrenees is 900km long. I'm approaching half-way and the focal point, the Pic du Midi de Bigorre. First, backtracking to Luz-Saint-Sauveur (a town that's worth a look for its castle ruins and knights-templar church), is a climb up the **Col du Tourmalet,** possibly the most famous of all the cols in the Pyrenees for its historic connection with the Tour de France over decades. Cyclists the world over come here to make the ascent.

It would be difficult to say to a cyclist who has accomplished the Tourmalet pass after a punishing climb in the saddle that, from the neighbouring summit of

↑ Waterfall at Pont d'Espagne (Caroline Mills)

the **Pic du Midi** – reached by a less gruelling gondola ride from **La Mongie** – the Tourmalet doesn't look quite so demanding!

There's more to the summit of the Pic du Midi than a 12-minute gondola ride and it's a fitting closure of a Pyrenean tour to see the mountains all laid out, stretching as far as one can see from east to west, and south. The summit houses a futuristic-looking observatory that does internationally renowned work. There's a fascinating multi-lingual exhibition, suitable for families, exploring factors of the solar and lunar systems, astrophysics, and topics such as the issues of light pollution. For a small additional fee, visitors may also visit the planetarium though by far the most popular attraction appears to be the Sky Walk, which protrudes to hang in mid-air from its rocky base.

I'm sorry to be leaving the high peaks behind but I'm not quite done with them yet. A drive north along the **Vallée de Campan** takes me to an area of the Pyrenees known as the **Bigorre**. Sitting between the Campan and Aure valleys, which run north to south, this tangled web of roads climbs up and down amid wooded foothills interspersed with open hillsides crammed with wildflowers, and remote villages in the valleys. The area is known for its gorges and caves – the Gourgue d'Asque and Esparros.

My route connecting Gerde, Marsas, Asque, Bulan, Espèche and Tilhouse is exalting; the wildflowers are some of the best representations I've seen throughout my tour of the Pyrenees. The Bigorre is fabulous countryside for walking or cycling (if you like hills) to explore further. As I climb up to **Tilhouse**, I stop for one last glance at the high peaks of the Pyrenees behind me. There, in an otherwise empty blue sky is the Pic du Midi, its landmark antenna jabbing at the firmament as if to deflate any puffs of cloud passing by.

↑ Immense views over the Pyrenees from the Pic du Midi. The gondola ride to the summit is pretty good, too! (Caroline Mills)

ESSENTIALS

GETTING THERE & AROUND
Saint-Jean-de-Luz is easily accessible on the A63 motorway from the north or, from Spain and the ports of Santander and Bilbao, the E70 (effectively the same motorway). From Saint-Jean take D918/D4 to Sare, D305 to Ainhoa, D20 to Cambo-les-Bains and then D918 to Saint-Jean-Pied-de-Port. Next is the D933 to Saint-Jean-le-Vieux, then D18/D19 to Larrau. Head north on D26/D113 to Arette-la-Pierre-Saint-Martin, and then on D132 to Arette. From there take D918 to Arudy, D934 to Laruns, and the D918 south to Argelès-Gazost. Continue south on D920 to Cauterets and Pont d'Espagne, backtrack on D920 and then take D921 to Gavarnie (D922 peels off to Cirque de Troumouse). Again, backtrack to Luz-Saint-Sauveur where you head east on D918 for La Mongie, then continue on D918/D935 towards Bagnères-de-Bigorre. For smaller 'vans and cars/bikes, take your pick of roads to explore the Bigorre area – there are plenty from which to choose! Extreme care and concentration should be taken on all mountain passes, taking into account that many of the high mountain roads do not have any form of crash barrier. Drivers that know the roads well are likely to want to drive considerably faster than you; there are plenty of places to pull off, so allow them to pass, allow your engine and brakes to have a breather, and enjoy the view! One particular mountain pass, the Col d'Aubisque, has signs stating it is not suitable for motorhomes owing to the occasional narrow section or overhanging rocks; I saw plenty of coachbuilt 'vans on the road, despite this, so use your own judgement of driving skills and nerve.

I cannot, however, recommend the roads around the Bigorre area of the Pyrenees for large vehicles. Many of the lanes are narrow and, unless your reversing skills uphill on single-track roads are top-notch, you'll only annoy the local residents. These lanes are best left to cars and small campervans or, better still, park up and explore them by bike.

Bulan, a village in the Bigorre area (Caroline Mills)

I saw no problems with **parking** anywhere, except Ainhoa where only small campervans will manage to park (or stop overnight at the campsite within walking distance of the village; see below).

All the mountain passes have large car parks to stop and enjoy the view or to head off on walks. There are a huge number of *aires*, useful for motorhomes to park in when visiting towns, including Saint-Jean-Pied-de-Port, even if not stopping overnight.

ACCOMMODATION
I stayed at: *aires* in Sare, Arette-la-Pierre-Saint-Martin, Cauterets, Gavarnie and La Mongie.

There are more than 100 *aires* in the Pyrenees and the foothills between the Atlantic and Mediterranean coasts, including all the main tourist towns and sites. There are also more than 30 France Passion sites.

Recommended **campsites**: Camping Harazpy, Ainhoa; Camping Ibarra, Sainte-Engrâce; Camping Mialanne, Arrens-Marsous; Camping d'Irati, Iraty Forest (the most gorgeous back-to-basics site beneath the trees in the forest); Les Gleres, Cauterets; Camping Bergerie, Gavarnie; La Ribère, Barèges.

Overnight parking/camping is not allowed officially within the Hautes-Pyrénées National Park, ie: at Pont d'Espagne (although I saw some 'vans that had stopped overnight in the main car park and some wild tent camping by experienced hikers at the southern end of the Lac de Gaube).

FIND OUT MORE
Hautes-Pyrénées Tourist Board
⚕ pyrenees-holiday.com
Pays Basque Tourism
⚕ saintjeanpieddeport-paysbasque-tourisme.com

Saint-Jean-de-Luz ⚕ saint-jean-de-luz.com

22 TWIN PEAKS

CROSS FROM THE PYRENEES TO THE ALPS, VIA THE MOST BEAUTIFUL VILLAGES IN FRANCE

WHERE	Occitanie & Auvergne-Rhône-Alpes (Hautes-Pyrénées, Haute Garonne, Ariège, Aude, Hérault, Tarn, Aveyron, Lozère, Ardèche, Drôme, Isère, Savoie, Haute-Savoie)
DISTANCE/TIME	780 miles (1,255km) from Pont d'Espagne (for Vignemale)/6 days
START/FINISH	Pont d'Espagne or Saint-Bertrand-de-Comminges (if you make this route a continuance of Route 21)/Chamonix-Mont-Blanc

The curtains are tweaked, inched back to peek at the sliver of dawn. When I arrived yesterday afternoon, Mont Blanc didn't exist; it's white cloak was accompanied by a matching shroud of fog and all that could be seen was a skirt of ice, draped down the mountainside towards Chamonix. Now, hurriedly half-dressed, I stand in the half-light awed by Western Europe's highest mountain. It gleams. My hot chocolate takes a long time to drink.

If you cross France with purpose to reach B from A, you'd take the autoroute and be there within a few hours. What a waste of scenery! I chose to cross the country from west to east by back roads linking Vignemale, the highest mountain on the French side of the Pyrenees, with Mont Blanc, the highest in the Alps. It's a journey of epic and ever-changing landscapes and, in the process, visits several villages recognised as France's most beautiful.

My tour begins in early morning as I climb from the **Pont d'Espagne** on foot to the Lac de Gaube, a mountain lake high in the Pyrenees National Park. Beyond the restful lake – a morning mirror as the sun rises from behind the enveloping peaks –

↑ Minerve, a Cathars village in the Languedoc (Cedric Weber/Shutterstock)

is Vignemale, sharp and stripy grey. Despite its distance, there is a deference to be shown so I sit for a while and watch as the day dawns on the mountain.

From the national park, my trip continues through the Pyrenees to the **Bigorre region** in the foothills (page 193). Once there, I follow the Neste River to **Saint-Bertrand-de-Comminges**, the first of the 'most beautiful villages of France' along the way. The hillside village, reputedly the exiled home of King Herod, is dominated by its 12th-century cathedral church; turn a corner in the road and it looms large. The walled settlement is tightly packed with a jumble of exceedingly pretty stone houses defining narrow streets not wide enough for a car. A selection of cafés, an art exhibition and museum, coupled with the UNESCO World Heritage Site-designated cathedral easily sees half a day gone, especially as I add a stroll around the remains of the Roman forum at the foot of the village.

I leave on the road to **Valcabrère** and come to the conclusion that I prefer this village; it has a similar collection of stone dwellings but offers a more open prospect. I cross the rivers Garonne (which ends up 310km northwest in Bordeaux) and Ger to follow the road to **St Lizier**, which looks very attractive on its hillside, and **Saint-Girons**, which looks equally scruffy, and cross into the **Parc Naturel Régional des Pyrénées Ariégeoises**. The Ariège is the most southeastern area of the Pyrenees and my stop overnight in the foothills near Baulou offers lovely views of fields and farms, jagged mountains and wooded hills with the distant choir of church bells and cow bells.

By misty morning all the views are gone; there's no rear-view mirror moment when I leave the Pyrenees altogether and the scenery flattens out around **Camon**.

This, too, is a Plus Beau Village though it doesn't come across as a tourist attraction like many of the other villages under the umbrella. There are no cafés, no shops except one tiny artist's studio, not even a bakery. The château and former abbey are privately owned (by an English couple that run an upmarket *auberge* and evening restaurant) and the houses appear charismatically shabby.

It's all very lovely, if a little melancholy looking in the silence of the day, made prettier still by the hundreds of rose bushes that climb façades along every street. There's a *roseraie*, too, a rose garden that borders the River Hers, which encloses the village in its defensive bend. The village is also on a *voie verte*, a former railway line that's now a 'green route' taking cyclists and walkers on traffic-free treks through the Cathar countryside.

As I continue through Cathar country by road towards **Carcassonne**, in place of wooded foothills are wide open plains, hummocks of sunflowers, wheat and ultimately vines as I drive along avenues of plane trees with khaki camouflage trunks.

There are two parts to Carcassonne: the bustling city centre; and 'La Cité', that feels much like a Disney-designed medieval theme park whose immaculately preserved ramparts hem in many tourists and much tat. Even the 'knight' standing outside the entrance to the drawbridge gates manages to remove two euros from the pockets of passers-by to have their photograph taken with him – and he does a handsome trade!

I continue on through the vine-growing **Minervois**, crossing over the distinguished Canal du Midi and follow, briefly, the Route des Vins du Minervois. With views of Corbières to the south and the Black Mountains to the north, I'm surrounded by vines, rotund pine trees, spindly cypress trees and bulging rocks as I pass through **Olonzac** (one of the Minervois' best-known wine villages) and

↑ Camon, a Plus Beau Village on the edge of the Pyrenees (Superstock)

the extraordinarily pretty village, **Azillanet**. Vibrant oleander bushes leap out of the landscape as I climb towards my next Plus Beau Village, **Minerve**. It's a landscape that takes me by surprise.

Salmon-pink Minerve is perched on the edge of two deep limestone canyons, through which flow the rivers Brian and Cesse; the latter runs underground, leaving gaping holes in the terrain. Portly pines and cypress are joined by olive trees, wild figs, and the acid yellow of shrubby hare's ear. A pungent scent of wild dill and curry plants permeate as swifts and house martins divebomb the foliage-filled Brian gorge.

Only one octagonal tower remains of the 11th-century castle that stands menacingly tall above the old gateway to this village that's immensely beautiful despite its grizzly past. 180 'heretic' Cathars were burned at the stake here when the town fell to Simon de Montfort in the 13th century; there's a modern memorial beside the church to commemorate the former residents.

Minerve and its neighbour **La Caunette**, which appears no less beautiful, are in the **Parc Naturel Régional du Haut Languedoc**. The vegetation as I head north through the park changes; the vines begin to disappear, the trees become wilder and more wooded and the terrain ever more hilly. The road climbs and as I approach **Rieussec**, I reach the top of a plateau from where are huge vistas of the Pyrenees – and the Mediterranean Sea.

It's raining heavily by the time I reach **Olargues**, the next town-sized, Plus Beau Village. Thunder rattles through the valleys, lightning vanishes speedily into the wooded hills making the hillside village, and its multi-arched stone bridge across the Jaur, appear all the more animated in the dark and temporarily hostile environment.

At **Hérépian**, I turn north along the Orb valley to a karst landscape of limestone cliffs and pavements. Pretty villages line the route, the best of which is **Lunas**,

↑ La Couvertoirade was built first by Knights Templars, then Hospitallers (Superstock)

attractively smart in a grand parkland setting. At **Vasplongues**, I head due north again after a brief spell running east, as the road climbs through and above the treetops. There are notable views of the massif – so many hills and mountains. So many trees! In every direction are the many limestone cliffs and causses. At **Les Rives**, the landscape changes unexpectedly and suddenly – now gentler pastures and arable fields, albeit wild and windswept, begin.

Crossing the A75 motorway, the surroundings change once more as peculiar rock formations appear amid open plains and stunted trees. As I arrive at **La Couvertoirade**, a road sign tells me I'm now in the **Cévennes**.

Those wide open plains are that of the **Causse du Larzac**, and there are excellent views of it from the ramparts in La Couvertoirade. I came across the Plus Beau Village by chance on a previous trip driving north when I pulled off the motorway to find somewhere to stay. I'm thankful that I did; it is one of the most extraordinary villages I've come across in Europe.

On the outskirts of the 12th-century walled village, which was created by first the Templars and latterly the Hospitallers, are large farmhouses with tumbledown yards filled with hardy sheep that otherwise graze the moors. Inside the rampart is a warren of confined streets and passageways faced by medieval houses. At night, it's disconcertingly dark, fingertip-feeling your way along the narrow alleys, all the while with an exciting sense of adventure, like trying to find one's way out of a maze.

Grey skies greet the morning as I run alongside the motorway and drop down into **Millau**, with views of Sir Norman Foster's famous viaduct – the 'bridge in the

↑ Kayak on the River Tarn (Jack Jelly/Shutterstock)

sky' – soaring above the Tarn valley and connecting Les Grands Causses. Millau is a gateway to the **Gorges du Tarn**, a UNESCO Word Heritage Site. The shallow river, with its sheer limestone cliffs, is loved by kayakers; there are rental places every few yards, including at the multitude of riverside campsites.

But the river is not only about kayaking; the gorge offers some of the most sublime villages along its length, like **La Cresse**, **Rivière-sur-Tarn**, **Les Vignes**, **La Malène** (one of the main locations for kayak rental) and **Saint-Chély-du-Tarn**, devoured by a bend in the river.

In between these villages, are the tiniest and remotest of perched hamlets, which hug the south/east bank of the river, often surrounded by troglodyte dwellings. There's no road to them; the only access is by water or zipwire across the river. They are extraordinarily beautiful. In fact they are quite extraordinary in every way. Yet, they're not regarded as *les plus beaux*. **Sainte-Enimie**, however, tucked into the gorge below the giant Sauveterre and Méjean plateaux, is.

Sainte-Enimie is one of the main stopping points for tourists along the route of the Gorges du Tarn. Indeed, the village has long been a stopping point for

pilgrims to the former Benedictine abbey and the hermitage once occupied by Enimie, by merchants on trading routes and by transhumance migration routes. Consequently, the crossroads village became extremely prosperous and the hillside houses represent this. It's a pleasure to amble through the cobbled medieval streets and envisage its social history.

The road to Mende climbs out of Sainte-Enimie on to the Sauveterre plateau. It feels dizzyingly high at times and, after some time constricted by the narrow gorge, I appreciate the wild and open space of the grassland plateau, dotted by tiny pine trees and protruding limestone rocks.

I had not anticipated a stop in **Mende**, situated in the valley of the Lot, but the town appears so attractive as I drive through, I have to pull over and take a look. Grand municipal and religious buildings central to which is the twin-spired cathedral, congregate next to narrow streets not much wider than those in some of the much smaller villages I've been visiting. Tall townhouses with colourful shutters give the centre a bijou feel. There's a Circuit du Patrimoine (Heritage Circuit) walking route that takes visitors on a tour of the town; it's one I certainly plan to revisit.

The road continues to climb out of Mende and once at the top of the **Col de la Pierre Plantée** – so called because of the giant boulders that litter the landscape – I'm at 1,284m, with 360° views. It's not long before I can see the bold red figure of Nôtre Dame towering above the little village of **Pradelles**, my next Plus Beau Village.

I'm not quite sure what to make of the hilltop village. The farmland views over the Haut Allier valley and distant mountains (some of which I've come through) are impressive, just as the view of Pradelles is on approach from the southwest. But Pradelles seems to look a slightly sad sort of village. Robert Louis Stevenson came here on his celebrated travels with a donkey through the Cévennes and

↑ Pradelles (Caroline Mills)

there's a hiking trail in his name that runs through the centre. But, today, everyone seems to be simply driving through, no-one is stopping and there are numerous *À vendre* (for sale) noticeboards stuck to crumbling houses.

Just north of Pradelles I turn southeast into the **Parc Naturel Régional des Monts d'Ardèche** towards Aubenas before heading northeast again to **Privas**. Ever since I left the Canal du Midi in the Minervois, I feel as though I've been climbing; now, in stages, begins the long descent to the Rhône valley. I cross over the River Ardèche when it's a baby mountain stream and, as it gets ever wider, criss-cross back and forth a further four or five times.

I'm unsure whether it's because I'm tired – I realise I should have stopped overnight in Mende – but I don't enjoy the Ardèche as much as I should. The road twists and turns through mountains that, today in drizzly rain, appear dull and dark with shaly grey bluffs and without the enormity of the views of, for example, the cols of the Pyrenees from where I began. The villages appear run down, the houses decayed, without any particular rustic chic. I'm grateful for the flat terrain of the Rhône valley when I reach it and, parked up for the evening at a tranquil fruit farm near **Grane**, I look at the distant Ardèche mountains scornfully.

It's a very gentle morning drive along country lanes, over lowland hills, between a smattering of small farms and fruit trees to reach **Mirmande**, my penultimate

↑ Mirmande (Franck-A/Shutterstock)

SOUVENIR

Les Plus Beaux Villages de France (🖥 les-plus-beaux-villages-de-france.org) is an association, that, as its name suggests, brings together a network of more than 160 of the most beautiful villages in France. There are strict criteria that must be met by villages in order to be considered for inclusion, with quality control to ensure that member villages help protect and promote the most exceptional of France's heritage. Aside from those featured here, more than 20 *plus beaux villages* are included throughout *Camping Road Trips*, and many others are within a few kilometres, worthy of a detour or reroute.

Plus Beau Village. The scenery has changed dramatically from the previous day's journey crossing the wild massif and I muse over the views of the, now rather attractive mountains to the west – those of the Ardèche – as the early morning light brightens their aspect.

It feels a privilege to share the peace of the hillside village with its residents early on a Sunday morning as I wander aimlessly through the narrow, stone-paved alleyways. Only the call of a dove and some gentle shimmying music coming from the little boulangerie breaks the silence. A café owner sits in a covered courtyard sipping an early cup of coffee, the heady fragrance of a rose blends with the whiff of someone's first Gauloise of the day as it drifts along the alley. A gentle breeze blows.

The village is so compact I feel as if I'm wandering through people's gardens. I avert my observations to the wonky wooden shutters in mushroom, avocado and pigeon blue that soften the shrieking pink of oleander bushes and flamboyant Provençal lavender. There are plenty of cafés and restaurants and Mirmande clearly attracts artists – painters, potters, jewellers and textile galleries all throng the little stone houses. It feels a harmonious place and I leave refreshed ready to begin 'The Alps'.

The first of the Alps (or PreAlps) – the mountains of the **Vercors** – are already in view as I venture northeast towards **Valence** and cross the Isère River. But they're largely being ignored. Why? Walnuts! All along the Isère valley, and as I turn north on my way to Saint-Antoine-l'Abbaye, the last Plus Beau Village I visit, there are fields and fields of walnut trees. In nearby **Chatte**, there's even an agricultural institution devoted to the walnut. The short-cropped orchards with refined rows of black trunks and lustrous leaves are a resplendent sight, topped in **Saint-Antoine-l'Abbaye**, by the equally glossy glazed tiles that adorn the roofs of many of the buildings.

The village centres around its enormous abbey, where Benedictine monks and, more recently, Hospitallers, would 'cure' pilgrims of 'St Anthony's Fire', a poisoning of the blood. There's a fascinating exhibition – in English and French – in the museum housed in the abbey about the gradual advancements in medicine and medical procedures. It's free to enter and also includes a visit to the abbey's medieval gardens and exhibition on medicinal plants. In fact, there are 11 'museums within a museum', including one on the French Revolution and one about the composer Hector Berlioz (who was born in nearby La-Côte-Saint-André). It's quite a find for such a remote village.

My journey continues through the lusciously green **Chartreuse** – renowned for its monastery and green liqueur made by the monks to replicate the colour of the hillsides. At **Chambéry**, I circumnavigate the Massif des Bauges to visit the Olympic park at **Albertville** and to run along the beautiful valley of the **Morte** and the western shore of **Lake Annecy**.

The glacial mountain lake is as blue as a swimming pool and very inviting for a potential dip. But as I wander around Annecy's eye-catching canals and streets, thunderous clouds form and I have to make a dash for cover. The storm is torrential and I decide to abandon my chosen route to Chamonix over the mountains in favour of the longer but safer route on the 'White Motorway'.

In **Chamonix** I resign myself to pictures of Mont Blanc hung on the wall of a restaurant in town. I'll at least celebrate my crossing from the Pyrenees to the Alps with hearty Savoie fare. My resignation is premature.

As I walk back to the campervan, I see signs of the mountain shroud dispersing. Mont Blanc becomes Mont Rose as night falls and takes on its sundown blush.

Le Plus Beau? Right now, yes.

↑ Mont Blanc, viewed from Chamonix (Caroline Mills)

ESSENTIALS

GETTING THERE & AROUND If starting the route from the car park at Pont d'Espagne (on Route 21), follow the instructions from there to Saint-Bertrand-de-Comminges on page 197. Saint-Bertrand is on the D26, 65km southeast of Tarbes. I used the D8, D21, D117 and D625 to Laroque-d'Olmes before minor roads to Camon and then the D18 to Carcassonne. There I took the D610 to Olonzac and D10 to Minerve. Then: D907 north to Saint-Pons-de-Thomières; D908 to Olargues and then Bédarieux; D35/D142/D609/D55 to La Couvertoirade. D809 to Millau; D809/D907/D907B to Sainte Enimie; D986/N88 to Mende and Pradelles; N102 to Aubenas; D104 to Privas and Loriol-sur-Drôme; Mirmande is on the D57, 8km southeast of Loriol. A7/N7/N532/A49 (J9) to Saint-Marcellin; Saint-Antoine-l'Abbaye is 11km northwest of Saint-Marcellin. A49/D520/D1006 to Chambéry, A43/A430 to Albertville; D1212/D1508 to Annecy. A41/A410/A40/N205 to Chamonix-Mont-Blanc (owing to poor weather); otherwise, head cross-country on D16 to Thônes, D909 to La Clusaz, D909 and D1212 to Saint-Gervais-les-Bains then pick up N205 to Chamonix.

    Parking is paid by the hour/day at Pont d'Espagne (Parc National des Pyrénées), to reach the Vignemale. There is dedicated motorhome parking/*aires* at all of the 'Beaux Villages' locations, except Saint-Bertrand-de-Comminges; coachbuilt 'vans are best parked at the foot of the hill beside the Roman ruins. There are also motorhome *aires* at Carcassonne (and lots of car parks; larger 'vans can use Parking La Narbonne), Mende, Annecy and Chamonix.

↑ Lake Annecy (PHILIPIMAGE/Shutterstock)

ACCOMMODATION I stayed at *aires* in Cauterets (near Pont d'Espagne), La Couvertoirade, Annecy and Chamonix-Mont-Blanc. I also stayed on **France Passion** sites at Baulou, near Foix in the Ariège department, and at Grane, in the Drôme.

There are **campsites** at all of the Beaux Villages visited here, except Olargues (use Camping Caroux at Mons) and La Couvertoirade (use Les 4 Templiers at Le Caylar). Other locations: Camping Les Glères, Cauterets (for Pont d'Espagne/Vignemale); Camping la Cité, Carcassonne; Camping les 4 Saisons, Grane; Camping Le Semnoz, Annecy; Camping de la Mer de Glace, Chamonix. There are campsites every few metres along the Gorges du Tarn; one I particularly recommend is Camping Le Peyrelade at Riveière-sur-Tarn.

FIND OUT MORE
Chamonix-Mont-Blanc ⊘ chamonix. com
Hautes-Pyrénées Tourist Board ⊘ pyrenees-holiday.com

Les Plus Beaux Villages de France ⊘ les-plus-beaux-villages-de-france.org

TOP TIP: EXTEND THE TRIP Add the tour of the Pyrenees (page 182) to the beginning of this tour, and you'll visit further villages within the Plus Beaux Villages de France association, including Sare, Ainhoa and Saint-Jean-Pied-de-Port. There are also many other villages within the association within a few miles of this particular route, all worthy of a visit.

GERMANY

Kaiserstuhl (cityfoto24 Shutterstock)

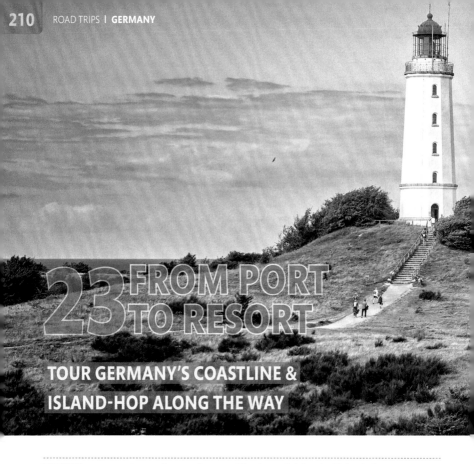

23 FROM PORT TO RESORT

TOUR GERMANY'S COASTLINE & ISLAND-HOP ALONG THE WAY

WHERE	Lower Saxony, Bremen, Hamburg, Schleswig-Holstein & Mecklenburg-Vorpommern
DISTANCE/TIME	1,094 miles (1,760km)/21 days
START/FINISH	Papenburg/Ahlbeck

As we begin our ascent, leaving Hiddensee's tiny harbour at Kloster behind, the cloudless sun beats heavily upon the dusty, hard-baked footpath and our beaded brows. With a vastness of soft sandy Baltic beaches upon which to stretch out on the island, it was not our intention to climb the Dornbusch, the only high ground on Hiddensee. But the increasing splendour of the national park scenery appears to pull each limb magnetically one step further, and then another, and another.

Past expanses of sandoorn bushes, laden with golden orange berries. Past wind-sculpted deadwood that, smoothed by time, lies like silver treasures among the grassy heathland. Past wafts of pungent pine trees that offer the occasional dapple of shade from their needles, and a chorus of cicadas that chatter vociferously among the spiky grass.

↑ Dornbusch Lighthouse, Hiddensee (DR pics/Shutterstock)

Not anticipating our hilltop hike, foolishly, we are short of water. But, as we reach the first viewpoint, all thoughts of hydration dissipate. Before us is a vista of green and blue. The seahorse-shaped island spreads out before us, fashioned by lowland pastures in which is a blissfully remote farmstead and, above, gentle pine-clad slopes. By the time we reach the lighthouse, on the highest point of the Dornbusch, our thirst is quenched from an oasis-like café hidden amid the expansive clifftop woods.

Hiddensee is not the first island that we visit, though, as we zigzag our way along the coastline. From Germany's border with the Netherlands and the North Sea, in the west, to its border with Poland and the Baltic Sea in the east, we hop offshore no fewer than six times.

We begin our tour of northern Germany slightly inland at the riverside town of **Papenburg**, close to the Dutch border. As we approach, intense curiosity gets the better of us as incomprehensibly colossal buildings dominate the skyline. They belong to Josef Meyer, a cruise-ship builder whose gigantic headquarters operate a fascinating tour to watch some of the world's largest and most renowned cruise ships under construction before they're tugged – backwards – nearly 50km downstream along the River Ems to set sail on the high seas.

Papenburg, with its rich nautical history set within the very flat, fertile lands of East Frisia, is also the focal point of the German Fen Route, a 100-mile (161km) signposted touring route through Germany's fenlands that's full of canals, verdant meadows feeding Friesian cows, windmills and little red-roofed villages. It's perfect cycling terrain but of the whole circular route, we found the 20 or so kilometres of quiet rural back roads between two handsomely decorative towns, Papenburg and Leer, to be the most rewarding.

Here the open fields, divided by dykes and avenues of birch trees, are plentiful and punctuated by the occasional farm or hamlets like **Völlen**, **Mark** and **Driever**, the prettiest with its aged red brick houses and cobbled roads. The road runs alongside the River Ems, the same route taken by the enormous cruise ships and, as we watch the sun set by **Leer's** highly ornamented *Rathaus* (town hall) on the banks of the river, we can only begin to imagine what the sight of such towering ships sailing through the town centre towards the sea would look like. It is, we are told, a momentous occasion for the local community that attracts hundreds of onlookers.

Ready for the sound of the sea, we drive northeast from Leer to the coast where we pitch up beside the historic fishing harbour at **Neuharlingersiel**. It's with purpose that we do – to catch the early morning ferry to **Spiekeroog**, one of Germany's eight East Frisian Islands.

The string of low-lying, sandy isles are located a handful of miles off the German coast, in the Wadden Sea. It's an area with a unique ecosystem that has been designated both as a national park and a UNESCO World Heritage Site. The sea is so shallow that boats must navigate a specific course to reach the car-free island of Spiekeroog.

Even bicycles are forbidden in the centre of the single village on the island, a popular summer destination for holidaymakers looking for the serenity of a place where walking is essential to get around. Most day trippers arrive on the mid-morning ferry and remain within the vicinity of the village so our early boat means we enjoy a couple of hours mingling with the locals over breakfast in the island bakery before setting off on a walk across the dunes to the vast and secluded beach.

Spiekeroog is a magical place, scented by wild briar roses that thrive on the dunes alongside rowan, oak and sea holly. Spending only a few hours helps relieve the stresses of daily life. We would gladly spend longer, but the last boat back to the mainland doesn't wait for stragglers.

Maritime life, naturally, plays a significant role in Germany's heritage and many of the towns and cities along the coast are architecturally rich, each with a historic port. Many once belonged to the Hanseatic League, an association of towns across northern Europe that existed in the Middle Ages to maintain the safe trading of

← **Top** The traffic-free island of Spiekeroog, in the Wadden Sea **Below** Papenburg (both Caroline Mills)

goods. As trading ports, these towns thrived. Consequently, medieval warehouses and wealthy merchants' houses sprung up, many of which survive today.

The first of these towns that we visit is **Stade**, which has an elegantly preserved medieval centre, focused around the *Alter Hafen* (old harbour). Here, overlooking the highly ornamented, gabled façades, is the place to sit and enjoy a summer drink.

Hamburg, which we visit by rail from Stade, also once belonged to the Hanseatic League. Lovers of architecture will enjoy the juxtaposition of historic and modern buildings side by side. The centre is a pleasure to walk around and our self-guided walking tour takes in the imposing *Rathaus*; St Michaelis Church, a notable landmark for arriving ships; the 17th-century merchant warehouses in the Speicherstadt district, a UNESCO World Heritage Site; and the Alsterarkaden, a romantic colonised arcade. Modernity is represented by the Elbphilharmonie, a concert hall of shimmering glass overlooking the harbour; rotund and leaning office blocks; and the sky-high television tower. However, for outstanding views of the entire skyline, we take a round-trip ferry journey that also allows us to see Hamburg's famous docks, one of the largest ports in the world. It's eye opening!

By morning, we're back on the road, skirting Hamburg altogether as we pass through the **Altes Land** (Old Land), the largest fruit-growing region in northern Europe. Fruit growing alongside the River Elbe dates back to the 14th century and every couple of kilometres, it's possible to stop at one of the many farm shops and roadside stalls to purchase fruit and associated produce.

↑ Elbphilharmonie at Hamburg (Caroline Mills)

However, we're aiming northeast towards the coast of the Schleswig-Holstein region, east of Kiel, another of Germany's notable ports. One-time fishing villages around the **Hohwachter Bucht** have become off-the-beaten-path hideaways, a place to enjoy sand and sea without the crowds. We can take quiet evening strolls around the extensive bay at Hohwacht and our first dip in the Baltic Sea away from the masses.

Little wonder, for the following morning the masses appear to be on **Fehmarn**, an island of large, open cornfields and horse studs off the northeast coast of Schleswig-Holstein. The island, which also serves as the arrival and departure point for ferries to and from Denmark, is far busier with road traffic than we've so far encountered and even our coastal walk at **Markelsdorfer Huk**, the most northerly tip of Fehmarn, appears to be not that remote. Where one campsite ends, another begins, the multitude lining the coast and we retreat back to the mainland in search of more peaceful surroundings.

We find them on **Poel**, another – smaller – island with a causeway-like road linking it to the mainland 8km northeast of Wismar. Where Fehmarn was cultivated and grandiose, Poel is wild, rugged and rural. We pass by tiny bays, windswept heaths and through becoming hamlets until we reach the village of **Timmendorf**, on the west coast. Here, with a large, informal *Stellplatz* (parking place) within a few metres of the harbour and beach, an ice-cream parlour and an excellent bakery, we enjoy a quiet evening watching mackerel skies and a soft evening light wash over the island as the sun sets.

It's only a small backtrack to visit **Wismar**, a Hanseatic city that, in 2002, was granted UNESCO World Heritage Site status for its well-preserved centre.

↑ Apples for sale at a farm shop in Altes Land (Caroline Mills)

The architecture of this small city is quite remarkable, the city's main square a place to simply stand in awe and appreciate the craftsmanship of the historic buildings that line it.

While the concentration of striking architecture in Wismar is almost preposterous – one visit cannot take it all in – we warm to the little town of **Barth**, about 120km east, where we stay at a secure *Stellplatz* overlooking its marina. The medieval town, with sections of fortifications and gates still visible, is situated in the former East Germany (DDR). The town combines beautifully renovated and brightly painted buildings in architectural styles from the Middle Ages to Art Deco with great brick warehouses that still bear the scars of occupation. There is plenty of character and charm, especially with the maritime location.

Barth sits on the edge of the **Vorpommersche Boddenlandschaft** (Western Pomerania Lagoon Area) National Park. Not dissimilar to England's Broads, the area is made up of a long, sandy coastline along the Fischland and Darß spit, behind which is a series of navigable rivers and huge, open lakes and lagoons. It's a popular summer destination, with watersports aplenty – the town of Ahrenshoop is a focal point for tourism – and lots of off-road cycle trails, too. A week spent here would not be disproportionate, but we're approaching the mainland's far east, with our eye on Stralsund.

Stralsund is a medieval city that, like Wismar, is so well preserved that it, too, has been granted UNESCO World Heritage Site status. In the 14th century, when

↑ Fishing huts on the island of Poel (clearlens/Shutterstock)

the Hanseatic League was at its height with more than 160 cities belonging to the association, Stralsund was regarded as the 'pearl' owing to its extravagance of exceptional buildings and its importance as a trading post. Today, there are more than 500 individually listed buildings and monuments within the city. A small, free exhibition on the city's UNESCO status is situated in the Oltholsche Palais in the Alter Markt (Old Market).

Some of the finest views of the city – with the exception of climbing the 366 steps to the 90m-high viewing platform of St Mary's Basilica – are from the harbour walls. And it's here that we begin our self-guided tour of the town. The large, brick warehouses on the harbourfront and the Gorch Fock windjammer in the harbour, offer a glimpse to Stralsund's recent past, when the town was under Soviet occupation as a naval port and the tallship was a training ship for the Soviet Navy. But, since the reunification of Germany, the harbour area has begun a gradual redevelopment to turn it into a stylish district of restaurants and bars alongside the OZEANEUM, Germany's national maritime museum.

As we wander into the city centre, the architecture becomes more astonishing with every turn. Its startling splendour reduces me to tears as the musical purity of two young musicians busking in the streets soars over the rooftops. Their handwritten note, rested precariously on an instrument case, informs passers-by of their 'dream' to study at London's Royal Academy of Music. A little girl stands beside them, watching and listening intently. Why, we ponder, would anyone wish to leave a city as outstanding as this? It's architectural beauty and culture, its coastal location, its surrounding lakes and parkland appears as perfect as any city could be.

↑ Stralsund (Marc Venema/Shutterstock)

Charmed by the place, we stay in Stralsund far longer than we anticipate. But our *Stellplatz* offers a grand view of the Rügenbrucke, Germany's longest bridge and it lures us to cross to Rügen, Germany's largest island.

Owing to its peculiar shape, with a collection of peninsulas and enormous sea inlets, **Rügen** has a vast coastline. The island's main town is **Bergen**, which lies roughly in the centre and forms an axis from which to visit all remaining areas of the isle. It's difficult to park a large 'van for the day here, though, so we continue on to the tiny village of **Schaprode** in the far west of the island, past small, cultivated fields and along graceful avenues of trees.

In Schaprode we're able to stop in the pleasant beachside *Stellplatz* and wander the 200m through streets of old brick and thatched cottages to the tiny harbour from where we catch the boat to **Hiddensee**. Leaving diners in quayside restaurants, we drift out to sea for the 45-minute crossing to **Vitte**, the largest and most centrally located of the three villages on Hiddensee.

What greets us, as the boat docks beside the car-free island, is a line of child-sized trolleys waiting for resident owners, and a horse and cart to transport

↑ Jasmund National Park on Rügen (ricok/Shutterstock)

visitors and residents. But the island is only a matter of metres wide and within a two-minute walk, we're soaking up the drenching sun on Hiddensee's long Baltic beach. The dry sand is exceptionally soft and hot to touch with every footprint vanishing in an instant on the fiery foreshore.

A sandy path takes walkers north and south so we wander at leisure to the village of **Kloster** in the north, a handsome village of yesteryear set amid shady woods. It's regarded as the cultural centre of the island with a couple of museums and a handful of places to eat. But we just keep wandering and find ourselves mesmerised by the beauty as we climb to the **Dornbusch lighthouse** for incomparable views.

The end to a miraculous day on a magical island ends no less remarkably, with a momentous sunset that turns the sea orange as the island fades into the distance on our return to Rügen.

By morning we take the five-minute ferry crossing to the **Wittow peninsula** heading for **Kap Arkona**, Rügen's most northerly point. All vehicles must park at Putgarten, 2km south of the cape, a pretty but popular tourist village. In place

of the miniature road train that transports passengers to the cape, we opt for a wonderful walk along flower-lined footpaths with magnificent views of the cape's two lighthouses and, latterly, the sea.

The cape has a bizarre mix of sinister ex-military buildings (including a Cold War submarine bunker) and wedding ceremonies at the top of the lighthouses so we wander on, around the headland, to the traditional herring-fishing village of **Vitt**. The thatched cottage settlement is only accessible on foot or bike, tucked

↑ Beech woods in Jasmund National Park (Caroline Mills)

at the foot of chalk cliffs but its charm makes its pebbly beach and makeshift fish smokery a popular place to visit.

From one cape to another, we pass along the string-like **Schaabe** that divides the sea and joins the Wittow and Jasmund peninsulas, to pitch up in the small, clifftop village of **Lohme**. Here, the private *Stellplatz* next to the village shop sits within 46m of the **Jasmund National Park**, Rügen's most famous sight.

The national park, also a UNESCO World Heritage Site, comprises immense chalk cliffs, sculpted into wavy formations through centuries of erosion and a vast swathe of airy beech woods with beams of sunlight, the trees with tall and skinny pedunculate trunks. We take the 13km signposted Hochuferweg walk that runs through the woods along the clifftop with continuous sight of the sea below. Despite the intense heat, our woodland walk is cool and refreshing, with the opportunity to stop and enjoy views of the park's most famous landmarks, such as the 188m-high **Königsstuhl** cliff formation.

Our walk ends in **Sassnitz**, which has a small, attractive promenade with a number of (expensive) restaurants but is, otherwise, an unremarkable town. On another occasion, we would opt to take the bus to Sassnitz and walk back to Lohme.

We spend five days on Rügen and in that time we barely begin to see all the island has to offer. But there's one 'attraction' we wish to visit before we return to the mainland – the **Colossus of Prora**.

Between 1936 and 1938, the Nazis built a 4.5km-long concrete building designed as a bathing resort. The first of five resorts planned for the Baltic Sea

↑ Vitt, near Kap Arkona, is accessible only on foot or by bike (or boat) (Caroline Mills)

area, it was the aim of the political party to provide accommodation for 20,000 citizens who could spend a ten-day supervised holiday here.

War broke out and the incomplete building was turned to military use. There is now a large museum in a small section of the building, near the 'festival hall'. The building is monumental in scale and its partly derelict state leaves one silent and shuddering. But the museum, which provides documentary exhibits of the planning and building of Prora and a separate museum documenting its military use by the DDR during the Cold War, is well worth a visit. In a slightly unsettling twist, other parts of the building are now renovated to create a luxurious bathing resort.

As if intentionally, huge grey clouds roll across the sky as we leave Prora, indicating our return to the mainland – briefly. For within an hour we are crossing the diminutive **Peenestrom** (the mouth of the River Peene) to the island of Usedom.

In the far northeast of Germany, **Usedom** is regarded as the country's riviera, with a string of rich and imperial bathing resorts along a 42km uninterrupted beach facing the Baltic Sea. It has attracted royalty, the fashionable and the wealthy

↑ V2 rocket at Peenemünde (Caroline Mills)

since the 19th century, with an abundance of smart and stylish villas to match. But before we sun ourselves on the riviera, we have one other must-see military institution to visit.

Peenemünde, in the north of the island, is synonymous with destruction but also space technology. For here, at the World War II Air Force Testing Centre, is where the technology for modern space travel was developed and the first long-range rocket was launched into space in 1942. A poignant and thought-provoking exhibition on the conflict between science and ethics and the ambivalence of technology (requiring several hours to really appreciate it) is housed in the old harbourside power plant at the Historical Technical Museum. We also visit a redundant Russian submarine moored in the harbour and there are several other museums and exhibitions to explore around the harbourside.

With the stirring history lesson over, it's time for fun and we spend the remainder of our trip exploring Usedom's various resorts. First, **Zinnowitz**, with its 315m Vineta-brücke pier (reputedly, the sunken Roman city of Vineta lies off the coast near Zinnowitz), at the end of which is a submersible diving capsule. Latterly we use a *Stellplatz* in **Ahlbeck** as the base from which to discover the **Kaiserbäder**, the three conjoined imperial resorts of Bansin, Heringsdorf and Ahlbeck.

↑ Elegant Imperial architecture and floral promenades of the Kaiserbäder (Caroline Mills)

The trio are chic and smart, each with a distinctive pier; at 508m long, Heringsdorf's pier is the longest in continental Europe. Large Italianate villas and 'French' châteaux overlook the Baltic, all in a parkland setting along which runs the 13km-long promenade from Bansin to Swinemünde in Poland.

Sipping cool, summer drinks at the end of Heringsdorf pier, squelching the softest sand beneath toes and taking a dip in the Baltic seems a fitting end to our 1,609km tour of Germany's coastline. But we're not quite there yet.

With a 3km walk along the pine-tree promenade from Ahlbeck, we walk across the border into Poland. The sand is no different, the footpath continues. But we have come to the end of our journey as we stand in no man's land between brightly painted border posts in the respective flag colours of the two countries. The soft swish of the Baltic lapping at our toes is calling us. It feels good.

ESSENTIALS

GETTING THERE & AROUND Papenburg, from where we begin our circular tour of the German Fen Route, is 16km from the Dutch border, on the B70. Thereafter, we follow minor roads to the coast and Neuharlingersiel. From Bremerhaven, we take the B71/B74 to Stade and cross country through the Altes Land via Hollern, Jork and Neuenfelde. We use the A1 autobahn from Harburg to skirt around Hamburg and cross through the Holsteinische Schweiz (Swiss-Holstein) Lakeland region to reach the Hohwachter Bucht coast.

The 104/105 leads to Wismar, Rostock and beyond; at Ribnitz-Damgarten, we follow the coast road to Ahrenshoop, Zingst and Barth, then minor roads to Stralsund. The 96 crosses to Rügen, while the 105 continues to Greifswald before taking the 111 to Wolgast, where we cross (road bridge) to Usedom.

Foot passenger ferries to Spiekeroog depart from Neuharlingersiel and to Hiddensee from Schaprode, on the west coast of Rügen. There are also ferries to Hiddensee from Stralsund, on the mainland. Public transport on Hiddensee is a horse and cart or one bus that connects the three villages.

All major towns and cities that we visited (except Hamburg) have a *Stellplatz* for motorhomes to **park**. On-street parking is difficult in the Kaiserbäder area; using *Stellplätze* is essential for motorhomes.

ACCOMMODATION We stayed on **Stellplätze** along the entire length of the route. Many are as well organised as a good campsite, often with security. Almost all include electric hook-ups. In particular, the following were excellent: Papenburg, Neuharlingersiel (perfect for catching the early ferry to Spiekeroog), Stade (excellent for visiting Hamburg), Wismar, Timmendorf, Barth, Stralsund, Schaprode (ideal for catching the ferry to Hiddensee), Altenkirchen, Lohme, Prora, Peenemünde, Ahlbeck.

   Campsites: Campingplatz Papenburg; Ems-Marina-Camping, Leer; Nordsee-Camping, Neuharlingersiel; Campingplatz Nesshof, Guderhandviertel (for Stade and Altes Land); Camping Jipp, Blekendorf (for Hohwachter Bucht); Campingplatz Leuchtturm, Timmendorf; Ostsee Camping Ferienpark, Zierow; Campingplatz Am Fresenbruch, Zingst (for Barth); Sund Camp Altefähr (for Stralsund); Campingplatz Am Schaproder Bodden, Schaprode; KNAUS Camping Park Rügen, Altenkirchen; Krüger Naturcamping, Lohme; Camping Prora, Prora; Zeltplatz, Peenemünde; Nandalee Camping, Heringsdorf.

FIND OUT MORE

German Fen Route ⌀ deutsche-fehnroute.de

Hamburg ⌀ hamburg-travel.com

Hiddensee ⌀ seebad-hiddensee.de

Lower Saxony Tourism
⌀ niedersachsen-tourism.com

Mecklenburg-Vorpommern Tourism
⌀ off-to-mv.com/en

Papenburg ⌀ papenburg-marketing.de/EN

Peenemünde ⌀ museum-peenemuende.de

Prora ⌀ proradok.de/en

Rügen ⌀ ruegen.de/en

Schleswig-Hostein Tourism
⌀ sh-tourismus.de/en

Spiekeroog ⌀ spiekeroog.de

Stade ⌀ stade-tourismus.de

Stralsund ⌀ stralsundtourismus.de/en

Usedom ⌀ visitusedom.com

TOP TIP: GROUP TICKETS To visit **Hamburg** we purchased a one-day group rail ticket (from ⌀ hvv.de) for up to five people (available at weekends and bank holidays before 09.00) and, for €19, enjoyed a smooth and punctual 50-minute ride from Stade to the city centre plus unlimited travel on all public transport. The ticket is also valid on the ferries that ply the Elbe and, while there are many harbour tours, the number 62 ferry offers an excellent, free (with a day ticket) 90-minute circular boat trip around the harbour.

↑ The beach and Baltic Sea at Ahlbeck (Caroline Mills)

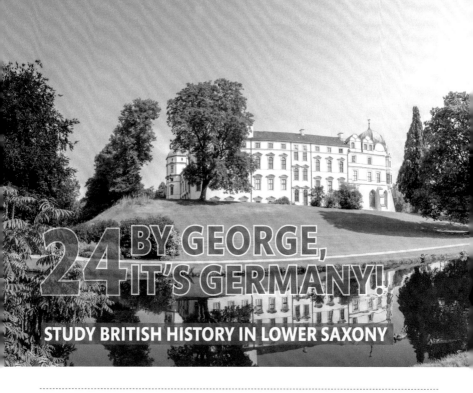

24 BY GEORGE, IT'S GERMANY!

STUDY BRITISH HISTORY IN LOWER SAXONY

WHERE	Lower Saxony
DISTANCE/TIME	263 miles (423km)/6 days
START/FINISH	Celle/Bad Iburg

It's a story that would rival any script from a soap opera. There's scandal, murder, exile, mental illness, love affairs, illegitimate children and political drama, and all this in a pre-modern era when society was not so liberally minded. While children study 'The Tudors', 'The Stuarts' and 'The Victorians' in school history lessons, 'The Georgians' is not part of the curriculum. Little wonder, for it's they that I am referring to, and their history is enough to make a schoolgirl blush.

It's a little over 300 years since the accession of George I to the British throne, in 1714. He was not British-born, but a German who, by the Act of Settlement in 1701 – and a series of advantageous marriages to gain European power – found himself in London wearing the Crown. I, meanwhile, am sat in Hannover, trying to make sense of it all.

George Louis (or Georg Ludwig to quote his German name) was the first of five generations from the House of Hannover to rule Britain – spanning 123 years to the coronation of Queen Victoria in 1837. But it's necessary to come to Germany to make head or tail (or indeed tale) of all the Georges.

↑ Celle Castle (Sina Ettmer Photography/Shutterstock)

There are many places across Germany associated with the Hanoverian Kings – from summer residences to Ducal courts, ancestors' upbringings to exiled queens. I had only five days to learn of the Georgian kings so I stuck to a small area around Hannover.

I began in **Celle**, 40km northeast of Hannover, and an architecturally rich town of half-timbered houses, beautifully decorated and ornamented by inscriptions, dating back to the 15th and 16th centuries. It's a place that is buzzing with activity and, as I discovered, simply enjoying a coffee and croissant to watch the town go about its business is a great introduction.

Celle, founded in 1292 by Otto the Strict, was one of the richest and most important principalities in the Holy Roman Empire. Otto was a part of the Welf (or Guelph) family – from which the Hanoverian kings descend – and, still in existence today, is the oldest surviving royal family in the world.

With the town palace originally built in the 13th century, Celle became the seat and official residence of the Guelphic Dukes. The striking, moated palace, now more Baroque and Renaissance in style than its origins, was the home of George I's father (whose wife, Sophie von der Pfalz, was half-British owing to her mother being the daughter of James I and sister of Charles I) and is also the birthplace of George I's future wife – and cousin – Sophie Dorothea. Theirs was an arranged marriage for gains of land and power. It didn't last owing to adultery on both parts.

When George became King of Great Britain in addition to Elector of Hannover, Sophie would have become the first British Queen from the House of Guelph but, as I discovered by visiting an exhibition in the palace showing the Guelphs' route to the British throne, was banished for her adultery to a small, hidden-

↑ Climb the belltower of St Mary's Church for outstanding views of the numerous half-timbered houses in Celle (GagliardiPhotography/Shutterstock)

away castle at Ahlden, 40km northwest of Celle. Here she remained for 30 years until her death without ever being able to see her two children – the future George II and a daughter, also Sophie, who politically married the King of Prussia and became mother to Frederick the Great. Two generations later, George III's sister Caroline Mathilda, who married the schizophrenic King Christian VII of Denmark, suffered a similar fate and was imprisoned for life in Celle Castle after she had an affair with his doctor.

But the scandal doesn't begin there. George I's dad, Elector of Hannover and a Guelphic duke, was betrothed to a charming French actress. He, meanwhile marries George's mum for gains in power, and asks George's uncle (also father of George I's wife) to take the French actress off his hands and marry her, giving over some land to get him out of the hole he's dug himself. Scriptwriters would struggle to come up with a better plot!

Whatever the royal scandal, there's a fantastic view of picturesque Celle Castle and the town from the tower of St Mary's Church, though the 234-step climb is not for the faint-hearted. Also while in Celle, I visited legacies left by King George II, firstly, within the palace, the stunning Baroque theatre still in use today, and after, the Celle National State Stud. A keen horseman, George II founded the stud in 1735, bringing English thoroughbreds to breed impressive stallions. These days,

↑ The Baroque theatre in Celle is a legacy of Great Britain's King George II (Caroline Mills)

the stud is considered one of the leading organisations for horse breeding in the world. There's an annual Stallion Parade held every September, with royal carriages and dressage presentations.

With an introduction to the Personal Union covered, I took the train to **Hannover** to continue my history lesson, initially at the Palace and Royal Gardens of Herrenhausen. Built as a summer residence for the Guelphs, the palace succumbed during World War II and reopened in 2013. In the Palace Museum, an exhibition recounts the time leading to the accession of George I and the dual reign in Britain and Hannover.

Following his coronation in England, George I travelled from London to visit his summer residence at Herrenhausen five times. He built the elegant orangery and the remarkable 35m fountain in the garden. The vast and sumptuous Baroque gardens, which were lovingly laid out by his mother Sophie von der Pfalz (and where she later died), had been a favoured rendezvous for the love affair between Sophie Dorothea, George I's wife, and Philip Christof Graf von Königsmarck. It was an affair that cost Philip his life.

George II stayed at Herrenhausen many times and organised glittering garden parties with fountains and fireworks for the social elite. His grandson George III, however, never visited Herrenhausen and contemplated demolishing the palace.

↑ The gardens of Herrenhausen (clearlens/Shutterstock)

The palace exhibition reveals a further scandal – that George II had an illegitimate son named Johann Ludwig von Wallmoden whom he refused to accept. The mistress-mother was born in Hannover but later became a naturalised citizen of Britain in 1740 and Countess of Yarmouth. Growing up in England Johann developed a taste for British country houses and gardens; he collected a wealth of artworks and sculptures, some of which can be seen in the Herrenhausen Palace Museum. He built Wallmoden Palace, a five-minute walk from Herrenhausen through the English-landscaped Georgengarten, also developed by Wallmoden.

Wallmoden Palace is now home to the Wilhelm Busch-Deutsches Museum für Karikatur und Zeichenkunst (William Busch German Museum for Caricature and the Art of Drawing), which houses an excellent collection, including the portfolio of Britist satirist Ronald Searle. Some of the caricatures and cartoons on display depict social and royal life through the ages.

Returning to the heart of Hannover, I explored the city centre on foot. To do this I picked up a useful, free, English guide from the Tourist Information Centre (opposite the main railway station). 'The Red Thread' takes you on a 4km self-guided tour through Hannover – simply follow the red-painted line on the pavement as the pocket guide tells you about the highlights along the way. In doing so, I passed the State Opera House, Georgsplatz (obviously named), the Waterloo Monument (with British connections), the Lower Saxony State

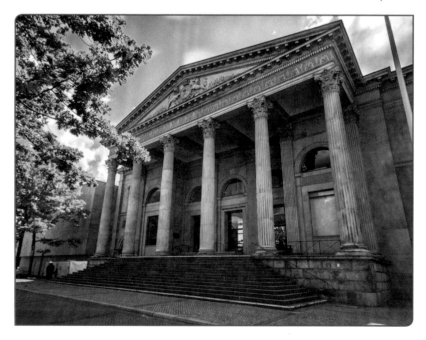

↑ Leine Palace, Hannover (Lepneva Irina/Shutterstock)

Museum, and the very fine Neo-Renaissance New Town Hall. Here, for rooftop views over the city, I took a glass-lift to the top of the dome on an unnervingly curved journey as the lift moves sideways while rising.

With feet firmly back on the ground, I moved on to Hannover's Old Town quarter, with half-timbered houses and a view of the Leine Palace. This was the Guelph seat in Hannover and is the palace in which, in 1701, the Earl of Macclesfield presented Electress Sophie von der Pfalz, George I's mother, with the Deed of the Act of Succession, declaring that she would succeed Queen Anne to the English (and ultimately British) throne. She died just before Queen Anne and therefore her son, George I, became King. The serene, pale stone frontage hides other deeds though.

Leine Palace is where, on a visit to his lover Sophie Dorothea (George I's wife), Duke Königsmarck was murdered for the affair. With the princess banished to Ahlden, George made his way to England – with his mistresses!

And it was **Ahlden** that I visited next. It's a pretty little village, made up of old timber-framed farmhouses bedecked with roses, one after the other along the main street, and the *schloss* more of a half-timbered manor house than

↑ Houses in Ahlden (KaMay/Shutterstock)

grand statement. Privately owned, visits to the castle are limited but there are wonderful opportunities for walking, especially along the banks of the rivers Aller, which flows through the village (from Celle), and the nearby Leine, which flows through Hannover.

From a poor marriage to a good one, it was time to head south to **Schloss Marienberg**, 29km south of Hannover. The castle is a romantic gem in every sense – fairytale in design, Marienberg was built by King George V of Hannover for his wife Marie, to declare his love for her publicly.

This King never became King of Great Britain because the British laws of succession allowed Queen Victoria on to the throne, though he was the nephew of George IV and William IV of Great Britain, and Queen Victoria's cousin. He dearly loved his wife and proved it with this building. The castle is still owned by the Guelph family; with its beautiful stellar vaulted ceilings and monastic arches, tours are well worth it. Lunch in the old stables is rather good, too!

Feeling slightly punch-drunk by multiple Georges, Sophies and Ernests, I took a drive deeper into the countryside to the **Weser Valley**. Crossing the

↑ Bad Pyrmont (Mano Kors/Shutterstock)

river at **Hameln** (of Pied Piper fame), my route took me to **Bad Pyrmont**. Exploration uncovered a moated *schloss*, visited by distinguished guests such as Frederick the Great (nephew of George II) and Queen Louise of Prussia (George III's niece).

Alongside the graces and lacy elegance of a spa town, the rambling gardens are quite something for a leisurely stroll, with water fountains everywhere and the sub-tropical Palm Gardens, next to the *schloss*, a distraction from regal history.

But, with six springs in the town each providing a different mineral combination, it's drinking water that visitors flock here for. I went to the domed pump rooms, where the six waters are provided on tap like a bar. My first tasting, Friedrichsquelle, slightly petillant, was ok; my second – Der Hyllige Born – tasted of iron girders and I felt the need to 'down it' like a drinks-shot before rushing for a strong coffee to remove the taste – not the idea, I'm sure.

Driving north over the western hills of the Weser valley, I stopped in **Rinteln**. By the banks of the Weser, the charming old town is on the south bank; it's worthy of a visit to enjoy the many old buildings, Gothic Rathaus and church square. It's not a regal town, though, so I moved on to **Bückeburg**, which has links to both George I and George II.

↑ Schloss Bückeburg (hydebrink/Shutterstock)

Schloss Bückeburg sits on an island right in the centre of town. I happened to be visiting during the annual Land Partie, a mammoth country show that takes over the castle and its grounds, it offers a different way in which to view the lavish rooms. One-time owner Count Schaumberg-Lippe, who was the grandson of George I, and a close associate of George II during the Seven Years War, links the castle to the Hanoverian kings. King George II thanked the Count for his allegiance with a gift of thoroughbred horses – the castle and *Hofreitschule* (riding school) has been a centre for equestrian arts ever since.

You can visit the stables here to see the prestigious 'Royal Hanoverian Creams', and watch artistic, costumed displays of prancing horses; the creamy-white equines used to pull the British state carriages of the Hanoverian kings.

I had time for one last stop – the town of **Bad Iburg**. Some 16km south of Osnabrück, its *schloss* is where King George I grew up as a child, and where his sister was born. There is a small museum though access to the castle is limited to guided tours at weekends.

It seemed fitting to end here, where the Personal Union began, long before the Act of Succession was signed. In 1664, the Protestant castle church of Bad Iburg was inaugurated. It was initially the court chapel of the first Protestant prince-bishop of Osnabrück, Bishop Ernst-August I of Brunswick-Lüneburg. He married one Sophie von der Pfalz, a half-English Protestant princess, and they had a son – the future King George I. And the rest, as they say, is history.

ESSENTIALS
GETTING THERE & AROUND
Celle is on the B3, 43km northeast of Hannover, easily accessed off the A2 autobahn. Ahlden is 47km northwest of Celle, approached via the B214. To reach Bad Pyrmont from Ahlden, I used the A7 autobahn A3 to Schloss Marienburg, heading west cross-country to the A217 for Hameln and B83/L431.

From Bad Pyrmont, I used the L426/L758 to Rinteln, crossing the A2 autobahn to Bückeburg. I took the A30 autobahn, leaving at J18 and heading south on the A51 to Bad Iburg.

I opted to stay in Celle and take the train to Hannover, it's a 15-minute walk to the railway station from the *Stellplatz* and a 30-minute rail journey into the centre of Hannover. This also avoids driving into Hannover's Umweltzone. An alternative is to park/stay in the *Stellplatz* at either Laatzen or Garbsen, both on the outskirts of Hannover and each served by trams to the city centre.

With the many *Stellplätze*, I had no problems **parking** anywhere; motorhomes are widely accepted and accommodated. You'll find directional signs for motorhome parking in most towns.

ACCOMMODATION I stayed on *Stellplätze* in Celle (Schützenplatz), Bad Pyrmont and Bückeburg. All three are very close to the respective town centres, well used and provide a pleasant and convenient stay, each with a motorhome service point. Bad Pyrmont and Bückeburg both have hook-ups.

   Campsites: Campingplatz Winsen, Winsen (for Celle); Campingplatz Ahlden, Ahlden; Campingpark Schellental, Bad Pyrmont; Camping Park Kalletal, Kalletal (for Rinteln and Bückeburg).

FIND OUT MORE

Celle & celle.travel
Hannover & visit-hannover.com/en
House of Hannover & britroyals.com/hanovertree.asp

Schloss Bückeburg & schloss-bueckeburg.de
Schloss Marienburg & schloss-marienburg.de

TOP TIP: HANNOVER CARD

If staying for two or three days around Hannover, purchasing a HannoverCard gives 'free' use of all trams, buses and trains in the Greater Hannover Transport area in addition to many discounts on attractions and restaurants.

↑ King George I spent his childhood in Bad Iburg (Yannic Niedenzu/Shutterstock)

25 AN EIFEL LOT TO SEE

TOUR GERMANY'S EIFEL REGION, A LAND OF ANCIENT VOLCANIC ACTIVITY

WHERE	North Rhine-Westphalia & Rhineland-Palatinate
DISTANCE/TIME	130 miles (209km) of the 175-mile long route/4 days
START/FINISH	Monschau/Mendig

Quietly, and alone, we sidle into Germany as if through the back door. No roar of engines on the autobahn, no queues at aging, disused border checkpoints; only us on a tranquil, minor road carved through a block of densely planted beech trees in **Belgium's Hautes Fagnes-Eifel Natural Park**.

We're on our way to explore the Eifel region, and in particular the Deutsche Vulkanstrasse (German Volcano Route), a linear tourist route that takes in some of the area's extraordinary scenery. For the Eifel region is a geological wonder, an ancient volcanic area.

The Vulkanstrasse connects 39 geological sites related to the Eifel volcanoes, including the remains of craters, cinder cones, lava flows and volcanic sources. The driving route is a good introduction to the area; follow it to every signpost and it takes you along roads and to places one might otherwise miss, or use it simply as an introduction from which to divert and discover further. In all, we cover 209 of the 282km, but discover more of this breathtakingly beautiful region along the way.

↑ Eifel National Park (Superstock)

Our first stop is the stupendously pretty town of **Monschau**, close to the Belgian border. Tucked into a steep-sided, wooded valley, the town has a history of cloth-making and mustard; its collection of timber-framed buildings clusters around the River Rur with flower-decked bridges and the romantic ruins of a 13th-century castle above. It all creates a scenic setting for a drink in the town square.

Umpteen gift shops and cafés later, we drive the short distance to the village of **Rurberg**, on the banks of Rursee, one of three conjoined ribbon-shaped lakes, that are the Rur (the same that flows through Monschau), Ober and Urft dams. Here we pitch in the campsite-like *Stellplatz* merely a few steps from a lifeguarded bathing lake.

We explore the lakeland area further, and take off for a hike in the Eifel National Park, a tiny area by comparison to the vast Eifel region but covering 108km² nonetheless. Walking in the shade, first alongside the dark and mysterious Urftsee (Urft Dam), we turn 'inland' to climb under the canopy of trees that covers the Kermeter, a steep hill that sits between Urft- and Rursee. Into hot sun at the top, brushing past the sweet scent of broom, we gain inspired views of both lakes sparkling below.

After an early-morning dip in the lake the following day, we take a quiet, velvet-smooth boat trip into the national park along Urftsee, through the fjord-like valley

lined with beech, oak, silver birch and pine. Upon arrival, the peace is sublime, and a walk across the towering dam wall provides a display of interconnecting wooded valleys. The walk back to Rurberg along the lakeside foot and cycle track is accompanied by the sound of silence and a kaleidoscope of butterflies plus exquisitely striped tiger moths bathing on hemp-agrimony.

A drive across the expansive **Dreiborn Plateau** above the lakes takes us to **Blankenheim**, the second timber-framed town we come across in as many days. Like Monschau, it too has a towering-high Rapunzel-like castle. We park up in the *Stellplatz* by the pretty River Ahr, little more than a bubbling stream and, with supper concluded and spying signposts for a 8km circular walk from our pitch, head out on a stroll through woods, over hills and along riverside pastures to see more of this beautiful landscape.

It's not until our third day in the area that we actually take to the Vulkanstrasse; picking it up in places for short stretches and not following the route in exact linear order. The route officially begins in Laacher See in the northeast of the region and finishes at Manderscheid to the south, looping north and south numerous times; we pick up the route at **Hillesheim**, nearer to the finish than the start, and drive initially southwest, passing through gentle, cultivated countryside and pretty villages along empty, rural lanes. Crossing the River Kyll at **Birresborn**, the road takes us on an incredibly picturesque climb through the **Salm Forest**, thronging with butterflies and with occasional views through open glades of the valley below.

↑ Monschau (Caroline Mills)

Passing through **Manderscheid,** the official end of the Volcano Route, we see two medieval castles hugging wooded hilltops within yards of one another. The town was once a border post between two warring principalities within the Eifel region; the Upper Castle (and the town) belonged to Trier while the large Lower Castle, to Luxembourg as the ancestral seat of the Counts of Manderscheid, one of the most powerful aristocratic families of the region. Guards in the huge stone towers eyed one another suspiciously for centuries across the forested ridge.

We continue (following the route in reverse order) along the Vulkanstrasse to **Holzmaar**, a lake created from a volcanic crater – obvious by its roundedness. It only takes a few minutes' walk to circumnavigate lakeside but, surrounded by woods in a nature reserve, its serenity is hypnotic. Some 5km further, beyond **Gillenfeld**, is the larger **Pulvermaar**. Also a volcanic crater, this lake is popular with bathers and has a campsite adjacent.

We stop off in **Bad Bertrich**, accessed down a steep, hairpin hill. This ribbon town, surrounded by dark, densely covered cliff-like mountains, is lined with decorative villas and hotels. It is a restful spa town with health clinics and large thermal baths, though it seems that, of the seven ages of man, those visiting Bad Bertrich are of the latter. The children appear very much out of place, so we move on. The climb out of town towards **Lutzerath**, our stopping place for the night, provides wonderful views of wooded crevices.

↑ Manderscheid (Caroline Mills)

Our final day in the region continues along the Vulkanstrasse in reverse order, with a minor detour to visit the **Nürburgring**. Known to millions as the venue for Formula One Grand Prix motor racing (including, in 2020, where racing driver Lewis Hamilton equalled Michael Schumacker's record for the most-ever Grand Prix wins), we're able to wander around at our leisure, and could visit the **ring°werk** centre on site for lots of motor-racing based activities. Instead we stop at one of the large spectator areas to watch adrenalin-fuelled cars hurtle around the Nordschleife 20km circuit, described as, 'the world's most beautiful country road without oncoming traffic.' With speeds that involve screeching brakes, I'm not sure how much of the scenery the drivers actually see – including the red squirrel that dices with danger as it scampers across the tarmac – while they twist and turn on hairpin bends, blind corners and frightening cambers. Suffice to say, the immediate area around the track (you can walk right alongside) is indeed beautiful.

Passing **Hohe Acht**, the remnant of a volcano and the region's highest 'mountain' at 747m, we venture on through the scenic villages of **Weibern** and **Brenk** before finishing our tour at **Laacher See**, the largest of the volcanic lakes, next to which sits the attractive Benedictine Abbey of Maria Laach.

As we sit overlooking the lake, chatting to a friendly baby coot dabbling at the water's edge, we contemplate all that we've seen. There were no fiery explosions upon our journey, no earth tremors or giant eruptions of ash clouds in this ancient volcanic landscape. What we did see was a remarkable rural vista, worthy of a return visit.

ESSENTIALS

GETTING THERE & AROUND We arrived in the area on the N67 from Eupen (Belgium) to Monschau then the L246/L166 to Rurberg (with steep descent). The route to Blankenheim from Rurberg (northeast of Monschau on the shores of Rursee), includes the 266 and 265 to Schleiden, then 258 to Blankenheim: note the *Stellplatz* can only be approached on the 258; do not turn off at signs for the town centre, which has a pedestrianised zone. We used the 258 south and L115/L26 to Hillesheim, where we picked up the Vulkanstrasse.

The Vulkanstrasse is signposted along its length in both directions. We found all roads in the region to be quiet, easy and very pleasant to drive along.

We had no problems with **parking** anywhere, though you may find issues in Monschau during summer; the town has a series of car parks to avoid traffic in the historic centre – motorhomes should not attempt to drive through, or into, the centre – the entrance to the dedicated motorhome *Stellplatz* is off the Burgring, opposite the Vennbad swimming pool; there's possible daytime parking at the Laufenstrasse parking area, too.

Aside from specific events, there's free parking at the Nürburgring; we pulled up at viewing areas alongside the track, on the road to Kempenich.

ACCOMMODATION We stayed on **Stellplätze** at Rurberg, Blankenheim, Lutzerath and Mendig. All are well signposted upon entering the towns and villages. There are further *Stellplätze* at Gerolstein, Andernach, Mayen, Gillenfeld, Monschau and Nürberg and Simmerath.

Campsites: Campingplatz Lutterbach, Rurberg am Rursee; Campingplatz Perlenau, Monschau; Eifel-Camp, Blankenheim; Campingplatz am Pulvermaar, Gillenfeld; Camping am Nürburgring, Nürberg; Camping Laacher-See, Wassenach.

FIND OUT MORE
Eifel National Park ⬦ nationalpark-eifel. de
Eifel Tourism ⬦ eifel.info

German Volcano Route ⬦ deutsche-vulkanstrasse.com/en
Monschau ⬦ monschau.de/en

TOP TIP: EXTEND THE TRIP Having completed the Vulkanstrasse, you could add on a tour of the Rhine and Mosel wine routes, as these rivers run within a few miles of Laacher See (the end of the Vulkanstrasse).

↑ A silver-washed fritillary and Jersey tiger moth in Eifel National Park (Caroline Mills)

26 MANNHEIM & WOMAN

FOLLOW IN THE TYRE TRACKS OF BERTHA BENZ ON THE FIRST EVER LONG-DISTANCE MOTOR CAR JOURNEY

WHERE Baden-Württemberg
DISTANCE/TIME 212 miles (341km) including route & local driving/4 days
START/FINISH Mannheim/Pforzheim

Despite all the antiquated, stereotypical jokes about women drivers, it was a woman who, in 1888, undertook the world's first-ever, long-distance car journey. Had it not been for Bertha Benz, the courageous young wife of car inventor Carl Benz, the popularity of motor vehicles might never have taken off.

The story goes that Dr Carl Benz invented the first functioning two-stroke engine in 1879 followed by the first patented automobile in 1886. Few believed the vehicles to be useful, regarded as functional only for short journeys. In a major marketing exercise, Bertha took the car without his knowledge or permission and, accompanied by her two teenage sons Eugen and Richard, drove from Mannheim, where the Benz family lived, to Pforzheim to visit her mother. It was a round trip of some 140 miles, one of tremendous courage by Bertha who, besides the unknown risks of the journey, potentially faced stigma for her social non-conformities. As it transpired, her journey made headlines and it sparked a revolution in car manufacture.

To celebrate the first-ever, long-distance car journey, a signposted tourist route has been created from the roads that Bertha and her sons took – the Bertha Benz Memorial Route. The entire journey glides through gentle countryside, though

↑ Heidelberg (mapman/Shutterstock)

to avoid unnecessary descents on the return journey (the car had no brakes until Bertha 'invented' them), the first woman of motoring took a slightly different route back to Mannheim. We follow her tracks north to south from Mannheim to Pforzheim, with the occasional detour to visit other locations from the signposted return journey.

We pick up the route in **Feudenheim**, on the southeast outskirts of Mannheim, the one-time home of the Benz family. Here, close to the giant concrete supports of gargantuan flyovers and the hum of motorcars, we become instantly charmed by the greenery of the suburbs – fields of sunflowers through which titanic storks wander nonchalantly beside the willow-lined River Neckar.

As the sun throws sparkles across the water like exploding fireworks, riverside **Ilvesheim**, with its decoratively painted houses provides an indication of what's to come, but it doesn't prepare us for the preposterously pretty **Ladenburg**, the first true rural location on the route.

Sitting beside the River Neckar, Ladenburg's town centre – a ten-minute walk from our first *Stellplatz* – appears like something from a book of fairy tales. Its marketplace, lined with captivating ancient timber buildings and the allure of umbrella-shaded restaurants, is playing host to a farmers' market when we arrive. The tantalising array of just-picked vegetables sold from giant woven baskets, the scent of fresh-cooked bread and rainbow of summer fruits is as much as we can bear before our initial explorations of the town are curtailed, returning to the 'van laden with a feast of local produce. Walks through the riverside park and admiring the views of the vine-clad Odenwald hills nearby have to wait until evening as the sun begins to pale.

Ladenburg is also where Dr Carl Benz lived with his family until his death and where, having fallen out with the company he'd originally set up in Mannheim, he began manufacturing under a new company name with his son Eugen. His car-making factory is now a museum, the Automuseum Dr Carl Benz, displaying glossy specimens of Benz, Mercedes-Benz and Daimler motor vehicles.

The collection includes a working replica of the very first automobile in the world (Benz's 'Model One') and, alongside, the vehicle that Bertha Benz drove on her now celebrated journey, the three-wheeled Benz Patent Motorwagen 'Model 3'. The exhibition is brought up to the present day with a Mercedes Petronas Formula One car.

Bertha Benz was known to take the trip from Mannheim to Pforzheim quite regularly but, prior to the first car trip, her usual mode of transport for the journey was the train. On her car journey she continued her drive by going east from Ladenburg to Heidelberg, simply because there was a straight Roman road without any hills. As many of the once-small towns that she drove through on her route are now cities of industrial size, ironically, we leave our motorhome at the *Stellplatz* and, for ease, take the train to Heidelberg!

↑ Ladenburg (mapman/Shutterstock)

We have no qualms about 'cheating'. Ladenburg's train station is a picturesque 15-minute riverside walk from the *Stellplatz* and a train journey of equal length. A return ticket to the city is cheaper than the cost of parking – or indeed the hassle of finding somewhere to park.

Heidelberg is one of Germany's most popular tourist cities but with limited time, we take off immediately for the Altstadt, the old town, a good 30-minute, fast-paced walk from the Hauptbahnhof. Approaching the Hauptstraße (High Street) – a mile-long pedestrian zone – we appreciate the draw. Pictorially rich in architecture, the high street provides an abundance of places to eat and up-market brand-name shops occasionally punctuated by a handsome square. Alluring narrow thoroughfares lead off the main street either down towards the River Neckar that flows through the city or up to the forested hillside, where timber villas perch amid the trees.

Heidelberg is an ancient university city We come across statues of academic celebrities such as Mr Bunsen – he of Bunsen burner fame – amid flower-filled courtyards, and reminders of Heidelberg's contribution to the printing industry before we stumble across the city's castle. Of mammoth proportions, the rust-brick *schloss* dominates the hillside behind the city.

Back in the 'van, we follow Bertha's route east, directly into wine-growing territory at the foot of the **Odenwald hills**. **Schriesheim** and neighbouring **Dossenheim** are renowned for their wine production. Both villages offer a brief, attractive wander with a romantically ruined *schloss* on the hillside behind for company.

↑ Benz Patent Motorwagen 'Model 3', the car used by Bertha Benz (Caroline Mills)

It's at this point that we choose to make a detour to **Hockenheim**, a place that Bertha Benz drove through on her way back to Mannheim. It's apt that the once small village has become one of Germany's most celebrated motor racing circuits.

The gates to the circuit are open as we park up beside the Hockenheimring Motor Sport Museum, and we're lured trackside by the thunderous scream of engines. With evidence of the German F1 Grand Prix having taken place the previous week, a motorcycle race is now on and we can watch free of charge. Such is our ignorance, we cheer for our favourites – 'the orange one in the lead' or the 'extra loud one'!

Rejoining Bertha's official route south, we continue on to **Wiesloch**, a town that honours 'the first petrol station in the world.' Bertha faced several problems with the Model 3 along the journey, including a blocked fuel line, which she fixed with her hairpin, and a broken ignition, mended using her garter. Most notably though, her husband's calculations for fuel consumption were incorrect and she ran out of fuel at Wiesloch. She had to ask for Ligroin (a detergent used as a fuel at the time) in the town's Stadt Apotheke.

The historic pharmacy has been restored to its original state and outside the entrance, now within a pedestrian zone, a sculpture depicts Bertha and the boys on their journey. The town sits on a modest hill, the old quarter tucked behind fortress-like walls. Below are tiny allotments brimming with sunflowers, tomatoes, chilli peppers and soft summer fruits.

A captivating sight, they are the first of several we see as we make our way through open countryside and old apple orchards to the spa village of **Bad Schönborn**. Church bells greet us as we pitch up for the evening in the village *Stellplatz*; after-dinner walks along various waymarked circular trails in the countryside prove popular.

With the most cerulean of mornings following, it's only a handful of miles to **Bruchsal**, a town of two halves. The modern, pedestrianised town centre is not especially becoming but within yards are the vast grounds of a Baroque *schloss*. As we wander past erupting fountains, gleaming white chivalrous statues and giant tubs of electric-blue agapanthus in the sculpted gardens, the colossal church bells boom and the organ resonates against the powder pink walls of the castle.

It's a place to linger a while – the *schloss* houses a museum that's open to the public – but we're on our way to **Karlsruhe**, by train. The fan-shaped royal city is regarded as one of the most classically designed in Germany and is the birthplace of Carl Benz.

We walk through the landscaped Zoological Gardens from the train station to the city centre. The formal parkland and riotous flowerbeds offer plenty of places for a picnic, boating lakes and places to escape the ferocity of the midday sun. The pastoral scene lies juxtaposed beside academic museums and the elegant

→ **Top** Schloss Bruchsal (Sina Ettmer Photography/Shutterstock) **Below** Karlsruhe Zoological Gardens (Caroline Mills)

Corinthian columns of Classical buildings gracefully towering skywards before the commanding *schloss* is approached. Walking everywhere, we don't feel the need to take a guided tour but there is a Hop-on, Hop-off City Tour bus that visits the largest tourist attractions and is particularly useful for reaching those further afield.

Returning to the *Stellplatz* at Bad Schönborn overnight, we continue following the Memorial Route along the Pfinztal, a tiny river valley that offers ancient orchards and wildflowers hugging the roadsides. The farming landscape isn't the most dramatic scenery but is pleasant enough with gentle undulations to break up the vistas.

We stop at **Kleinsteinbach** to catch the train to **Pforzheim**, Bertha's final destination. Initially we can't decide what to make of the town with the apparent lack of a historical heart. In place, the town's imposing modern cathedral, theatre and polar-white congress centre cluster along the banks of the River Enz while its tributary, the Nagold, offers an attractive, pastoral scene within the city centre. When we come across a small section of stone wall close to the riverbank, all becomes clear – the entire town was destroyed in 1945 and virtually every building stems from the post-war period; we realise we're observing little of what Bertha Benz once saw.

Returning to the motorhome, it doesn't take long to drive the remainder of the route and appreciate the views from the road that we'd not long seen from the rails – some of the prettiest of the entire route. As Bertha would have begun her return journey we climb into the wooded hills of the **Black Forest**, offering our thanks as we leave to a remarkable woman and her courageous achievement.

↑ The River Nagold in the centre of Pforzheim (Caroline Mills)

ESSENTIALS

GETTING THERE & AROUND We approached Mannheim from the A6. Brown tourist signs are frequently located directing drivers along the Bertha Benz Memorial Route. We took trains to Heidelberg, Karlsruhe and Pforzheim: Heidelberg: from Ladenburg (where you can also reach Mannheim and other destinations such as Frankfurt); Karlsruhe: from Bruchsal – we parked at a large P&R (free parking) at Bruchsal-Gewerbliches-Bildungzentrum, an out-of-town train station on the N3 south of Bruchsal. The car park may be busy mid-week but at the weekend we found the 120-place car park empty with spaces for the motorhome to overhang. There is a campsite opposite the entrance. An alternative is the P&R at Untergrombach though there is not as much parking space. Pforzheim: from Kleinsteinbach – we parked at the P&R at Kleinsteinbach. The large car park has no marked bays and it is right beside the railway platform for the train to Pforzheim. None of the stations we caught the train from had ticket offices. Cash is required otherwise visit ⌀ bahn.com/en to obtain a barcode to buy tickets.

Rail travel is inexpensive and service is generally excellent. Regional day tickets offer superb value and are valid until 03.00 the morning after purchase for up to five people.

ACCOMMODATION We stayed on *Stellplätze* in Ladenburg and Bad Schönborn. Both are privately run, exclusively for motorhomes/campervans. **Wohnmobilstellplatz Ladenburg**: (⌀ wohnmobilstellplatz-ladenburg.de) is a peaceful, tidy site on the edge of the town with rural views to the Odenwald. Adjacent is a large riverside park with tennis courts, a lido and restaurant. The town centre is a ten-minute walk, bakery five minutes. **WellMobilPark Bad Schönborn** (⌀ wellmobilpark.de) is a large site on the edge of the village and adjacent to TherMarium, a spa and wellness centre (⌀ thermarium.de), open to the public, and a large public park. There are many walking trails within the area and bike hire is available from the *Stellplatz*.

We noted *Stellplätze* along or close to the Bertha Benz Memorial Route at: Mannheim-Friedrichsfeld, Schwetzingen, Bruchsal, Bretten, Ruit, Karlsruhe Ettlingen, Pforzheim (this parking area is noisy and very suburban; when we arrived, we decided against stopping overnight and returned to the WellMobilPark at Bad Schönborn).

Campsites: Campingplatz Mannheim Strandbad, Mannheim; Camping Heidelberg, Heidelberg; Campingplatz am Eichelberg, Bruchsal.

FIND OUT MORE

Automuseum Dr Carl Benz
⌀ automuseum-dr-carl-benz.de
Bertha Benz Memorial Route ⌀ bertha-benz.de
Germany National Tourist Board
⌀ germany.travel/en

Heidelberg ⌀ heidelberg-marketing.com
Hockenheimring ⌀ hockenheimring.de
Karlsruhe ⌀ karlsruhe-tourismus.de
Wiesloch ⌀ wiesloch.de

27 MUSICAL INTERLUDE: THE HARMONY OF FOREST BATHING

COMBINE WINE & WALKS WITH A CULTURAL SANDWICH

WHERE	Rhineland-Palatinate/Baden-Württemberg
DISTANCE/TIME	196 miles (316km)/6 days
START/FINISH	Herxheim (bei Landau)/Baden-Baden

Descending a set of stone steps behind the Friedrichspa, we kneel and put our hands to the pavement. The cobbles are cold yet the manhole cover buried within the walkway is hot to touch. It warms our fingers to the core. It's an unseasonably cool summer day but, even in winter, when Baden-Baden's ice-cold temperatures are low enough to freeze thermal water dripping from the Fettquelle grotto, the manhole remains warm.

Through the latticework of the cover rises a welcoming hot steam though it distorts our vision of Baden-Baden's elegant skyline. For beneath the pavement is the gushing thermal water that helped to place this town on the world's stage. The Romans, scared of the Black Forest where they thought bad spirits might exist, dared not venture into the dark and brooding mountains, and settled in the foothills where they discovered the water ejecting from the bowels of the earth.

Unlike the Romans, we're quite happy to explore the Black Forest, which we do on foot. But first we discover another love of the Romans – wine, along part of Germany's 85km Weinstrasse (Wine Road), with a cultural interlude in Baden-Baden.

Everyone's heard of the River Rhine – that great, long river that flows from the Swiss Alps right along the border of France and Germany and up through the latter to the North Sea. It gives its name to one of Germany's most western states, Rhineland-Palatinate, also considered one of the most romantic with fairytale castles, ruins, medieval towns, forests and miles upon miles of vines. Less well known within the state is a small area just to the west of the Rhine, the Pfälzerwald (Palatinate Forest) that's designated as a Naturpark and UNESCO Biosphere Reserve.

To the west of the Pfälzerwald is Pirmasens, the largest town in this forested, hilly locale, close to the French border. To the east, lie the flat lands of the Rhine Valley, filled with vines and fruit trees. We begin our tour here, in the small town of **Herxheim bei Landau**. Ten kilometres west of the Rhine, the town is similar to many in the area – an extra-long main street that's filled with half-timbered houses and with a very pleasant central square in which to sit and enjoy a mid-morning coffee or a late evening glass of something. Kandel and Winden, to the southwest, and Rohrbach, just to the west, are much the same, surrounded by acres of attractive orchards, the village streets beset by homemade stalls selling locally grown apples, plums, potatoes, pumpkins – and wine. Indeed, it's the second-largest wine region in Germany and we find ourselves ducking to brush beneath many a pretty vine-clad decoration that drapes its way across village streets.

← View from the Ellbachseeblick in the Black Forest (Superstock)

We pick up the Deutsche Weinstrasse at **Klingenmünster**, a charming village with flower-decked houses and *Weinstubes* – places in which to sample the local fermentation alongside a hearty meal. It is a romantic village, with the sloping vines followed by steeply wooded hillsides erupting behind and the deep red ruin of Burg Landeck sitting atop.

The Weinstrasse wiggles its way northeastwards through one after another of pretty villages that hug the lower slopes of the Pfälzerwald. Before us, a green sea of vines, tinged with purple as perfectly formed bunches of grapes dangle tantalisingly. And every few miles, another red ruin pops up from the trees.

At **Neustadt**, we should, perhaps, continue north along the Weinstrasse to Deidesheim and Bad Dürkheim, two of the route's most picturesque settlements but, eager for nature, we turn west and climb into the forest. Here we find a forgotten world with quiet, winding valleys and hilltop roads. And trees – lots of them!

Our cross-country route takes us to **Dahn**, to follow the scenic – if you like trees – road to **Bad Bergzabern**. It's a road that stumbles across what the Palatinate, besides vines, is perhaps most renowned for – giant red rock formations that appear out of the trees at every turn. This is great walking and cycling territory – and there are plenty of cycling and hiking trails to explore, including the German Wine Route Cycle Trail, which runs parallel to the Deutsche Weinstrasse.

↑ Deutsche Weinstrasse on the edge of the Pfälzerwald (Caroline Mills)

Having come almost full circle, we take a short-cut through a tiny slice of France to cross the River Rhine west of **Baden-Baden** and a cultural stopover in the spa town. Friedrichbad, that by which we kneel besides to feel the warmth from underground, is the oldest working spa in the town housed in a resplendent building of domes and columns. It sits above the ancient pools of the Roman bathers. Their handiwork and hypocaust system of underfloor heating can be seen within the Römische Badruinen (Roman Baths). Neighbouring Caracalla Spa is the modern equivalent.

Today Baden-Baden, filled with cultural connections, thrives for a global audience all year round. But it was the period of the Belle Époque when the town became truly international. Then, Baden-Baden was the Summer Capital of Europe as royal and aristocratic guests came to see and be seen, promenading through the park sipping the health-giving spa water and lured by the theatre, Kurhaus, the famous casino, elegant French-designed hotels and the town's natural surroundings.

Composers, musicians, authors and poets joined them, congregating beneath the trees of the Lichtentaler Allee and mingling in the concert halls (and casino), gathering inspiration for works of musical and literary art. Russian Fyodor Dostoevsky wrote *Der Spieler* (*The Gambler*) here to pay off debts in association with his personal gambling habit. Composers Clara Schumann and husband Robert, Hector Berlioz and Johann Strauss all spent time in Baden-Baden, but none more so than the composer Johannes Brahms.

↑ Frieder Burda Museum in Baden-Baden (g215/Shutterstock)

As we approach Brahmshaus, strolling along the Lichtentaler Allee, the tumultuous sound of the composer's 2nd Symphony explodes into my head. Brahms put the finishing touches to this masterful composition in Baden-Baden and I begin to lose myself in his music as we wander beside the River Oos. In winter I've watched the ice-cold water struggle for movement, searching for ever-narrower channels as it coagulates into brittle icebergs and frozen sculptures; for now, the river has regained waterfalls once more and where, before now, I've questioned the harshness of nature as mallard ducks, feathers plumped, stand on frozen soil in 'bare feet', today the children make riverbank friends with them as I wander the gardens and admire the white lace bridges that fan the river.

Having already observed the grandeur of the town centre hotels, each ornamented with delicate balconies, I'm not prepared for Brahmshaus, a demure white-shingle villa perched on a rock at the southern end of Maximilianstrasse. This is the only surviving residence of Brahms, and his rented attic rooms are cosy with a quartet of visitors inside.

The house custodian flits between German and English with diligent speed to enlighten any listener about Brahms' time in Baden-Baden. But as she chatters I'm distracted by the intensity of the original wallpaper – a cobalt blue with a child-like potato print that exudes innocence and personality. Black-and-white photographs of the composer adorn the colourful walls and a small, upright piano stands waiting to fill the house with music once again.

↑ Brahmshaus, Baden-Baden (Caroline Mills)

Impassioned by the rudimentary living quarters of Brahms, we retrace our steps to follow Baden-Baden's 'Cultural Mile' through the Lichtentaler Allee Park. Locals are out making the most of the day – dog walkers, cyclists and a party of schoolchildren play by the river. I take notice of a riverside bench that must be the sunniest in Baden-Baden for yesterday I saw an elderly lady sitting there, wrapped in winter warmers, a blanket drooping over her knees. She was turned, like a sundial, towards the sun's glow. And now, same place, same bench, a smartly dressed gentleman, figured in a long black woollen coat, topped by a Trilby hat and gloves, sits with a book in hand beneath the golden rays, despite the rawness of the unseasonal day.

Our walk takes us from the serene Kloster Lichtenthal, a Cistercian abbey where the courtyard silence is occasionally invaded by musical performances, past the sculptures of Brahms and his friend Clara Schumann, and across the river to the golden-domed Russian church. Back in the park, we enter the Frieder Burda Museum that displays contemporary art exhibitions. The modern building is a stark white cube with white walls, soaring white columns, white, banded staircases and balconies to match. Colour is blended by nature through the glass box façade.

Beyond is the State Museum, the Theater Baden-Baden – modelled on the Paris Opéra and where Hector Berlioz premiered his work *Béatrice and Bénédict*. On the steps of the Kurhaus, used by Clara Schumann and Strauss for concerts, we turn our backs on its octet of Corinthian columns and look across the rooftops of the town. A radiant sky lights up the town's backdrop and the Florentinerberg on which sits the Altes Schloss Hohenbaden, a romantic sandstone ruin tucked amid

↑ Altes Schloss Hohenbaden above Baden-Baden (LiliGraphie/Shutterstock)

the trees. The sun glints on the giant slabs of mountain rock behind the Stiftskirche, the natural panorama illuminating the slender pink belltower of the church.

At the northern end of the Cultural Mile we reach the Festspielhaus – the festival hall, grand in scale and decoration. Its front entrance was a former railway station, used by the aristocracy in the days of the Belle Époque and lofty ceilings ornamented with soft frescoes show off the grandeur of the building. Behind is the concert hall, the second largest in Europe (only Paris' Opéra Bastille is larger). Creativity appears to seep from the walls as we climb the stairs with the vista of Baden-Baden before us.

Standing in the upper balcony, the auditorium appears vast. Riggers are on stage preparing for the night's performance, the musical instruments already in position, gleaming from the orchestra pit. In a separate part of the building, in cosy wood-panelled rooms, double basses, cellos, trombones and saxophones sit on stands waiting to be played. This is Toccarion, a children's adventure space of musical games and activities.

Overflowing with culture, we leave Baden-Baden and climb into the hills to drive along the **Schwarzwaldhochstrasse (Black Forest High Road)** towards Baiersbronn to clear our heads with walks in the mountains. Allegedly, hiking was 'invented' in the Black Forest.

↑ The Black Forest, or Schwarzwald (rawcapPhoto/Shutterstock)

It was Philipp Bussemer from Baden-Baden who, at the end of the 19th century, opened what was possibly the first tourist information centre in his haberdashery shop, publishing hiking maps and guides and signposting walking routes throughout the area. It's a task that's still performed by the *Schwarzwaldverein*, an organisation that looked after the Black Forest then and does today.

The Black Forest occupies Germany's second-highest mountain range after the Alps. Its name is fairly obvious for the densely wooded slopes of pine trees but there are luscious green meadows and heaths, too. Two separate areas of the forest are, collectively, one of Germany's most recent national parks, its status designated in 2014. We choose to base ourselves in the small town of **Baiersbronn**, on the park's edge.

Baiersbronn promotes itself as 'Hiking Heaven' and understandably so. It's a pretty town in even more appealing surroundings, with 483km of waymarked hiking trails. These are most often gravel tracks, not jaunts across muddy fields.

Our first stop upon arrival is the walking information centre where we pick up maps, an excellent free walking guide to the area and discover Baiersbronn's *Geniesserpfade* or 'Connoisseur Trails', a series of walking routes that connect mountain restaurants and farms producing regional specialities. We also pick up our Kinder-Wander-Pass, a series of walking trails suitable for children.

And so begins our first walk. A gentle climb above the town at the foothills of the Rinkenkopf, where the tree line provides summer shade as we watch a sinking sun dance and flicker across the bronzed rooftops.

In the morning, snack-filled rucksacks at the ready, we take off for a day's walking into the hills. Steps are steady initially, following the Sankenbach valley, a tiddly stream that enters the River Murg, which in turn trips its way over rocks past the *Stellplatz* in the centre of town (we had pitched our 'van right by the river). In a couple of miles we reach the Sankenbachsee, a glacial lake among trees – and a long way from any road so it's only walkers here – that provides the perfect stopping point for a dip into the rucksack. An energy boost is needed for no sooner as we've circumnavigated the lake we begin to reach dizzier heights, climbing steeply to gain views of the lake below and above the treetops of the forest. The climb includes passing by the Sankenbach Waterfall as the crystal waters plummet 40m into the lake.

Approaching the summit of the Uberzwerchberg, paths level out to provide smooth terrain into the little village of Kniebis, but not before a quick detour to the viewing point, Ellbachseeblick. At 921m, it's one of the highest points in the area around Baiersbronn and provides great treescape views of the northern forests even though a thick fog begins to enshroud the vegetation.

With lunch in Kniebis, we make our long and gentle descent back towards Baiersbronn, passing beautiful mountainside flowers and berries, approaching the town just as rattling thunder makes way for a biblical rainstorm. Snug and dry back in our 'van, hiking map spread out across the table, we begin to plan a walk for the next day, ready to explore one of the other four valleys that descend on Baiersbronn.

SOUVENIR

Black Forest Gateau is one of Germany's best-known regional specialities. In fact, it has become so universal that you may remember some pretty hideous commercial pub desserts derived from it in the 1970s/80s. A fresh, homemade cake, eaten 'on location', is a different thing.

One of the best places to try a slice is the **Sattelei Wanderhütte** (Hiking Cabin) between Mitteltal and Tonbachtal, near Baiersbronn. If you want to take some home, head to **Café König**, on Lichtentaler Strasse in Baden-Baden.

Baiersbronn also has three Michelin-starred restaurants in the town, plus you'll find numerous attractive mountain hut restaurants serving local produce and specialities.

→ On a walk from Baiersbronn through the Sankenbach valley (Caroline Mills)

Soaking in Baden-Baden's Caracalla Spa at the end of our stay in the Black Forest (with a return trip to the town on our way back north), I think of all the musicians, the literary giants, the artists and the hikers that have been inspired by the town, and by the forest. Like them, we too have become smitten by the town and forest's charms. We've seen exquisite beauty, pondered over pieces of contemporary artwork in the Frieder-Burda Museum, been drawn to the ornamentation of buildings, interior decoration and been seduced by the captivating sound of church bells echoing into the evening, the scent of pine and the colours of nature. Oh, and, we've succumbed to a piece of Black Forest Gateau.

↑ Ellbachseeblick near Kniebis (Caroline Mills)

ESSENTIALS

GETTING THERE & AROUND
Herxheim bei Landen is 31km northwest of Karlsruhe, on the L493. We drove west on minor roads to Rohrbach and Klingenmünster before picking up signposts for the Deutsche Weinstrasse north to Neustadt. Here we turned west on the 39, then minor roads to Johanniskreuz, then the 48, 10 and 427 to Dahn. The 427 continues to Bad Bergzabern, where we continued east to Winden and Kandel before turning south to cross the border into France. We used the French A35 autoroute to Junction 56, then southeast on the 500 to Baden-Baden. The 500 and 401 takes you to Baiersbronn.

Baiersbronn has a small train station, providing opportunities to take walks elsewhere within the area without having to drive. In particular, a visit to the neighbouring town of Freudenstadt is worthwhile; the town has an outstanding historic market place, the largest in Germany. [*]

ACCOMMODATION
We stayed on a ***Stellplatz*** in Herxheim. There are many others around the Deutsche Weinstrasse, including at Rohrbach, Bad Bergzabern and Neustadt. We also stayed on *Stellplätze* in Baden-Baden and Baiersbronn.

Campsites: Campingplatz Rülzheim, for Herxheim; Camping im Klingbachtal, Billigheim-Ingenheim; Campingplatz Pfrimmtal, Sippersfeld; Campingplatz Zum Neudahner Weiher, Dahn; Campingplatz Adam, Bühl – for Baden-Baden; NaturCamping Langenwald, Freudenstadt – for Baiersbronn.

FIND OUT MORE
Baden-Baden Tourism ⊘ baden-baden.com

Baden-Württemberg Tourist Board ⊘ tourism-bw.com

Baiersbronn ⊘ baiersbronn.de

Black Forest National Park ⊘ nationalpark-schwarzwald.de/en

Black Forest Tourism ⊘ schwarzwald-tourismus.info

Deutsche Weinstrasse (German Wine Route) ⊘ deutsche-weinstrasse.de

Rhineland Palatinate Tourist Board ⊘ rlp-tourismus.com/en

TOP TIP: WILDERNESS EXPERIENCE
For a more independent wilderness experience, there are nine hiking camps where, from May to October, tents can be pitched and permission granted to sleep overnight in the Black Forest Nature Park Central/North, the Black Forest Nature Park South and in the Black Forest National Park. The camps are all away from villages and towns, can only be reached on foot and have space for up to three tents, a fireplace and a small toilet cabin. Hikers must take their own food and water, and take their rubbish with them when they leave. Sites must be pre-booked at ⊘ trekking-schwarzwald.de.

28 EUROPEAN UNION

TOUR THE RHINE VALLEY AND SEE EUROPE IN A DAY

WHERE	Baden-Württemberg
DISTANCE/TIME	145 miles (234km)/3½ days
START/FINISH	Sasbachwalden/Blansingen

Some people scream with fright, some because it's part of the fun. Some hold their arms in the air while others cling on for dear life. As we climb, ever so slowly to the ridge peak of the Poseidon aquatic rollercoaster, in anticipation of what's to come I'm gripping my adrenalin-fuelled daughter sat beside me until the blood drains from my fingertips – and her arm. I have my eyes closed, much to the disgust of my son sat one row in front, who cackles at my apparent terror.

By splashdown, I come to the conclusion that I'll leave the 130km/h, 73m-high Silver Star with 4G loops for my son to experience (consider it payback for laughing). And that I'm better watching the excitable screams of speed enthusiasts on the Megacoaster from the sidelines as they hurtle past me from zero to 100km/h in 2.5 seconds. I sense I've become soft with my increasing years.

No matter. For we're at **Europa-Park**, a multi-award-winning theme park in Germany, close to the border with France. And, to quote a cliché, there is 'something for everyone' here. It's frequently one of Germany's top-ranking tourist attractions (it always makes the top three) and has been voted the 'World's Best Theme Park' for six consecutive years at the leisure industry's annual Golden Ticket Awards. And while my three teenagers are keen to turn their tummies upside down, I'm happy to soak up the atmosphere of walking from one country to the next, all in the space of a day.

You could say that Europa-Park is an interactive tourist brochure for most countries in Europe. Exploring the cobbled street and timber chalets of Switzerland, the grand piazza of Italy or the gabled houses of the Netherlands is as much a part of our visit as the rollercoasters and rides. And the attention to detail – the buildings, the floral arrangements, the landscaping – is outstanding; we really do sense that we're wandering along the streets of whichever country we happen to be in at the time. Lured by the whitewashed houses of 'Greece', the shimmering blue of the Aegean Sea and the crumbling ruins of some Greek mythological temple is, I'm sure, how I ended up being persuaded onto a rollercoaster, after all.

If you don't like fast rides, or any rides at all, or even the notion of theme parks, Europa-Park is definitely different – and special. We all find our own level of activity, whether the greatest thrill-seeking rides, something a little tamer or simply watching high-rise divers perform daredevil stunts. For the youngest members of the family, including babies, 'Ireland' is the country to visit, along with Grimm's Enchanted Forest.

You can also taste your way around Europe, too. Eat *crêpes* in France, *Wiener Schnitzel* in Austria, *Poffertjes* and coffee in the Netherlands or freshly prepared

smoked fish in Iceland. We choose to go loopy and have our food delivered by rollercoaster in the Food Loop restaurant, watching as our dishes twist and turn towards our table. Gimmicky, maybe, but the food is delicious.

We stay to the very end of the day when people are running to the rides for one last go – including my son who opts for the Timburcoaster, a vast contraption of timber scaffold that echoes as the wooden carts rattle by and flaming torches erupt into the dusky sky. I try to remain impassive towards theme parks as we wander to the exit, but it's very difficult when the golden onion domes of 'Russia' glow and the starry lights of 'Germany's' main street lead you to sugar-pink puffs of candyfloss. We've had a fabulous time.

And the most convenient aspect of all? Our motorhome is parked in Europa-Park's very own campsite ready for an overnight stay. Europa-Park Camping and Camp Resort is a vast complex with an American Mid-West theme; if you don't have your own tent, caravan or campervan, you can stay in a tipi or covered wagon. The campsite also has its own restaurant, the Silver Lake Saloon. As we return to the site, guests are toasting marshmallows around campfires, the flames flickering hypnotically.

Our day of action-packed fun is sandwiched between a couple of gentler days either side, exploring the foothills of the Schwarzwald (Black Forest) and the countryside of the Rhine Valley. The trip had begun in **Sasbachwalden**, some 40km northeast of Strasbourg and 48km from Europa-Park. A small and perfectly formed village, Sasbachwalden is perched on the edge of the Black Forest, just as the road begins to climb away from the Rhine Valley, so providing beautiful

↑ Mummelsee (Juergen Wackenhut/Shutterstock)

views of the plain, and the Vosges Mountains in France, further west. Staying on a small *Stellplatz* in the romantic village, we took advantage of the numerous footpaths and trails through the vineyards that smother the hillsides to enjoy the views of the fairytale-style, flower-decked houses tucked among the vines.

With the copper clanging of church bells in the morning, we began our climb up through the forest pines to **Mummelsee**, a small, glacial lake that's popular as a stopping off point for those driving along the panoramic Schwarzwaldhochstrasse (Black Forest High Road). This mountain road runs from Baden-Baden to Freudenstadt and is one of the most celebrated routes in Germany.

Descending back to the Rhine Valley via the spa town of **Bad Peterstal-Griesbach** and **Oberkirch**, we made our way along the flat to a delightful, private *Stellplatz* in **Meißenheim**. Surrounded by sunflowers and fields of maize, the village is perfect for accessing numerous cycle routes, including the 520km Rheintal-Weg (Rhine Valley Way), and walks to Meißenheim's nature reserve beside the river. The village is also a mere 20-minute drive from **Europa-Park**.

The day after our visit to Europa-Park and our mammoth 'tour' of Europe on foot, we continue with our driving tour of the Rhine Valley. Taking the back roads south of **Rust**, we pass through a land of fruit trees and sunflowers, with views of both the Vosges Mountains and the Black Forest at all times. At **Weisweil**, we turn up the **Rheinstrasse**, arguably one of the prettiest of little-known roads in Germany – an avenue of trees beside the extraordinarily blue River Altrhein.

↑ Fields of sunflowers are a regular sight in the Rhine Valley (Tanja Midgardson/Shutterstock)

The river is one of many in a network of streams and waterways that flow through a vast, forested nature reserve beside the River Rhine.

Quiet and far removed from the clatter of rollercoasters and screams of excitement, we feel we could happily stay all day amid the wildflowers, electric blue damselflies and fish basking in the dappled sunlight. We find a shady spot to sit and absorb the solitude, enjoying a walk to view the regal Rhine. Oh, what a sight! The river appears as smooth as silk, graced by silent swans and laced by banks of wildflowers. In the middle of the river is the border between Germany and France, not that there's any markings to determine exactly where.

Continuing on our way through **Wyhl**, **Sasbach** and **Königschaffhausen**, each village grows ever prettier. That is until we climb the **Kaiserstuhl**, a noticeable volcanic hump in the otherwise flat landscape, when a view to surpass all others appears: terraced vines and small, heath-like undulations of calcareous limestone give way to unstoppable panoramas across the Rhine Valley.

Halting for a picnic lunch just outside **Oberbergen**, we set off on foot to climb **Badberg**, a notable grassland ridge that, in the sunshine, produces clouds of butterflies with every step. We count at least a dozen or more different species; the area is known for several rare varieties otherwise only found in the Mediterranean, owing to the microclimate. From the top, the scenery appears even more striking. It's one of the least expected and most underrated areas of Germany we've seen.

We cross the small ridge of hills known as the **Tuniberg**, no less pretty than Badberg, to head back towards the Black Forest. Just before **Freiburg im Breisgau**,

↑ We count at least a dozen different species of butterfly on Badberg (Caroline Mills)

considered one of Baden-Württemberg's most historic cities, we turn south keeping the river valley on one side and the ridge of Black Forest hills on the other as we pass through lively wine villages, fields of sunflowers and asparagus beds. This area is reputedly the sunniest in Germany and, today at least, it doesn't disappoint.

By evening we park up beneath plum trees in the orchards of a private *Stellplatz* in **Blansingen**, one of the last villages overlooking the Rhine Valley before the river turns east. With our overnight stay free of charge, I return the gesture by purchasing a couple of bottles of wine, produced by the owner Claudia Straub who is a notable winemaker in the area. But before I pull the cork to toast the end of our trip, a village walk to view the river offers up one last surprise: it's not noticeable when driving, but the Rhine is entirely shrouded by trees. There is no river to see, until you're right beside it!

We look forward to a return visit to this part of Germany – to see more of the river, hike further amid the vines and attempt another rollercoaster … with my eyes open this time.

↑ Views of the Kaiserstuhl from Badberg (Caroline Mills)

ESSENTIALS

GETTING THERE & AROUND
Sasbachwalden is on the L86, 4.5km east of Achern and 29km south of Baden-Baden. Mummelsee is to the east, on the B500, which is also known as the Schwarzwaldhochstrasse (Black Forest High Road). From Oberkirch, on the B28, we took the A5 autobahn south for one junction, then the B36 to Meißenheim, followed by the L104 to Rust (Europa-Park).

The Rheinstrasse is a dead-end road to the west of Weisweil. Then, from Weisweil, take the L104 to Sasbach, the L105 to Königschaffhausen followed by the K5127 to Oberbergen. Badberg lies north of the L115, with a small parking area (though large enough for motorhomes to park). We then travelled east towards Freiberg im Breisgau on the B31, to pick up the B3 south to Blansingen.

We had no issues with **parking** anywhere; Europa-Park has a vast dedicated parking area for motorhomes. This does get busy and it's not possible to pre-book parking. There is lots of space to park beside the River Rhine at the end of the Rheinstrasse near Weisweil.

View from Badberg over the village of Altvogtsburg and the vineyards of the Kaiserstuhl (movit/Shutterstock)

ACCOMMODATION
We stayed on *Stellplätze* in Sasbachwalden, Meißenheim and Blansingen (listed in *Bord Atlas* under Efringen-Kirchen). We also stayed at Europa-Park Camping.

Campsites: Camping Grässelmühle, Sasbach (for Sasbachwalden); Camping Schutternsee, Friesenheim; Europa-Park Camping, Rust; Camping Lug ins Land, Bad Bellingen.

FIND OUT MORE

Baden-Württemberg Tourist Board ⌀ tourism-bw.com

Black Forest Tourist Board ⌀ schwarzwald-tourismus.info

Europa Park ⌀ europapark.de/en

TOP TIP: VISIT SWITZERLAND
Fancy a trip to Switzerland? Blansingen, where we end this road trip, is only 20km from Basel, in Switzerland. There are several small railway stations between the village and the border, with direct trains to Basel, each with a car park. Catch a train from Bad Bellingen, Rheinweiler, Istein or Eimeldingen.

29 A NATURAL QUARTET

VISIT FOUR REGIONAL NATURE PARKS FROM EAST TO WEST

WHERE	Bavaria
DISTANCE/TIME	455 miles (732km)/5 days
START/FINISH	Passau/Bad Brückenau

A good signpost can be a thing of beauty. One that informs you wild boar might dart across the road at any moment suggests you might be somewhere quite special. I am. I'm in the Bavarian Forest, which, 50 years ago, became Germany's first national park.

I began from **Passau**, a town in the far southeast of Germany, bordering Austria. Here the mighty Danube meets the rivers Ilz and Inn. The Ilz has its origins in the Bavarian Forest, a forest that spans both Germany and the Czech Republic (known there as the Bohemian Forest) and is the largest in Central Europe. I follow, very crudely, the Ilz north to the town of **Grafenau**, a gateway to the national park.

Climbing lowland hills, initially with that glorious combination of 'alpine' meadows and pine, then latterly all trees, my first stop is **Lusen National Park Centre** at **Neuschönau**. It's a good base from which to begin exploration of the park, with an exhibition about the forest, a treetop walk and information about the 500kms of marked hiking and cycling trails, including guided tours. I'm eager to get out there, so I pick one of the circular, signposted walks and head into the forest.

On the lower slopes are swathes of beech, silver birch, rowan and spruce. It has recently rained and the fresh woodland scent is glorious as I soak up the peaceful

↑ Bavarian Forest National Park (StGrafix/Shutterstock)

atmosphere and contemplate the sheer scale of the forest – and the wildlife that lives here, including lynx, wildcats, beavers and… wild boar. Popular with families in the forest is the 200ha of animal enclosures, where species that naturally inhabit the area are brought together.

There's also a short trail that leads out of the forest to the village of Neuschönau itself; walkers follow a guided route, with informative boards about the forestry industry and local traditions such as Bohemian dances like the Polka.

Back in the 'van, I climb ever-higher, to **Waldhäuser**, one of the highest villages in the mountains. My amble is brief and low-level by comparison to the hiking possibilities; from here, one can pick up paths to climb Lusen, at 1,373m, one of the highest mountains in the region, or the Goldsteig Trail, a historic 660km path over the mountains to the Czech Republic that, as its name implies, was a trading route for, 'white gold' – salt.

There's nothing golden about the sun today and, with cloudy skies, the forested hills appear intensely blue, almost violet, as I wander about the slopes. I find more colour as I drop back down the hillside by road and head north to first **Spiegelau** and, latterly, **Frauenau**.

The area around these villages is concentrated with glassware manufacturers, from factories on an industrial scale to artisan crafters creating colourful art. It's a centuries-old industry, using wood ash to make the glass. Up and down the valley are slender chimneys, telltale signs of a glass workshop. Many are open to

the public, be it a factory tour and have-a-go glassblowing sessions, to warehouse shops (Spiegelau is not only the name of a village, but also a brand of glassware). JOSKA, further north at Bodenmais, is a large tourist attraction, described as a *Glas Paradies* (glass paradise). I visit the **Glass Garden** in Frauenau, where 21 glass sculptures are set amid the grounds of the Glass Museum.

I continue north, with a detour to **Frauenau Reservoir** (Trinkwassertalsperre) just outside the town, from which there are scenic walks through the forest and around the water's edge. It's the first of two 'lakes' I visit in the forest; while the first is manmade, the second, **Arbersee**, 23km northwest, is glacial, dark and brooding, tucked among the pine trees. It's a well-loved beauty spot; there's a lakeside restaurant, pedalo rental and the start of numerous walking trails, including to the summit of Großer Arber, the highest mountain in the Bavarian Forest. Those that don't wish to walk are whisked to the mountain top by cable car.

Finishing at the highest point seems apt, so I leave the Bavarian Forest and drive west through the foothills, 35km west of Bodenwöhr, into open countryside of the **Regen valley** with an overnight stop at Bodenwöhr, ready to begin my exploration of the next nature park.

While the Bavarian Forest is grand in scale and status, the **Hirschwald Nature Park** covers a tiny area of Bavaria – only 280km². It's triangular in shape, bordered by the Lauterach valley in the southwest and the Wils valley in the east. It's not so exceptional to warrant an exclusive trip but is, nonetheless, a quiet, rural landscape of agricultural plains and woods that's undisturbed by the trappings of mass tourism.

I enter the park at **Schmidmühlen**, in the Lauterach valley. I'm instantly captivated by the beauty of the valley, the curving river channelled narrowly between water meadows and wooded hills. The Lauterach is regarded as one of the most scenic aspects of the Hirschwald, though as I criss-cross the park, turning this way and that along country lanes, the variety of landscape strikes me. There's nothing overly dramatic, no majesty or pomp to the setting. But there's escapism in the pastoral plateaus, the pine woods, the farm-and barn hamlets and the empty roads, decoratively edged with lemon-tinted common toadflax.

I pass through onion-domed villages like **Hausen** and **Reusch**, some so small they don't make it on to the road atlas, and the namesake village of **Hirschwald**, whose onion-domed church tops them all for plumpness. I drop back down from the Hirschwald plateau to the Lauterach valley again from where there are handsome views of **Kastl** and its former Benedictine abbey poking above the trees from its hilltop position. The town, on the western fringe of the nature park, justifies a hike to the hilltop to take a look around the abbey church. Its internal, whitewashed simplicity, decorated with little more than rows of heraldic emblems frescoed on the walls, is very attractive.

← **Top left** The Treetop walk at Lusen National Park Centre (precinbe/Shutterstock) **Top right** Woods in Hirschwald Nature Park (Caroline Mills) **Bottom** Glass Garden at Frauenau (Caroline Mills)

I cut back over the plateau towards **Ensdorf**, on the eastern edge of the nature park. A little beyond Hirschwald village, the road peters out and becomes a gritty track through the woods, with plenty of places to pull off and walk or cycle. It's quite beautiful and, as the tarmac picks up again, I come across a remote pilgrimage church on one of the many Jakobsweg (St James' Way) routes through Germany; if I set off from here on foot, I could be on Spain's Santiago de Compostela some 2,300km later!

Instead, I enjoy my last remnants of the nature park and sit for a while looking at the eastern views. The sirens of Ensdorf's weekly fire station drill crank up eerily through the woods and wake my daydreams as if to tell me it's time to leave. So I make my way northwest along the Wils river valley and on to my next destination some 50 or so kilometres northwest, the **Fränkische Schweiz Naturpark** (Franconian Switzerland Nature Park).

The cities of Nürnberg (Nuremberg), Bamberg and Bayreuth are all renowned, well-visited urban beauties. The trio feature along the Castle Road, one of Germany's themed and signposted road trips and all three are don't-miss destinations. Except on this occasion. For, what's less well known is the nature park that lies in between this cultural triangle.

Franconian Switzerland has nothing to do with the country of Switzerland; it's a tag given by 19th-century Romanticists who likened the landscape to those of its namesake, and it has remained ever since, much like other 'Switzerland' attachments given to places with a vaguely hilly topography. I don't share their association; the Fränkische Schweiz Naturpark has a character of its own.

Approaching from the southeast, near **Pegnitz**, clues begin to appear as I pass through a tiny corner of the **Veldenstein Forest**; a sign for a grotto, then a protruding rock emerging from the undergrowth. By the time I've crossed the A9 autobahn, heading along the Weiherbach valley towards **Pottenstein**, it's clear I've arrived in Franconian Switzerland. Suddenly before me are towering sculptures,

↑ Rock formations in the Fränkische Schweiz Naturpark (Caroline Mills)

moulded limestone rocks shaped by eternity. Some emerge precariously balanced among leafy birch trees, which cling on by their shallow, rockbed roots. Climbers, looking for the best overhang, cling on, too.

While some folk climb the rocks, others delve deep at Teufelshöhle (Devil's Hole), a giant underground cavern that offers concealed beauty. At 1,500m-long, it is the longest cave in Germany, and is also one of the most visited attractions in the area, although there are other notable caves to visit locally, including Sophienhöhle and Binghöhle.

The Weiherbach valley is fabulous for walking and cycling – as is much of the nature park – while Pottenstein offers a plentiful supply of reasons to remain, especially for families: a boating lake, summer toboggan run, lido, a *Kletterwald* (woodland ropes course), an exhilarating SkyWalk not to mention a medieval hilltop *Burg* – and an ice-cream café.

The projecting rocks keep coming, though, and at neighbouring **Tüchersfeld**, enigmatic formations and symmetrically patterned houses combine to create a weirdly wonderful mix. Also here is the Fränkische-Schweiz Museum. It's presentation is a little old-fashioned but there are some nuggets of information about the region and the collection of buildings, including an original 18th-century synagogue, merit time spent.

I turn off at **Behringersmühle** for a short circuitous route, initially northeast along the small Ailsbach River valley to **Oberalsfeld**. The dell feels tight and enclosed owing to the gorge-like cliffsides and there are castles and chapels perched high above. Up and over a narrow ridge northwest towards **Waischenfeld**, I have elevated views of the valley as I climb, before descending to the parallel

↑ Pottenstein (Animaflora PicsStock/Shutterstock)

Wiesent valley. Waischenfeld, sat on the river, is a gorgeous little place. Despite its relative remoteness, it buzzes with daily life, has an attractive town square and enough shops to stock up on provisions.

My return to **Behringersmühle**, alongside the Wiesent, is sublime, with steep, wooded cliffs one side and the open valley on the other. It's slightly misty as I follow the river and the lush, green water meadows take on an ethereal quality.

I continue to follow the Wiesent west to **Streitberg**. The route is no less uplifting than that from Waischenfeld, with rocky ledges, old mill houses, ruined burgs and the river always in view. Alongside the road and river is a single railway track, used only at weekends by the Franconian Switzerland Steam Railway for trips up and down the valley. I determine it would be a lovely sight to see the steam train toot-tooting its way through such idyllic countryside.

There are footpaths and viewpoints in abundance accessed from the village of Streitberg offering excellent panoramas of the Wiesental. After an early morning wander to castle ruins above the village, I head the 124km northwest by road to **Bad Kissengen** for the start of my final nature park.

I'm now in the heart of Germany, on the northwestern edge of Bavaria where it meets two other states, Hesse and Thuringia. Bad Kissengen is a southern gateway to the **Rhön UNESCO Biosphere Reserve**, which crosses the three states and covers an area of some 1,850km². Such recognition focuses on people and conservation coming together in order to develop a sustainable future that maintains the special character of the landscape, that of wide open moors and lowland mountains. A part of the biosphere reserve is also designated as the **Bavarian Rhön Nature Park**; it's this that I focus on.

From Bad Kissengen, I head north alongside the Fränkische-Saale River to **Bad Bocklet**, a spa town that hugs a wooded hillside. I find it a strange town; its front

↑ Waischenfeld (Superstock)

face shows off a beautiful meadow-like parkland, the KurPark, that's attached to the spa. There's an elegant formal garden and it's free to wander around and 'take the air'. But that's it; behind, I couldn't find any heart to the town.

I move on, first northeast to Bad Neustadt and then west to Bischofsheim, along wide open valleys through which flow diminutive streams flanked by gnarled crab apple trees, shored up by steep wooded slopes and with a heady scent of cow dung. Slate church spires, like witches' hats grace the villages and towns; I find the architecture more austere and less comforting than the half-timbered dwellings of the Fränkische-Schweiz region.

At **Bischofsheim**, a pretty town with a manageable-sized centre and the furthest north that I venture, I turn back south and begin to climb the **Kreuzberg**, the highest of the low-level mountains within the Bavarian Rhön Nature Park. The summit, on which there's a monastery brewery, is a fine place from which to begin numerous walks. Views above the village of Sandberg are of open hillsides studded with trees and wooded hills; it's a classic view of a typical Rhön landscape. As I pass through, first, **Sandberg** and, latterly, **Waldberg**, I find both villages unremarkably remarkable – the houses are nothing extraordinary, but the way in which they're lined up along the road are; each one detached, one after the other without fault.

I descend to **Gefäll** and determine that the villages look better within an overall panorama than they do at close proximity. At **Bad Brückenau**, I climb up for the last time – and away from Bavaria.

In my time carving a diagonal line across Germany from the Czech and Austrian borders to the very heart of the country, I've witnessed forest, moorlands, river valleys and the most peculiar rocks. I've seen heather and harebells, trout and trickling streams. The wild boar? They'll have to wait until next time.

↑ River Wiesent (Caroline Mills)

ESSENTIALS

GETTING THERE & AROUND The 85 runs from Passau to Grafenau, where I then used minor roads around the Bavarian Forest National Park (all ok for coachbuilt motorhomes), finishing back on the 85 around Cham and Roding to Bodenwöhr. I then head cross-country on minor roads to Burglengenfeld and Schmidmühlen before criss-crossing the Naturpark Hirschwald, all on minor roads. I join the A6 autobahn south of Amberg at junction 66, Theum, and travel west for two junctions before heading north to Sulzbach-Rosenberg and picking up the 85 again towards Pegnitz. The 470 is the main route through the Fränkische-Schweiz area, though I also used minor roads to explore. I go cross country on the 2188 to Bamberg then the 26 to Schweinfurt and 286 to Bad Kissingen. In the region of the Rhön, I take the 2292 to Bad Bocklet, the 2292 (with a short return detour on the 2267) to Bad Neustadt and 279 to Bischofsheim, before returning south via Sandberg and Burkardroth on the 2290/2288 before taking the 286 to Bad Brückenau.

All of the places mentioned here are suitable for **parking** large motorhomes.

Burkardroth, in the Rhön UNESCO Biosphere Reserve (Caroline Mills)

ACCOMMODATION I stayed at *Stellplätze* in Passau, Bodenwöhr-Neuenschwand (Gasthof Zum Troidlwirt, where you can also have an evening meal), Streitberg and Bad Bocklet.

Campsites: Camping Passau, Passau; Camping Heiner, Bayerisch Eisenstein; Campingplatz Ludwigsheide, Bodenwöhr; Campsite Bärenschlucht, Pottenstein; Rhön Camping, Bischofsheim.

FIND OUT MORE

Bavaria Tourism ⚓ bavaria.by

Bavarian Forest National Park ⚓ nationalpark-bayerischer-wald.bayern.de/english

Bavarian Rhön Biosphere Reserve ⚓ biosphaerenreservat-rhoen.de

Franconian Switzerland ⚓ fraenkische-schweiz.com

JOSKA Glasparadies ⚓ jwoska.com

Naturpark Hirschwald ⚓ naturparkhirschwald.de

Passau ⚓ tourism.passau.de

Rhön ⚓ rhoen.de/en

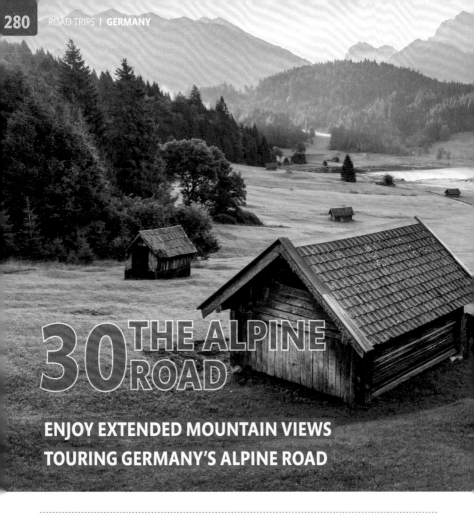

30 THE ALPINE ROAD

ENJOY EXTENDED MOUNTAIN VIEWS TOURING GERMANY'S ALPINE ROAD

WHERE	Bavaria & Baden-Württemberg
DISTANCE/TIME	280 miles (450km)/5 days
START/FINISH	Berchtesgaden/Lindau

What is it about the smell of freshly mown grass? Especially when it's on a gently sloping mountain pasture and you can hear the sound of cowbells merrily tinkling as their brown and white-patched owners tear at luscious green turf. There's an emerald lake that sparkles in the sunshine, its cool water fed by precipitous waterfalls that tumble from a craggy mountain backdrop.

This is, in effect, Germany's Alpine Road, or Deutsche Alpenstrasse, all rolled into one. The signposted tourist route gently meanders through blissful Alpine countryside between Königsee, close to the Austrian border, and Lindau, on the northeastern edge of the massive Bodensee that divides Germany from Switzerland and, again, Austria.

↑ Wagenbrüchsee (Geroldsee), between Krün and Garmisch-Partenkirchen (Stefano Termanini/Shutterstock)

We begin our tour at **Berchtesgaden**, a popular tourist town central to a small pocket of Germany that juts into a predominantly Austrian landscape. The town is famous for its proximity to Königsee, Germany's highest lake, and the Kehlstein upon which is Kehlsteinhaus, otherwise known as Adlerhorst ('Eagle's Nest'). This was a Third Reich headquarters close to Adolf Hitler's private retreat from which he could survey both Germany and Austria; the Kehlsteinhaus is now a restaurant overlooking an immense panorama.

Within an instant we're in the **Berchtesgaden National Park**, deemed one of the most beautiful areas of Europe, despite the rolling mist hampering far-reaching views on our initial visit (we've since returned and they are, indeed, outstanding). Our route takes us through **Ramsau**, the first of dozens of enticing villages we encounter, and a winding road to **Hintersee**. Milk churns left for collection, floral decorated houses and neatly stacked log piles create decorative patterns against the mountain vista; it's a good start.

Through woodland that's excellent for walking, we begin a long descent towards the River Schwarzbach. It fits into a gorge far below the road, with a waterfall that appears to descend from the Gods, filling the air with noise. The landscape begins to change noticeably approaching **Ruhpolding-Waich**, as it becomes open parkland with stunted trees pinned to rustically fenced fields.

Here we come across the **Chiemgau Arena Ruhpolding**, at first glance only a couple of ski jumps on the hillside until we take a wander around the horseshoe bowl of hills. The arena is home to the German Ski Club Biathlon team (an Olympic sport with a combination of Nordic skiing and shooting), and we see many athletes training along the numerous tracks, also usable as public footpaths for lovely mountain walks.

We opt instead for a walk through the Weitsee Nature Reserve to a trio of lakes – Lödensee, Mittersee and Weitsee – but heavy rain prevents it being long and we shelter at our first *Stellplätz*, in **Reit im Winkl**, listening to the thundering rush of the River Lofer outside our door.

Leaving Reit (a popular Nordic skiing and walking centre) as glimpses of sun and wispy clouds hug the hilltops, we approach nearby **Unterwössen** with a small glider circling above us. Intrigued, we follow a sign for the German Alps Gliding School through the village to a small open valley where we sit to watch these graceful 'birds' winched into the air, circle around the mountains (including a

↑ Berchtesgaden (canadastock/Shutterstock)

large one hidden in the clouds!) then land. It's an ideal distraction as we wait for the skies to clear; ultimately a deep blue sky emerges that makes the Alpine scenery look all the more resplendent.

Our next planned stop is **Aschau**, a beautiful town (from the windows of our 'van at least) with a vast castle on a hill – **Hohenaschau**. But, with limited places to park, we have to move on. We choose to take the autobahn for a few miles, but we find the junction closed for roadworks and we're rerouted back to the Alpenstrasse, thankfully. For had we taken the motorway, we would have missed one of the prettiest parts of the route, between Achenmühle and Nußdorf.

Our stop for lunch among fields at **Törwang** allow us to take a 3km waymarked circular walk through meadows that, but for the wildflowers and butterflies, seem un-Alpine like, with only the odd glimpse of a mountain from a rise in the terrain.

↑ Walking at Törwang (Caroline Mills)

In charming **Nußdorf (am Inn)** we pass between fruit orchards and along an avenue of walnut trees before crossing the River Inn and turning west again. The narrow, but magnificent, road through the village of **Wall** and the tiny hamlet of **Seebach** takes us to another type of Alpine landscape; a darker, more rugged pine-clad world before we descend steeply to **Bayrischzell** in a large, open valley below.

Stopping for a breather at **Schliersee**, with yet another scenic lakeside town, our journey takes us through **Rottach-Egern** (the route passes through Rottach, not Egern) to follow a long, straight road among the **Bayerwald pine forests**. We climb to the **Achenpass** and a tiny, 1km corner of Austria before the road passes beside – and across – the ever-so-blue **Sylvenstein-Stausee**, a large natural-looking reservoir that provides an impressive backdrop for the road-bridge that crosses it.

We follow the River Isar north, to overnight in **Bad Tölz**. A prettier Baroque town you'd be hard-pressed to find. With the dropping sun making the Old Town glow, we take the 400m riverside walk from the *Stellplatz* to find the main street crammed with a swathe of astonishing decorative buildings.

We rise early to appreciate the town centre bathed in morning sunlight and begin with a diversion through marshland, north of **Kochel am See**. It takes us into a wall of thick fog, which makes the mountains disappear altogether. With **Kochelsee** left to our imagination, we climb to discover a different day ahead of

↑ Painted buildings in Bad Tölz (FooTToo/Shutterstock)

us, the intense sky reflecting into the electric blue **Walchensee**. Deep and clear, with a panorama of peaks, it isn't long before the children are swimming in the mountain-cold water. And it isn't long before they climb out again! Blue the sky may be, but the water is not a summer temperature.

Nonetheless they have time to recover and appreciate the lake once more as a gondola transports us the 1,731m up Herzogstand. From above, the lake looks even more inviting, with views over the tops of, what feels like, the entire Alpine range. Spotting glaciers from the panorama point and wildflowers all around, it's necessary to sit a while in the mountain-top restaurant and enjoy lunch amid such beauty.

↑ Walchensee (Caroline Mills)

↑ Schloss Hohenschwangau, neighbour of Schloss Neuschwanstein (kunmingzijin/Shutterstock)

Continuing on the Alpenstrasse to **Wallgau**, we latterly pass through **Garmisch-Partenkirchen**, world-renowned for its ski facilities, and climb once more into an area of the Alps that feels utterly remote. It's the start of the **Ammergauer Alpen region** and a change in character again; we feel far from civilisation one moment before we're suddenly thrust into the beautiful mountain town of **Ettal**, which is dominated by its vast Benedictine monastery, now a luxury hotel.

At **Steingaden**, as the views turn from craggy mountain to open farmland and gentle undulations, the Deutsche Alpenstrasse combines with the last few miles of the Romantische Strasse (Romantic Road), another of Germany's long-distance waymarked tourist routes. It's a fitting finale for this fairytale road, with the unbelievable spectacle of Schloss Neuschwanstein. Built by 'Mad King Ludwig' towards the end of the 19th century (and recognised by fans of the film *Chitty Chitty Bang Bang*), the building is theatrical inside and out. It is one of two prominently positioned castles; the other, Hohenschwangau, belonged to Ludwig's father and is understated by comparison to his son's turreted flamboyancy. Having visited before, we bypass on this occasion – this is one of the most-visited attractions in Germany and it's rare to find it without a mass of visitors.

The neighbouring town of **Füssen** is no less beguiling. At the southern tip of Forggensee and lying within a bend in the River Lech, the medieval town is filled

↑ Füssen (Nella/Shutterstock)

with crooked streets and photogenic buildings, such as Hohes Schloss (High Castle), a Benedictine monastery, a clock tower and the colourful Reichenstrasse, or main street.

It's possible to stay overnight in the town's *Stellplatz* but we opt for the countryside of the **Allgäu Alpen**, the next stage of the Alpine range. With views in the rear mirror of Zugspitze, Germany's highest mountain at 2,962m, we approach **Nesselwang** where we can enjoy walks in the fresh mountain air; the *Stellplatz* sits at the foot of the ski slopes and there's a lovely walk up the mountain.

↑ Alpsee Bergwelt (Caroline Mills)

After all the ups and downs of mountain passes, dramatic peaks and deep gorges, the final stage of the Alpenstrasse becomes something of a welcome change. It moves away from the drama encountered in the early stages of the route, and winds around open countryside; the peaks turn into cushioned hills and the valleys widen. Though less glamorous, it is arguably prettier for being more soothing.

Our route takes us to **Bühl** and the picturesque Alpsee, where I wave the children 'goodbye' as they hop on to a moving chairlift that climbs the Eckhalde. Half an hour later, they reappear – at greater speed than when I left them, as they hurtle down the mountainside on the Alpsee Bergwelt; at almost 3km in length, it's Germany's longest toboggan run. Like a rollercoaster through the trees, there are, I'm told, some impressive views on the descent, though I'm more than impressed with those that can be seen from the foothill.

Farmers are bringing in the hay when we reach our final overnight stop in **Scheidegg**. We lie back in the sunshine and listen to cowbells as the scent of fresh-cut grass wafts over us. For us, the combination becomes symbolic of alpine meadows. It's our lasting memory as we descend lakeside to Lindau and the completion of our route. As roads go, the Deutsche Alpenstrasse would happily be my daily commute of choice.

ESSENTIALS

GETTING THERE & AROUND We began our tour along the Deutsche Alpenstrasse at its eastern end, close to Berchtesgaden and finished at Lindau, which, on the edge of Bodensee (Lake Constance), is the official end (or start) of the route. The whole route is signposted in both directions.

We found no problems with **parking** anywhere (except Aschau), especially with the excellent network of *Stellplätze*. In Füssen, we parked on the side of the road on Route 16 (towards Rieden/Marktoberdorf); there is a *Stellplatz* on the edge of town (a 20-minute walk from the centre), however.

ACCOMMODATION We stayed on *Stellplätze* in Freilassing (the evening before the start of the tour), Reit im Winkl, Bad Tölz, Nesselwang and Scheidegg.

Campsites: Camping Resort Allweglehen, Berchtesgaden; Campingplatz Ortnerhof, Ruhpolding; Campingplatz Demmelhof, Bad Tölz; Camping Hopfensee, Füssen-Hopfen am See; Camping Alpenblick, Weiler-Simmerberg.

FIND OUT MORE

Deutsche Alpenstrasse ⊘ deutsche-alpenstrasse.de/en

German National Tourist Board ⊘ germany.travel/en

INDEX

Entries in **bold** refer to major entries; those in *italic* refer to photos

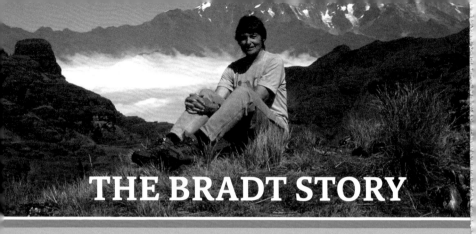

THE BRADT STORY

In the beginning

It all began in 1974 on an Amazon river barge. During an 18-month trip through South America, two adventurous young backpackers – Hilary Bradt and her then husband, George – decided to write about the hiking trails they had discovered through the Andes. *Backpacking Along Ancient Ways in Peru and Bolivia* included the very first descriptions of the Inca Trail. It was the start of a colourful journey to becoming one of the best-loved travel publishers in the world; you can read the full story on our website (bradtguides. com/ourstory).

Getting there first

Hilary quickly gained a reputation for being a true travel pioneer, and in the 1980s she started to focus on guides to places overlooked by other publishers. The Bradt Guides list became a roll call of guidebook 'firsts'. We published the first guide to Madagascar, followed by Mauritius, Czechoslovakia and Vietnam. The 1990s saw the beginning of our extensive coverage of Africa: Tanzania, Uganda, South Africa, and Eritrea. Later, post-conflict guides became a feature: Rwanda, Mozambique, Angola, and Sierra Leone, as well as the first standalone guides to the Baltic States following the fall of the Iron Curtain, and the first post-war guides to Bosnia, Kosovo and Albania.

Comprehensive – and with a conscience

Today, we are the world's largest independently owned travel publisher, with more than 200 titles. However, our ethos remains unchanged. Hilary is still keenly involved, and **we still get there first**: two-thirds of Bradt guides have no direct competition.

But we don't just get there first. Our guides are also known for being **more comprehensive** than any other series. We avoid templates and tick-lists. Each guide is a one-of-a-kind expression of an expert author's interests, knowledge and enthusiasm for telling it how it really is.

And a commitment to wildlife, conservation and respect for local communities has always been at the heart of our books. Bradt Guides was **championing sustainable travel** before any other guidebook publisher. We even have a series dedicated to Slow Travel in the UK, award-winning books that explore the country with a passion and depth you'll find nowhere else.

Thank you!

We can only do what we do because of the support of readers like you – people who value less-obvious experiences, less-visited places and a more thoughtful approach to travel. Those who, like us, take travel seriously.

TRAVEL TAKEN SERIOUSLY